Into the Guns of
PLOESTI

Leroy W. Newby

Motorbooks International
Publishers & Wholesalers

First published in 1991 by Motorbooks International Publishers &
Wholesalers, P O Box 2, 729 Prospect Avenue, Osceola, WI 54020 USA

Library of Congress Cataloging-in-Publication Data
Newby, Leroy W.
    Into the Guns of Ploesti / Leroy W. Newby.
      p.   cm.
    Includes bibliographical references.
    Includes index.
    ISBN 0-87938-494-8
    1. Newby, Leroy. 2. Ploesti, Battles of, 1943–1944. 3. World War,
1939–1945—Aerial operations, American. 4. World War, 1939–1945—
Personal narratives, American. 5. United States. Army Air Forces—
Biography. 6. Bombardiers—United States—Biography.
I. Title.
D764.3.P57N48 1991   90–48367
940.54′4973—dc20

On the front cover: A B–24J owned by the Collings Foundation. This liberator is a former Indian air force patrol plane. Tom Reilly orchestrated the
restoration that took 90,000 man hours. *Michael O'Leary*

Printed and bound in the United States of America

Contents

To the many thousands of US fighting men in their twenties in the
1940s—at sea, on the ground and in the air—who came face to face
with adversity, and were the better for it; some of whom paid the
ultimate price to preserve the freedom for all who follow.

Organizations dedicated to perpetuating the efforts of those who served in the Army Air Forces in World War II

Air Force Association
1501 Lee Hwy.
Arlington, VA 22209-1198

American Ex-Prisoners of War,
  Stalag Luft IV
8103 E. 50th St.
Indianapolis, IN 46226

Association of Former POWs in
  Romania
1077–B Blackshear Dr.
Decatur, GA 30033

Bombardiers Alumni Association
6 Redgate Ct.
Baltimore, MD 21228

Bombardiers, Inc.
200 Van Buren St. #2109
Daphne, AL 36526

Caterpillar Association of the US
P.O. Box 1321
Kenosha, WI 53141

The Eighth Air Force Historical
  Society
P.O. Box 727
Oldsmar, FL 34677

Fifteenth Air Force Association
P.O. Box 6325
March Air Force Base, CA 92518

Friends of the U.S.A.F. Museum
P.O. Box 1903
Wright-Patterson AFB, OH 45433

International B–24 Liberator Club
P.O. Box 841
San Diego, CA 92112

Second Air Division Association
P.O. Box 727
Ipswich, MA 01938

Foreword

Leroy "Ted" Newby has done a masterful job of catching the full flavor of the 26–month bomber war on the oil refineries at Ploesti, Rumania (during the war Romania was spelled Rumania). Because of his own harrowing experiences in 50 missions as a bombardier, Ted Newby has been able to write a convincing and compelling dramatic account of the two-year battle to knock out the oil refineries that were so vital to Hitler's mechanized and mobile war machine.

Newby's personal experiences on 50 missions were effectively covered in his first book, *Target Ploesti: View from a Bombsight*. That book was for the most part confined to Newby's bomber crew and their experiences on high-level strikes on the Ploesti refineries in the five-month period from April through August 1944. Those bombing strikes were made from southern Italy.

Through remarkable extensive research on the history of World War II, coupled with extensive correspondence with other survivors of the Ploesti bombing raids, Newby has put together a comprehensive story covering the entire 26–month period and including the famous low-level mission—code name TIDAL WAVE—from air fields in North Africa.

Extensive correspondence with other survivors of the Ploesti bombing runs and war record research made it possible for Ted Newby to write with authority and drama on the details of the experiences of others who took part in those earlier raids that consistently disrupted the oil supply of the Nazi war machine.

Because of the depth of research, and because of the skillful manner that Newby has used this research material, I felt, as a reader, that I was on the bombing missions from Africa and from Italy. The reader is caught up with the combination of boredom and fear as bombers droned toward the Ploesti targets. He has the feeling of exhilaration and then of despair as unexpected weather, crew adjustments, or bad timing upset the precise planning time table. The reader feels the elation when luck, and occasionally planning, results in all or part of a mission being accomplished.

Only someone who has experienced the fears, the frustrations, the failures and the occasional successes could have written this book. But simply experiencing these raids would not be enough unless those experiences were followed by years of systematic research on the Big Picture of World War II and the hundreds of little human dramas that were involved with death and survival in the long battle to cripple or destroy Hitler's oil supply.

Newby's *Ploesti* reads like a fast paced novel. It is clear and direct, and Newby has a good ear for authentic dialogue of the bomber crews.

—*Clark R. Mollenhoff*
Pulitzer Prize winning reporter

Preface

War is often thought of as steel and gunpowder; death and destruction; pain and suffering; lingering injuries and mind alterations; and ultimately, victory and defeat.

War is usually fought over freedom: between an aggressor seeking to destroy another's and a defender trying to preserve theirs.

John Stuart Mill, a nineteenth century English philosopher, wrote about freedom:

> War is an ugly thing, but not the ugliest thing; the decayed and degraded state of moral and patriotic feelings which thinks nothing is worth a war is worse.
>
> A man who has nothing which he cares about more than his personal safety is a miserable creature who has no chance of being free, unless made and kept so by the exertions of better men than himself.

Behind the horror of war is the human drama of bravery and compassion; self-discovery and revelation; and even humor in and between battles, those lighter moments that help one survive the terror of the times.

Ploesti, referred to as the "Taproot of German Might" by Churchill, was the major source of oil for Hitler's tanks, aircraft and motorized army.

The Battle of Ploesti was one of the most significant battles in US military history. It lasted twenty-six months, and the prize was oil: denied or sustained.

This is the story of the human drama behind that deadly struggle over oil; the key to maintaining the Nazi war machine. While the story is limited to a relatively few individuals, the human aspect is fairly representative of the millions of young men who left their civilian jobs, farms or classrooms, willing to pay the price of freedom when called.

The events recorded here are all true. Many were my own experiences, and many were related to me by others who wrote in response to their reading my earlier book, *Target Ploesti: View from a Bombsight.*

One compelling letter from a young Michigan reader, John Cooper, stated: "There is a verse from Edward Fitzgerald's [translator] poem, 'The Rubáiyát of Omar Khayyám' that ran through my head as I read your story. It goes as follows:

> I sent my Soul through the Invisible, Some letter of that After- life to spell;
>
> And by and by my Soul return'd to me, And answered 'I Myself am Heav'n and Hell.'"

In the introduction to his edition of *The Rubáiyát* (New York: Random House, 1947), critic Louis Untermeyer discusses the poem's meaning. His depiction of Khayyám's earthly hereafter may be in conflict with many, including my own, basic religious beliefs about the hereafter.

It would, however, be difficult to convince anyone who has flown through a flak barrage that he wasn't experiencing hell on earth; heaven when he emerged alive. For that reason some of the battle scenes at Ploesti are metaphorically couched in Khayyám's language solely in an effort to portray the emotions of the moment to a reader who has not been there.

My research included other books and articles on Ploesti, Air Force historical microfilms, letters from readers, and interviews with a Ploesti resident who was under the bombs and with the son of a manager of a Ploesti refinery during the bombings.

For the purpose of increased clarity and interest, most conversations have been dramatized, under artistic license, and are intended to show the general nature of such dialogues under conditions portrayed.

—*Leroy W. Newby*

Introduction

The future lair of the legendary Count Dracula was under siege in 1598 as Michael the Brave set out for Transylvania, far across the Wallachian plains.

The warrior paused as he reached the entrance to the beautiful Prahova Valley, virtually impassable with its narrow gorges and untrodden forests, cutting and twisting its way through the Carpathian foothills and mountains. Impressed with its beauty and topography, he set up camp there.

Underneath the Prahova Valley lurked one of the world's best kept secrets. An abundance of latent energy in the form of crude oil had lain hidden there for millions of years.

Nature had tried to advertise the oil's existence, but the local stained-black sheep were ignored. They had been lolling around in the gullies of Pacureti where the crude gushed out in mud volcanos. Unquenched flames leaped out of the several crevices in the area and shouted a silent "Why?" No one saw the shout. The secret was safe.

The following year Michael the Brave was crowned Prince Michael the Brave.

Two years later the Prince would be defeated by the Polish forces commanded by Zamoski, but his campsite survived, and one day would become the world's first oil boom town. Ploesti was its name (pronounced Plo-ES-tee).

Many consider the significant birth of Ploesti to be 1856 when that first oil refinery was built (three years before Drake struck oil in Titusville, Pennsylvania).

Oil's commercial possibilities were evident when nearby Bucharest became the world's first city to be lighted by gas.

Fifty years later there would be a dozen oil refineries ringing Ploesti, with names like Romano Americana, Concordia Vega, Steaua Romana, Astra Romana and so on. These names were unknown to young Americans at the time, but would be well known to thousands of their sons who would shudder at the very mention of them.

As the emerging city of Ploesti entered the oil age it was called the white town of black gold. Oil was always in evidence. In summer, the fragrance of flowers competed with the aroma of oil. In winter, the snowflakes smelled of oil. Thus its presence impregnated the air night and day; and when the evening sun fought its way through the oily atmosphere a phenomenon occurred, unique in all the world: Twilight was always purple in Ploesti.

Phantom Quartet

Life never offers this kind of metaphor.
—Ioan Grigorescu

A man long dead lives, and a brave young man dies on a fiery day in August. A frightened boy discovers a rarely offered metaphor of life. A quarter of a world away a bugle sounds and a young man tumbles from his bunk, not knowing he too would join the emerging group.

Four men, a phantom quartet thousands of miles and centuries apart, unknowingly bonded that day in a manner not to be revealed for many years to come.

This unusual foursome, defying time and distance, had its subtle roots in 1599; surfaced in the summer of 1942; flowered in the incredible land-air battle of Aug. 1, 1943; and bloomed some forty years later in Iowa.

An American victory in the August battle had offered the potential of preventing the future loss of millions of lives: soldiers on battlefields, civilians in cities and Jews in the Holocaust still hidden from the world.

The metaphor's dénouement dramatized the words of the master who had told us all the world's a stage.

Part One

The Players

Chapter 1

Summer of 1942

Some are born great, some achieve greatness, and some have greatness thrust upon them.
—William Shakespeare, *Twelfth Night*, act II, scene 5, lines 157–159

June 11, 1942 was a balmy, sunny day, very pleasant by Ploesti standards, and it brought out crowds of strollers and shoppers.

The war had not yet come to their city, but German soldiers in evidence all around added some tension to the oil-impregnated atmosphere. The citizens knew the oil and high-grade aviation fuel their dozen refineries produced for the German armed forces made them partners in the war effort.

Mrs. Grigorescu and her two sons had just spent an enjoyable few hours in the magnificent sprawling Palace of Culture, the largest building in this city of 100,000. The several museums within the palace covered almost any subject one would like to explore, and the children were in their glory as they came out onto the street.

Their enthusiasm was bubbling at capacity as they reached the *Statue of Liberty*, standing in the square in front of the palace. The statue represented the goddess Minerva in bronze, mounted on a stone pedestal.

"Mama," said young Ioan, "this is a great lady. She stands for freedom."

The other son spoke up saying, "She was dedicated Sept. 1, 1879, and was made in Paris."

"My, my, you children have been paying attention in school," replied the proud parent.

"Mama," persisted Ioan, "my newest book in my home library tells all about the *Statue of Liberty*, and how our country fought long and hard for freedom. We aren't free anymore, are we?" A German soldier rounded the corner; his mother wiped a tear from her eye.

His brother hastily spoke up, "Ioan's library is better than any of his friends'." Then, in an aside to Ioan, "*Watch your tongue!*"

That night, the first American bombs fell on Ploesti. Just a few, and they landed harmlessly outside the residential area, but near the Astra Romana refinery, the largest in Europe. Few citizens were aware of the unsuccessful incursion.

A new smell was in the air. The smell of war, and of death. Ioan Grigorescu awoke the next morning unaware of his future role in history.

On the other side of the world, the only bomb dropped on Crafton, Pennsylvania, that June evening was the booming home run off the bat of Josh Gibson, the legendary catcher of the Homestead Grays of the Negro National League. Gibson, the Babe Ruth of his day, was considered by many Major Leaguers as being Ruth's equal.

His bomb cleared a row of poplar trees and a house located beyond the 440 ft. center field fence.

One young fan who witnessed the long homer was sitting behind third base that evening watching his Church League All-Stars battle the Grays, when he heard a high-pitched whine over his right shoulder.

Three P–38s in formation were buzzing the field. As they passed low over the diamond a batter hit a towering foul ball destined to land in the third base stands. Fans all around the enthralled youth leaned away from him as he sat erect and watched the Air Forces's advertisement disappear like the baseball over the poplar trees, shaking the top branches on the way by.

"Look out!" someone shouted.

"Not one chance in a million will it hit me," announced Ted Newby, with eyes only for the disappearing planes. The confident young man should have been holding an Irish Sweepstake ticket; the ball hit him on the shoulder. He was serving notice of the can't-happen-to-me attitude that would be a way of life two years later, as he flew into the flak-filled skies of Ploesti, Rumania.

No bombs were dropped on Dayton, Ohio, either, that evening in June 1942, but the newspaper headlines were telling of Royal Air Force (RAF) bombs falling on the German industrial city of Essen; Cologne and Bremen had shared the headlines a few days earlier.

These were exciting and frightening times. The RAF bombing campaign was encouraging, but our naval forces were fighting for their lives in the South Pacific, and Rommel's Afrika Korps, aided by Italian troops, were marching toward their eventual capture of Tobruk in Libya. Fortunately, British Field Marshal Montgomery stopped Rommel at El Alamein, Egypt, and drove them back to Tripoli and Tunis. This was a major turning point of the war, and permitted the later Allied invasion of Italy and the subsequent bombing of Hitler's oil source at Ploesti.

Dayton's Howard L. "Larry" Dickson was built like a football player, but his interests were stronger along scholarly lines. Dickson's frequent visits to the library took him past the local post office, where the ubiquitous recruiting poster always haunted him. As he would near the poster, Uncle Sam's eyes and pointing finger would pick him up like it had radar and follow him until he was beyond it. Sometimes as he neared the end of the surveillance he would peek back. The eyes and fingers were still on him. The graphics that shouted "I want you!" were redundant. The eyes and finger said it all.

His idea of a big evening was to immerse himself in one of the master's tomes; Shakespeare was his favorite. He was married and had a new son, so was exempt from the draft, but he was uncomfortable with that status. He wanted his son to be proud of his dad when the war was over. He wanted to become a combat pilot and shoot down the planes of those who would jeopardize his son's freedom.

One summer evening, as he passed by the post office, Uncle Sam pointed his finger at him for the last time. The next day he went back, waived his dependent deferment and signed up for the US Army Air Forces (USAAF).

Across the Atlantic, the quiet English market town of Stratford-upon-Avon was conducting its annual summer Shakespeare festival, with some of England's leading actors performing in the theater section of the Shakespeare Memorial. Wartime conditions were reflected in the sparcely occupied 1,000 seat auditorium.

The townspeople had only recently celebrated the 378th birth anniversary of its most famous citizen.

Shakespeare, at eternal rest under the floor of the chancel of Holy Trinity Church, was oblivious to all of the attention being paid him. He knew not of the war taking place all around him, nor of his forthcoming entrance as a player on the world stage.

American military forces around the world had been reeling under Japanese attack ever since Pearl Harbor, suffering defeat after defeat. Bataan and Corregidor in the Philippines were about to fall. Gen. "Vinegar Joe" Stillwell's forces were in retreat in Burma. The German army was advancing in southern Russia. And American home front morale was near the breaking point.

Suddenly there was hope. On Apr. 18, 1942, Lt. Col. Jimmy Doolittle led sixteen B-25s from the deck of the carrier *Hornet* straight to the heart of Japan—the famous Thirty Seconds over Tokyo that served notice America wasn't dead. Americans everywhere responded as if their city had just won the World Series.

In early May, the Navy followed up with a striking victory at the Battle of Coral Sea, and then began its slow, relentless advance, island by island, toward the Japanese mainland.

Later in the month, against this backdrop of anticipated victory, the United States went for another morale booster when twenty-three B-24 Liberator bombers were dispatched from a Florida air base—destination Tokyo, nearly 13,000 miles away.

The enormity of this undertaking, considering the state-of-the-art navigational and bombing techniques of the day, is mind-boggling. The bombers all carried two bomb bay fuel tanks, spare airplane parts including a nose wheel, and three months' food and clothing supply. *No bombs*. Navigation would be by *National Geographic* maps.

It was known as the Halvorsen Project No. 63, or HALPRO for short, and was named after its fiery leader, Col. Harry A. "Hurry Up" Halvorsen.

The basic plan was to fly a circumnavigational route via Brazil and over Africa to Khartoum in the Sudan; then on to Chekiang, China, from which the bombing attack on Tokyo would be made. This added about 4,000 miles to a direct northwest route, but offered better security for a surprise attack.

Except for the Tokyo raid, the USAAF had not yet conducted a bombing mission anywhere in the world. In addition, the B-24 Liberator had yet to make its maiden bombing attack under US colors, although lend-lease B-24s were being flown by the RAF.

While few Americans had ever heard of Ploesti, Rumania, US military planners had been planning an attack on that oil complex since the early days after Pearl Harbor. A paratroop assault was one of the options considered, but a long-range bombing attack by the new B–24s was most favored.

Even as preparations were being made for the unprecedented HALPRO mission, US military planners were certain Chekiang would fall before our forces arrived.

In mid-May Gen. George Marshall, with the backing of the Air Ministry in London, had convinced President Roosevelt of the importance of a Ploesti attack. It was then determined that HALPRO would bomb Ploesti from the Sudan area.

On May 22, HALPRO took off; twenty-three B–24s containing 231 flyers, technicians, reporters and observers who thought they would be the second contingent to drop bombs on Tokyo.

When the detachment arrived in Khartoum, nearly half of the planes were not combat-ready due to mechanical trouble and lack of real maintenance. At that, British commanders were vying for the deployment of the bombers for the defense of Malta and convoys in the area, and even a British paratroop drop was under consideration. US military people resisted such requests, and the Ploesti attack was set for a June 11 late-night takeoff for a dawn assault on the largest oil refinery in Europe, Astra Romana, on the southern edge of the city of Ploesti.

On June 5 the United States declared war on Rumania, Bulgaria and Hungary in order to make the attack legal. Those countries had previously declared war on the United States, but had been ignored up to this point.

The dwindling HALPRO force, down to thirteen operational planes, was sent to Fâyid, Egypt, on the Great Bitter Lake, just north of the Suez Canal. There it was briefed on a 2,600 mile round trip that took it *around* neutral Turkey—a route insisted upon by RAF officials. The bombers would fly at 30,000 ft. en route and bomb from 10–12,000 ft. and return to Fâyid.

Colonel Halvorsen's mother would have been proud of her son's arithmetic. He knew a fully loaded B–24 with two bomb bay gas tanks could not reach 30,000 ft., and could not stay aloft for 2,600 miles, especially if it suffered battle damage. He was willing to lead his men on the dangerous mission, but he would not commit them to impossible odds. He held a secret meeting with the mission crews, and drew a line on a map that went right through Turkey to Ploesti and right back through Turkey to an airfield in Iraq that was closer than Fâyid. His audience unanimously approved his plan.

HALPRO was facing the longest bombing flight in history, over unknown, blacked-out terrain at night, sans proper navigational charts, and was flouting avowed US daylight bombing procedures. None of the men had ever been in combat, dropped a bomb or seen an enemy plane. In view of this, Washington asked Moscow for permission to land in Russia, to shorten the total flight.

When the thirteen bombers took off at 2230 hours they had not yet heard from the Soviets. Shortly after they were airborne, word came back through channels with permission to land behind Russian lines, but it was impossible to advise the fleet due to a radio blackout.

As the planes flew through the night in loose tandem style they passed over an unsuspecting and sleeping Turkey. While crossing the Black Sea, crewmen were startled to see the siege of Sevastopol as the red-hot German mortar shells descended upon the city. They were seeing war for the first time, and they now realized that they were part of it.

13

Twelve of the thirteen planes reached the Ploesti area, but they were all above the clouds at the Estimated Time of Arrival (ETA) and could not see the target in the early light of dawn.

Though pioneers in the art of USAAF high-level precision bombing, they were forced to resort to a practice that all US bombing formations in the future would, on occasion, find to be a necessity. They simply bombed by dead reckoning navigation and ETA. When the second hand of the bombardier's watch reached a certain number, he hit the bomb toggle switch and the bombs fell out. Where they hit, nobody knows.

Later reports indicated a couple of bombs fell on Astra Romana's property, but did no damage.

They experienced a little inaccurate flak and a fighter attack. Seven planes landed in Iraq, two in Syria and four in Turkey. The crews that landed in Turkey were interned, but repatriated not too long afterward. They were all out of gas, and would not have made it back to Fâyid under the RAF plan.

While America's first bombing attack on Europe may be considered ineffective, it did have a dramatic effect on the war. It demonstrated to Luftwaffe Col. Alfred Gerstenberg, military attaché to the German Embassy at Bucharest, that Ploesti was destined to be a prime target.

Thence began the most comprehensive antiaircraft defensive program of World War II. They would be ready for the next full-force attack by the USAAF.

This historic moment was ignored in the world press. Washington issued no communiqué. Berlin was silent. Few Rumanians knew about the incursion, beyond the few who lived near Astra Romana and wondered about the explosions in the nearby farm fields while they slept. The war went on.

During that crucial summer a running battle ensued between Air Marshal Arthur T. "Bomber" Harris, Commander-in-Chief of the RAF Bomber Command, and USAAF's Generals Spaatz, Eaker and Doolittle over Allied bombing techniques against Germany.

Harris advocated area bombing of German cities at night, with no regard to civilian casualties. A worker in a German war factory was contributing to Allied casualties just as certainly as the enemy in uniform.

The USAAF generals argued for daylight precision bombing of strategic targets. A factory turning out planes, bombs, tanks or submarines to be used against our troops, however, should not be spared because of nearby civilian considerations. They also reasoned that concentrated three-dimensional boxes of thirty-six B-24s or B-17s, wielding 360 machine guns, offered a devastating barrage of firepower that would reduce losses from fighter attacks and preserve the integrity of pinpoint bombing accuracy available with the Norden or Sperry computer-like bombsights.

So was born the Allied dual bombing offensive: nighttime harrassment of the workers and daytime destruction of factories, transportation and oil production.

US daylight bombing began "officially" on Aug. 17, 1942 with an Eighth Air Force mission to bomb the marshaling yards at Rouen, France. The dozen B-17s landed fifty percent of their bombs on the target and held off a fighter attack with no loss or damage.

Reactions to this early victory were varied. The following day, American leaders wore an "I told you so" smile on their faces. German leaders understood the implications and took immediate steps to switch most of their night fighter production to day fighters, a fact that American bomber crews would soon notice. British leader Winston Churchill was unimpressed. He continued his relentless pressure on Roosevelt to abandon production of the B–17 and begin building the Lancaster, a British bomber capable of carrying up to nine tons of bombs compared to the B–17's three tons. He further implored the president to switch from daylight precision bombing and join the RAF in its nighttime area bombing campaign.

An interesting reaction was that of the HALPRO flyers interned in Turkey who heard the British Broadcasting Corporation (BBC) radio reports heralding the *first* US daylight mission to a European target. They were furious. Their little secret mission to Ploesti didn't seem to count.

The fall of 1942 marked not only the beginning of the US Eighth Air Force's reign in Europe but also the landing of Allied troops in North Africa on November 8, which paved the way for establishing the Ninth Air Force on the dark continent.

Ending of Axis North African resistance in May 1943 brought Ploesti 200 miles closer to American bombers. Bases were soon built in Benghazi, Libya— a threat not lost on Ploesti's General Gerstenberg.

Bombers of the Ninth Air Force, commanded by Gen. Lewis Brereton, helped pave the way for the British Eighth Army in its westward advance from Egypt into Libya. The British then built air bases of their own in the wake of this steady advance.

Indications were that Germany was under way with a widespread synthetic oil program and the need to destroy Ploesti oil capabilities loomed all the more important.

The road to Ploesti was littered with more than gas worries, flak and enemy fighters. It contained many obstacles in the form of special-interest groups who did not want a large number of bombers taken away from their pet projects.

Chapter 2

Summer of 1943

Franklin Roosevelt and Winston Churchill met in Casablanca in early January to discuss future landings in Europe once Germany was driven out of Africa. Joseph Stalin was not there in person, but he was there in spirit. He wanted an Atlantic landing that would establish a second front in the west and take some of the pressure off the battles on his western front.

Churchill came to Casablanca to sell three pet ideas. He wanted the USAAF daylight bombing converted to night bombing. He opposed an Atlantic invasion because the Allies lacked the strength for it, and instead, he wanted a Balkan invasion.

The decision to invade Sicily rather than an Atlantic site seemed to satisfy Churchill, as he gave up the Balkan plan and succumed to General Eaker's impassioned plea for "round-the-clock USAAF/RAF bombing of European targets."

The main announcement out of Casablanca, however, was the doctrine of Unconditional Surrender, a fist-shaking pronouncement that sounded good at the time, but one that later many believed probably prolonged the war in Europe.

A quiet and unannounced decision reached at that historic conference was to bomb Ploesti again with a large force of bombers once North Africa was secured. Col. Jacob Smart was assigned the task of developing a plan of attack. He was in the interesting situation of being told to achieve an objective, but was provided no known means of accomplishing it. The directive was in good hands, however.

Smart wrestled with his problem, and after much soul-searching and advice he concluded an attack at low level would be most effective. The reasons were many. A flight of 1,250 miles over enemy territory could best avoid radar by flying as low to the ground as possible. This tactic would also conserve fuel by avoiding the climb to 20,000 ft. for high-level bombing, and by eliminating the weight of oxygen equipment. A ground-hugging posture would cut down by one half the sphere of attack by enemy fighters.

A plus that would be appreciated by participants was that flak gunners would not have the luxury of long sightings, as the bombers would be coming by so quickly.

Another consideration that would not be lost on the flyers was the morale booster of being able to shoot back at the flak gunners—something they were powerless to do as sitting ducks at 20,000 ft.

Not the least of interest to the flyers was the chance of a successful skid-landing if hit, as opposed to bailing out at high altitude.

But the main consideration was the prospect for more precise and efficient bombing, along with minimum civilian casualties. More accuracy could be ensured by bombing on the deck. A typical oil refinery occupied an area of about a square mile, and within that confine were scattered several small critical installations such as a powerhouse, cracking towers, stills, boiler house and pumping stations. In addition, there were up to 100 or more large tanks for storing oil and gasoline. A force of some 200 bombers at 20,000 ft. could place all of its bombs on the property and not destroy the refinery. Ploesti had ten such major refineries surrounding the city proper, one about twenty miles northwest, and another about five miles south.

On May 17 at the Washington Trident Conference of Allied Chiefs, the Ploesti mission received its final blessing. STATESMAN was its code name.

At this conference Colonel Smart's plan for the low-level Ploesti attack was presented but received scant attention, as the thrust of the gathering was to discuss the invasion of Sicily and create another front for Germany to face.

Later General Brereton, Ninth Air Force commanding officer (CO), received Gen. Dwight Eisenhower's approval of the low-level plan, and set a new tentative date of June 23. The code name was changed to SOAPSUDS.

When the Sicily invasion was set for July 10, Eisenhower, US Army commander of the Allied Expeditionary Force, delayed Ploesti to the end of July, so the Ninth Air Force would have plenty of operational bombers for the invasion softening-up bombing. This appears to be an unspoken prediction of heavy losses and battle damage on the proposed Ploesti attack. Later it was firmed for Sunday, August 1 to minimize casualties to impressed Rumanian factory workers. The code name was changed for the final time, to TIDAL WAVE.

HALPRO was the opening move in a giant chess game destined to last for twenty-six months. It became the catalyst for considerable activity on the stage known as the world.

For the Allies, it kicked off the months of discussions on the *if* as well as the how and when of a second attack. This was followed by months of unprecedented preparation and rehearsal for a new type of battle never before witnessed in the history of military conflict.

For Colonel Gerstenberg there was no *if*. He knew it was the beginning of a new era. The American air armada would return—in force this time. The only unknown he pondered was the how and when, as he waited for the proverbial other shoe to fall.

Gerstenberg had been quietly building the Ploesti defense long before HALPRO, as he brought in more flak guns for the armed castle he called *Festung Ploesti*. He couldn't hide the refineries underground, so the city itself would become an unpenetrable fortress: a land battleship in the midst of the richest oil fields in German-occupied territory.

The two combatants, the offense and defense, were making simultaneous preparations in this giant game of wits.

The resulting next visible move on the world stage would later be considered the most thoroughly planned battle, offensively and defensively, the world had ever known.

Gerstenberg for the defense had the backing of Hermann Goering, his World War I combat flying buddy, and was being supplied most of what he requested for *Festung Ploesti*.

After HALPRO he began requesting fighters, and thus was born the air defense. Over 70,000 Slav prisoners and civilian slaves were put at the disposal of the Protector, as Gerstenberg was known.

He then laid out a master plan to counteract the coming air attack. It consisted of several elements designed to *find*, *fool* and *destroy* the enemy bombers; and also to minimize the inevitable bomb damage.

An elaborate network of bomber detection similar to the Kammhuber Line surrounding Germany was set up between Ploesti and North Africa. Freya early warning sets would pick up the bombers at a great distance, and Wurzburg radar would track the intruders. Direction-finding equipment was in place to home in on bombers foolish enough to use radio.

Two dummy Ploestis, built out of cardboard and wood, were located about a dozen miles from the city, but not south. An earlier concern had been an attack by Russia.

When the attackers reached the city they would meet batteries of 88 and 105 mm flak guns, manned by itchy-fingered gunners waiting to welcome them.

Hopefully the bombardiers, distracted by flak bursts, would be fooled by the camouflaged buildings and railroad tracks on the edge of the city. Rows of houses were painted on the roofs, and the highways from the city were seemingly extended, as dummy roads were painted over railroad tracks.

To further torment the bombardiers, smoke screens would be ready to flood the area with smoke up to 360 ft. thick, and covering a wide area.

The main concentration of flak batteries was south of the city, in anticipation that the bombers from North Africa would be at the extreme limits of their range and would come straight in on the bomb run. The largest oil prize in Europe—Astra Romana, located on the southern edge of the city—would be at the end of the long flight. Flak batteries were also in place to defend the other refineries.

Flak guns were mounted on railroad cars and located on tracks leading to several large refineries.

Over 100 barrage balloons, each anchored by long cables to a truck, were placed around the outskirts of the city, beyond the ring of refineries. They were lowered at night and could be raised in the day to heights up to 6,000 ft., and some to 10,000 ft. The long steel umbilical cords were intended to snag low-flying aircraft. Some cables had impact explosive charges attached at intervals. A plane hitting near a charge would tend to ride up the cable and set off the charge. Cables could snarl propellers and even cut off portions of wings.

Gerstenberg knew he could not stop the bombers. His flak guns could only shoot down a few planes, but a few hits in a formation at the bomb release point would disrupt the bombardiers and tend to split up and spoil the integrity of the formation and the group's precision bombing.

One of the Protector's greatest coups was the building of a pipeline around the perimeter of the city connecting all of the ten major refineries. Each refinery consisted of a production and a storage facility. If a given refinery had its storage facility badly damaged, but its production facility was still operating, it would feed oil into the pipeline and route it to another refinery's storage tank. Conversely, if a refinery's production facility was damaged, but its storage tanks were intact, it would accept product from the pipeline into its tanks. (Allied leaders did not learn about this pipeline until after Ploesti was captured.)

When asked why the pipeline was mounted in a ditch and *above* ground, Gerstenberg replied, "When the line is hit by a bomb it will be easier and quicker to repair if above ground."

The spirit of capitalism reared its head over the co-mingling of oil. The owners disliked the idea of sharing their oil with competitors, even though they were at war.

Circular cement and brick walls up to 20 ft. high and 4 ft. thick were erected around sensitive areas. Each oil storage tank was surrounded by a wall, cone shaped at the top, to contain its contents and resulting fire when the tank might be ruptured by bombs.

A crew of 500 highly trained firemen and policemen would be ready to spring into action once the bombers departed, so the slave and prisoner labor forces could begin the cleanup within any refinery damaged by an air attack. Special bomb disposal crews were on hand for the unenviable job of disarming dud bombs remaining after an attack.

Young Ioan Grigorescu was in awe of all the activity in his neighborhood, located on the southern edge of the city. The increased number of soldiers, walking the streets of his city, and the big trucks lumbering through town, with hordes of men aboard in dirty work clothes, bothered him. The frenzy in the air wouldn't leave.

One Sunday during the noon meal Ioan was deep in thought. Suddenly, he spoke up. "Pappa, are we going to be in the war?"

His father looked over sadly and said, "I'm afraid our great oil industry we have been so proud of will one day be our undoing, now that the Germans have taken over our country. It does look like they are expecting bombers, and that will put us in the war."

Ioan shook his head and said, "Every day I see one or two of those big sausages up in the air, like kites. In different parts of the city, too. My friends tell me they are intended to snag airplanes that try to bomb our city. Is that right?"

"That's what they are intended to do. They are just testing them. They take them down every night."

"Mama, do you think our house will be hit by a bomb?" asked Ioan's brother.

Mrs. Grigorescu looked around at the four walls and said, "Let's pray to God every night that our house and our family will be spared."

A few miles southeast of Ploesti there was a quiet, palatial estate consisting of many acres, located on a hill that overlooked the city and some of its oil refineries. Thirty-eight-year-old George Suciu had lived there with his family, a cut above the average Rumanian, since returning from the United States where he had worked for Standard Oil in 1931–32.

The Romano Americana oil refinery where he worked as assistant operating superintendent was located about a mile or so due east of the city. Both could be seen in the distance from Suciu's veranda.

The Suciu family often enjoyed their Sunday meal out on the veranda. On one such occasion that summer Suciu's wife turned to him and said, not as a question but fishing for an answer, "All of the Americans have gone home."

"That's right. Many good friends have left. They know what will be happening here one day," he replied.

"Do you think they will be back?"

"Yes, but unfortunately they will not be arriving by train, as before. They will be coming in bombers. Perhaps not the same men that were here, but their brothers or sons."

"Your refinery, Romano Americana, is owned by American interests. They surely won't bomb it." She paused, "Will they?"

"I would like to think so, but I'm afraid Ploesti, with its dozen major refineries, is too big a prize for them to be picky. And we are part of the prize."

"But our home is far enough from the refineries that we should be safe here," he added, for whatever comfort it might offer.

So much for the defense in this worldwide chess game.

The offense in the coming battle was faced with the difficult task of designing a means of sneaking some 178 four-engine B-24s across 1,250 miles of strange terrain, bombing several oil refineries from under 50 ft. altitude, and then returning to Africa. They had no idea of the reception being planned for them.

One year after the ill-fated HALPRO mission, Colonel Smart went to London to seek the aid of Col. Edward J. Timberlake, CO of the newly formed 201st Provisional Bomb Wing, to handle the operational details of the coming low-level mission.

The low-level bombing was foreign to bomber pilots trained and experienced in high-level precision bombing, so three Eighth AF groups were taken off combat status and sent on low-level formation practice runs.

There isn't a pilot alive who does not love to buzz ground objects, even though the military forbids such practice. The happy bomber pilots reveled in their newfound pleasure, despite having no clue as to why they were eating this forbidden fruit.

Speculation and rumors were blooming. Submarine pens were getting the most votes among the participants, with dams a close second. Then the real "Poop from the Group" surfaced. Their target would be the German battleship *Tirpitz*, trapped in some fjord up in Norway. The presence of two Norwegian naval officers hanging around the officer's club, PX and flight line could only mean one thing.

Unknown to the Norwegian naval officers, they were planted there to foster just such rumors. Neither understood why they were given the run of an American air base, free to roam the area with no questions asked. Certainly choice duty for any naval officer. Word of their presence spread to the other bases.

While the planes and pilots were getting prepped for the unknown mission, others were busy working on how they were going to find Ploesti and the specific targets.

No aerial navigational maps existed for the planned route across the Balkans, and they were to fly on the deck much of the way so as to stay under radar coverage.

No aerial photos of the refineries were available for the bombardiers, who also had never bombed at low level.

RAF officials were helpful in supplying these two missing visual elements. The Bodleian Library at Cambridge had previously appealed to citizens for any snapshots or picture postcards from their prewar European vacation travels. A representative visited the library and casually ordered the photo files on ten random areas of the world, including the Balkans.

Armed with the Balkans folder and selected pictures from the *National Geographic* archives, dedicated workers produced route maps and developed sequential oblique pictures of significant landmarks. Those producing the maps and route pictures had no idea of the areas involved, as there were no identifying words on the items they were handling.

The creation of oblique photos of the refineries, to be used by bombardiers, required even more ingenuity.

On the floor of a large room was a scale model of the city of Ploesti, built by the US Model Makers Detachment. Every house, street and tree was in place; ten oil refineries were located around the perimeter of the city proper. Railroad tracks, marshaling yards and the two other refineries were likewise reproduced. One man who viewed the model was astounded to find the house he once lived in.

They mounted motion picture cameras on children's tricycles and sent them on the bomb run to each of the seven largest refineries in the area. The resulting film duplicated what a bombardier would see as he raced toward his assigned target at over 250 mph, just 20 ft. off the ground.

Sequential still photos were made along the bomb run for use by the bombardier in recognizing his specific target, such as a cracking tower or power plant. No one knew what city they were working with.

Along with the silent bomb run movie, they produced a professional forty-five-minute sound motion picture on the entire mission for use at the

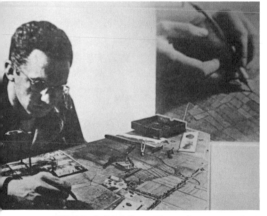

US Model Makers Detachment technician building a scale model of Ploesti and its ten surrounding refineries. All streets, houses, trees and hedges are put in place. Insert shows a hedging machine in use, where hedges, orchards and lines of trees are squeezed out of a nozzle not unlike a cake decorator.

Similar models were built for landings at Normandy, North Africa, Italy and other targets such as Peenemunde, Pilsen & Norway, Schweinfurt, Neuenbeken, and the Rhine and Moselle river valleys.

Vertical view (1:5000) of finished 5x5 ft. Ploesti model. The five White targets can be seen: WH-1 at extreme right of photo; WH-2 at top; WH-3 at lower center; WH-4 directly below marshaling yards; WH-5 at lower left.

21

briefing sessions. Never before had a motion picture been made in preparation for a coming battle.

The armed camps were not unlike two superpower football teams preparing for the big game, each trying to out think the other, and neither being allowed in the opponent's camp.

Timberlake had decided to use the two existing B–24 Bomb Groups of the Ninth Air Force, presently in the Benghazi, Libya, area, and augment them with two veteran Eighth AF groups and a newly arrived Eighth AF group, fresh from the States.

While the collateral map and photo materials were being prepared, pilots were scaring the contentment out of all the cows on nearby dairy farms as they perfected their new flying skills in low-level formation practice.

Finally, late in June, all three bomb groups set out on the first leg of an odyssey its survivors would never forget. They dared not fly across France for obvious reasons, and were forced to take the long way around, out over the Atlantic, to reach North Africa. Aside from a little ineffective flak at Gibralter, it was an uneventful transfer to the Ninth Air Force.

At Benghazi they joined two desert groups, whose flyers were equally puzzled by all the attention to low-level formation flying.

The veteran 44th Bomb Group "Eight Balls" moved in with the 98th, known appropriately as the "Pyramiders."

The other two, the seasoned 93rd "Traveling Circus" and the 389th, freshly arrived from the States and already sporting the name "Sky Scorpions," went to other airfields in the Benghazi area. The other desert group, the 376th "Liberandos," was located northeast of Benghazi, near the sea.

The three new groups were introduced to air war North Africa style. They thought they were in the minor leagues for milk runs to build up their mission count, away from the real war in Germany. This attitude was not well received by the men who had been eating desert dust and soaking up Italian flak for many months.

Flak knows no rank or league. The 44th would soon lose eight planes on one mission. A milk run?

While not yet announced as of early July, all of the flyers had the Italian invasion figured out. Their relentless pounding of the coastal area told them enough to spark the well-founded rumors. On July 9, several of the groups bombed the German General Staff headquarters at the base of Mt. Etna, Sicily, practically confirming the imminent invasion of the next day.

The five bomb groups picked to make the historic low-level attack on Ploesti were far from prima donnas in regard to the other bomb groups in North Africa. The Eighth Air Force men would be facing a combat regimen the likes of which they had rarely experienced in England's bad weather.

During the first nineteen days of July they flew eighteen high-level missions to Italian targets, culminating in the July 19 controversial bombing of Rome. On that sensitive bombing mission, all Catholic flyers were given the opportunity to stand down.

The following day the five chosen groups were pulled out of combat to concentrate on daily low-level formation bombing practice. The initial effort had no target involved; they were mostly trying not to run into each other in this difficult maneuver.

It doesn't take much to start a rumor, so this activity was a natural. Many of the votes went to the Brenner Pass in northern Italy, where ninety-five percent of all German war materials passed into Italy. The southern coast of France rated high in the official scuttlebutt nerve center's choice of the target. Ploesti began creeping up in the polls, and eventually shot to the top, as a result of repeated concentrated bombing attacks on a unique target.

A full-scale city of Ploesti, complete with the many refineries around its perimeter, was built out in the desert. The contours of the city were outlined by miles of whitewash and thousands of oil drums, covering a forty-square-mile area. The refineries were represented by replicas of key buildings, two-dimensional to minimize identification by German planes.

The city of Campina, some twenty miles northwest of Ploesti, was also outlined; its refinery, Steaua Romana, was properly identified in replica.

On the model Ploesti, Initial Points (IPs), where the bomb runs would start, were constructed thirteen miles northwest of "Ploesti," and about fifteen miles northwest of "Campina."

In a typical practice run the five bomb groups, numbering about 178 bombers, would assemble in the air near Benghazi and navigate to the respective IPs, from which they roared toward their seven targets just 20 to 30 ft. above the desert floor. One group of thirty planes attacked the Campina refinery. The others split into six attack units and bombed the other assigned refineries.

Several full-formation Ploesti missions were flown in this manner as the flyers rehearsed for the real thing. During the first few missions they dropped dummy flour-filled bombs that provided some degree of evaluation of the bombardiers' accuracy. Results on the early missions were disappointing, but improved with practice. The bombardiers were learning the new way.

All bombardiers had bombing tables on various types of bombs that showed their Actual Time of Fall (ATF) in seconds at various altitudes from 1,000 ft. up to over 30,000 ft. That information plus barometric pressure and temperature aloft was fed into the Norden bombsight prior to the bomb run on high-level missions.

The bombardier, through observation of the vertical cross hair and manipulation of the Course Knobs on the bombsight, would actually control the ailerons and rudders, literally flying the plane on the run in; he steered the plane. This part of the bomb run compensated for the wind effect on the plane, or bombing platform as it was known.

The bombardier also operated the rate (of closure) knobs as he strove to synchronized the movement of the horizontal cross hair with the speed of the bomber over the ground. This rate data was fed into the amazing computer that was the basis of the secret Norden bombsight.

The bombsight's computer, with all this input in place, would automatically calculate the precise point in space that the particular bombs on board should be released so as to land on the bombardier's aiming point (that is, the center of a factory building or cracking plant). The bombsight, not the bombardier as portrayed in early World War II movies, released the bombs via an electrical contact within the sight.

All this beautiful technology and training was for naught on a bomb run just 20 or 30 ft. off the ground.

The Nordens were removed from the planes and simple mechanical sights (little more sophisticated than the top of a bombardier's toe extended out in front of him) were installed on all planes.

The USAAF had little information on the characteristics of bombs dropped at low altitude. No one knew how a 500 or 1,000 lb. bomb would act

Famed Norden bombsight.

when it hit the ground while still in a fairly horizontal position. General Brereton asked Col. John R. Kane, CO of the 98th BG, to do some experimenting in this regard.

Kane dropped some fifty bombs on a nearby small island, at altitudes ranging from 10 ft. up to 250 ft. Each bomb had a forty-five-second delay fuse in the nose to permit the bomber to escape before the explosion. Accuracy was difficult at under 75 ft., but at over 75 ft. bombs would skid along the ground with a reasonable hope of hitting the aiming point, such as the front door of a power plant. It was also determined that some longer delayed fuses were needed for the first planes over a target. Fuses with only a forty-five-second delay would be cutting it too close for the last wave of planes to clear the explosions.

During one of the low-level practice runs on "Ploesti," one of the bombers was forced onto the ground by a plane above it. The plane skidded for 200 yards on the ground, engines still operating. Then the desperate pilot gave the engines full throttle and lifted his bomber back off the ground. That evening the pilot was given an award for the all-time distance record for taxiing with the wheels up.

On July 28 and 29, the bomber armada used live bombs with longer delayed fuses in full "dress rehearsals." Top officials were elated over the accuracy. They knew that if the bombers made it to Ploesti they would destroy all their assigned targets.

General Brereton, circling in a Liberator high above the desert stage, witnessed the final show and wrote in his diary: "The final test was a success!

They reached the targets on split-second schedule, and bombed with deadly accuracy, destroying the desert Ploesti."

Late in the rehearsal period the pilots, navigators and bombardiers were spending free hours studying the maps and target photos developed by the RAF in England. The scale model plaster cast of Ploesti had been brought to Benghazi and kept under heavy guard, and the key players studied it every day. Each of the seven refineries was there in minute detail. The cracking towers, power plants, boiler houses and distilling units were all there. The railroad tracks and marshaling yards were in place as well.

The flyers watched the 8 mm movie film made from the cameras mounted on the tricycles. They viewed it in slow motion, regular motion and fast motion to give them the illusion of approaching their refinery at different speeds.

Truly, no other military engagement in history had ever been planned as thoroughly as this one.

The enormity of their date with the unknown weighed on all of the combat crews. Ground crews were instructed not to engage any flight crews in conversation. Flight crews were isolated from all other personnel, both in sleeping areas and in mess halls. Conversation between the two was not allowed. They all knew whatever was up would happen soon.

The desert dust was the worst enemy of the bombers. Engines normally needed replacement after 350 hours, but here where they took off in clouds of dust they were usually replaced after just sixty hours. When many of the battle-weary bombers suddenly had all their engines replaced, it became a quiet announcement that *the* day was near.

While thousands of men were choking on the desert dust and wondering why, or building *Festung Ploesti* and knowing why, thousands of young men were back in the United States learning how.

Some were learning how to fly America's newest four-engine bomber, one that could fly faster, fly farther and carry more bombs than any other American bomber: the B–24 Liberator.

Some were learning how to navigate this inanimate behemoth from here to there at night, in soupy weather and in clear weather, while cooped up in its cramped nose compartment.

Some were learning how to fire .50 caliber machine guns from one of six gun positions on this dreadnought of the air.

Some were learning how to keep the airplane functioning while in the air, or maintaining radio contact with others.

Some were learning how to pick up a target in the eyepiece of a Norden bombsight, America's newest secret weapon said to be capable of dropping a bomb into a pickle barrel from 20,000 ft.

All of these specialists would soon become an integral member of a heavy bomber crew, just like the crews that were eating the North African dust. They would be flying a later model of the same B–24 aircraft, known affectionately as The Flying Boxcar, The Flying Time Bomb, The Flying Prostitute (no visible means of support) or simply the Baker Two Dozen.

When Ted Newby followed those P–38s over the center field fence to the Army Air Forces recruiting office in Pittsburgh, it began a whole new way of life for that young man.

All Aviation Cadets followed the same general path when Uncle Sam pointed his finger and his eyes commanded what the words said, "I want you!" Bomber crews were born this way.

While the dust eaters were softening up the defenses for our forces to storm the Sicily beaches, bombardier aspirant Newby and two other Aviation Cadets were storming the beach on Balboa Island in Newport Bay, California. The only defender was a pretty maiden standing alone on the beach, waving to them.

After a successful landing they drew straws to see who would take the sailboat back upwind to the rental dock. Newby, who was sailing for the first time, drew the short straw. Armed with hasty instructions on tacking he shoved off and began his erratic solo return trip.

Newby had not yet experienced evasive action on a bomb run, but he got a taste of it as he headed first for the shore on his left, and then reversed the sail to try to avoid capsizing a man floating on an inflated mattress in what he thought was the safety of the shore area. The man took a swim. The sudden reversal nearly capsized the sailboat too, as the neophyte sailor quickly learned a fundamental of sailing. Something about coordinating the rudder and sail reversal.

He somehow made it back, wondering if combat would be that tough. It of course would prove to be considerably worse, but in his own small way he was showing his disdain for the unknown—the hallmark of a combat flyer.

The young lady's parents, whose family name was King, provided a fine cookout for the three adventuresome cadets, and put them up for the night.

The Aviation Cadets attending Pre-Flight School at Santa Ana Air Base were treated to a nice banquet sponsored by the Masquers of Hollywood. The highlight of the evening was a show put on by Danny Kaye and the entire cast of the popular Jack Benny radio show. Claudette Colbert was a special guest.

After the show Cadet Newby went up to the head table to obtain Claudette Colbert's autograph on his program, and in his excitement he knocked over a tumbler of water onto Miss Colbert's satin-gowned lap. The location of the water stain indicated the aspiring bombardier had scored his first "shack," a bombardier term for a bull's-eye.

After the normal involuntary reaction and shriek, the lady mopped herself up with a napkin, looked at the conspicuous spot for a second or two, slowly shook her head from side to side, looked back up to smile at the embarrassed cadet and extended her hand for the program. As she signed her name she graciously said, "So you are training to drop bombs on the Japs. Keep up the good aim."

Jack Benny, long an idol of the bombardier, was sitting next to the inadvertent bombing, and may have been splashed. His response to the incident was a shocking, unfunny comment on the clumsiness of the chagrined cadet. Newby was crushed.

The bombardier-in-training was seeing a hint of what he would be facing in combat: victory juxtaposed with defeat.

As the men of TIDAL WAVE were departing from the heralded US doctrine of high-level precision bombing, and learning the strange new technique of low-level bombing, cadet Newby was embarking on just the opposite course.

He was going from a vivid demonstration of accurate low-level bombing at the Masquer's party to the bombardier school at Victorville, California, for training on the technique of high-level precision bombing with the Norden bombsight.

Bombardier cadets learned all about the Norden bombsight, inside and out. They learned to draw all of the inner mechanisms of the computer head that figured out when the bomb should be released, for existing conditions, so as to place the bomb precisely on the aiming point—or at least near it.

They learned how to operate the several knobs on the outside that enabled the inner workings to do their job.

The practice targets out in the Mojave Desert bombing range consisted of circular areas of level ground about 600 ft. in diameter. In the center of each area was a white 24x24x24 ft. pyramid, known as a shack. Asphalt roads circled the target at 100–200–300 ft. intervals.

All bombs dropped were photographed from the plane, so a pictorial record was available to confirm the impact point on the cadet's report. A cadet would never exaggerate the closeness of his bomb, of course, but the photo record was there to keep him honest. When a 7 lb. charge of black powder in the tail of the sand-filled, reuseable 100 lb. practice bomb exploded, it provided clear evidence of the impact point.

After making twenty-five practice bomb runs, a cadet began dropping his forty record bombs. Each bomb impact was scored as a Circular Error (CE). Bombs were dropped from 7,000 ft. and the results factored to 11,000 ft. A very good bombardier would keep his CE under 100 ft. When a cadet's CE average went over 230 he was given a "check ride" by another instructor. If he survived, he stayed in training. His regular instructor would work extra hard with him, as a "washout" reflected on the teacher.

A failed check ride entitled a cadet to a final check ride, and a chance to remain in training. A failed final check ride sent the cadet packing, usually to gunnery school, and from there quite often to membership on a bomber crew.

Newby and some friends hitchhiked up to Lake Arrowhead one weekend after the Saturday morning inspection and parade. There they met a nice family with a daughter, a motorboat and lodging for the three of them. The other two cadets were experienced with a toboggan-type board towed behind a motor boat, and were impressing the young lady.

Newby had never been on anything like this before, and even though a poor swimmer he decided not to be shown up by the others, and foolishly asked for a turn.

So there he was again in uncharted waters, this time in the middle of Lake Arrowhead, about 60 ft. behind a speedboat, and without a life jacket.

"Whatever you do, don't hold on to the rope if you take a spill," they shouted as he started out from the dock. "If you do the board may pull you to the bottom!"

All went well for a while, until they hit a little wake from another boat. The yachtsman-turned-skier left the board, but he was afraid to release the rope, as he didn't think he could stay up until they came around. He doubted if they believed how poor a swimmer he was.

"Let go! Let go!" they yelled.

He not only did not let go, but he managed to climb back up onto the board and resume skiing.

Later, his thoughts were: What's all this about the dangers of combat? They'll never get me. But I just hope and pray I never come down in the ocean. Third time might not be a charm.

Newby and the young girl hit it off quite well and the parents invited him back the next weekend. They were from Santa Monica and had a lodge along the lake where they spent most weekends.

It was difficult keeping his mind on bombing all week, but he managed to avoid any check rides, and when Saturday came he wasn't too concerned about it being his turn to be responsible for the room at morning inspection. All "gigs" for room infractions were charged to the cadet in charge that day. After all, the other two cadets were on-the-ball-type guys.

The inspecting officer rubbed the top of the door sill with his white glove, and it came up gig. Newby had already earned a couple of gigs on his own during the week, and this one put him over the top for allowable gigs.

Punishment for making the gig quota was to "walk two tours." Walking a tour wasn't all that tough. You strapped on a seat-type parachute and walked for one hour between two points about twenty yards apart. The seat pack of course bounced off your calves as you walked. Really not much fun.

One can put up with such punishment for several tours, but the painful part of a tour is that it can't commence until 6:00 P.M., and 8:00 P.M. was too late to try to hitchhike from Victorville to Lake Arrowhead some fifty or so miles up in the mountains.

Cadet Newby was crushed by his predicament. He knew he would have to stand up his date, but there was nothing he could do. He wrote a desperate letter of apology to her home address, hoping for a reprieve for a later date.

She never replied.

The lesson he learned there was responsibility and teamwork. Each member of a bomber crew is responsible to all the other nine members. Combat is a team effort. Cadet Newby was learning more than how to drop bombs.

Chapter 3

Men of TIDAL WAVE

While the cadets in training went off to Lake Arrowhead and other spas on their free weekends, the men of destiny would occasionally take a short "Flak Leave" (R&R) to Cairo, Egypt.

There was little else the flyers could do for diversion. A popular daily escape from the dust and heat was a swim in the Mediterranean. The Med became an even more popular retreat with increasing indications that the big day would soon be here, and Cairo street talk naming their target as Ploesti—and soon.

Rumors of a fifty-percent loss on the big one loomed as a serious threat to longevity, and sparked a letter-writing binge that included the regular non-writers.

The card games continued: poker, bridge and cribbage for the most part. Chess players were in evidence, and the stakes in the ever popular sport of crap shooting began to climb. Sort of a can't-take-it-with-you attitude among the betters.

Some of the men were intrigued by a new game they had learned. The new game actually had been around the Mediterranean area for quite a while—some 12,000 years. Flies were caught alive and held underwater until they became groggy. Then they were placed in a row on a table, and a house man covered each fly with a pile of salt. Betters chose their fly and backed their choice with money. Spirited rooting began for their unseen "horses." When a fly finally staggered out from under his pile of salt and flew away, his happy betters raked in their winnings. Certainly different.

A show put on by Jack Benny and Larry Adler helped boost morale. But it wasn't enough for one man, who was unable to shake the fear of the looming unknown. In spite of (or because of) numerous warnings not to eat the fruit available in Benghazi's outdoor markets, he purchased some and stashed it away for use at the appropriate time.

Others found more to contemplate than their fate as they sped over the desert a few feet off the ground. Earl Wescott, a waist gunner on Lt. Melvin Neef's crew, was fascinated by the huge mounds of ammunition left behind by either Rommel or Montgomery as they chased each other over the ground below him. He sensed he was a part of living history, even if a few months late.

On another such flight he experienced a different kind of history as they flew low over a farmer who was threshing grain the way he had studied it in geography class back in grade school.

It seemed as though the farmer had spread a huge tarp on the ground, with a stake or pole hammered into the center, and grain had been spread all over the tarp. Then an ox was tethered to the stake with a short length of rope and driven over the grain in ever smaller circles as the rope twisted around the pole. No doubt this was repeated many times until the grain was all shelled out.

Wescott was enjoying his history and geography lessons, but he knew he would soon be creating some new history of his own.

A uniquely American art form was adornment of US bombers with pictures and words, known as nose art. Nearly every bomber to be flown in combat would have some reflection of the crew's personality plastered all over the nose section on one side. Sometimes on both sides.

Most nose art was applied prior to the plane leaving the States, but some was done at the combat air base. The majority of nose art subjects were pretty girls—some directly connected with the pilot, and some just an eyeful with a clever caption alongside. They were all full-figured and most were bare-breasted.

Nose art sometimes was a contradiction with the purpose of its canvas. A four-engine bomber, laden with up to twelve 500 lb. bombs, ten machine guns, thousands of rounds of .50 caliber ammunition and ten men, on its way to dispatch destruction and death on the enemy had a pretty girl named *Sweet Sue* painted on its nose section.

A German fighter pilot with *Shoot, Fritz, You're Faded* in his gunsight crosshairs surely must have wondered what kind of enemy he was engaging.

No one ever wondered *why* they named their planes. They just did. Everybody did it. A bomber containing ten Americans 700 miles deep in enemy territory was a little piece of the United States.

The men inside that small island were still in America, even though they might be four miles above the muddy brown Danube, with an engine feathered, low on gas and an injured man aboard—hightailing it for home. The sign outside said so: *Boomerang, Sad Sack, Prince Charming, Wicked Witch* or *My Gal Sal.*

The USAAF condoned nose art, even encouraged it, although some examples were a little risqué. Permitting a crew to name its bomber was one way to speed up the process of turning ten young men, raised in an individualistic society, into a combat unit dedicated to teamwork. A bomber crew *must* work as a team, if only for survival, let alone performing its assigned task. Nose art was a psychological plus of which the flyers were unaware. They just thought it was nice of the brass to let them do it.

Parked out on the flight strip was a beat-up Baker Two Dozen named *Li'l Joe*, dressed in pink, as were all of the planes in the two North African bomb groups. The desert pink color of the fuselage and wings was an effort to blend them in with the surroundings and hide the large planes from the eyes of spotters high in the air.

Alongside the boldly painted name on the nose section of *Li'l Joe* was a pair of dice. They must have been lucky dice, as the bomber's pockmarked nose also had numerous small metal patches, covering flak and bullet holes. Badges of honor, as some called them. The fifty-three small bombs, painted in several rows, bragged of fifty-three combat missions against Rommel's desert troops and the flak-defended targets in Italy.

Li'l Joe was ready for Mission 54. The pilot, Lt. Lindley Hussey, scheduled to take this venerable war machine to battle again with Col. John R. "Killer" Kane's 98th Bomb Group, was also ready.

Another man was ready too, but he wore no silver wings. When Howard Dickson joined up back in Dayton, he had stars in his eyes like thousands of others. He wanted to fly in combat and shoot down enemy airplanes. But he did not make it through pilot training, and opted for Officer Candidate School.

He ended up as a gunnery officer in the 93rd Bomb Group commanded by Col. Addison Baker, and stationed in Hardwick, England. Their bombers were painted olive drab as they did not have deserts in England, and OD seemed to be a popular color for Army equipment.

While at Hardwick, Dickson decided he was not really in the war he joined up to fight in. As regular combat crews began building up their mission count to twenty-five for a completed tour of duty and a ticket home, Dickson started a little count of his own. He began going along on missions as an observer.

One day while visiting the Red Cross building on the base, the girl in charge, Dorothy "Mac" McDonald, asked Dickson, "Why do you fly on these dangerous missions when you needn't do so?"

"I have a son, and want to earn a medal so he will be proud of his dad's part in this war. I can't qualify as a crew member, but perhaps I can learn more about aerial combat than just hearing about it," replied Dickson.

Mac felt there was more to it than that. She believed Dickson admired the men who flew and wished to prove he could do their dangerous job as well as they did.

Dickson, always the scholar, had a penchant for reading the classics while on the missions. All the others had some pertinent job to do at all times in the air. They flew the plane, navigated, constantly looked for enemy fighters, looked after the many details of keeping a bomber operating properly while in flight, and dropped the bombs when they got to the target.

They at least had something to occupy their minds for that suspense-filled few hours it took to arrive at the main battle. Sometimes they had a skirmish with German fighters en route to enliven the trip.

Meanwhile, Dickson the passenger kept his mind occupied by reading Shakespeare, the *Iliad* and other classics—certainly not the normal fare for one flying in a bomber on the way to enter the flak skies over a sub pen or war factory.

Life photographers took a shot of a group of combat flyers squeezed together like sardines and looking up at the camera. Howard Dickson was proud to be right in the center of the men he admired and wanted to be like.

The photo later became the entire cover of the July 26, 1943 issue of *Life*, with the lower right corner of the title block pointing to the man who would fly into the enemy's fiercely defended *Festung Germany* reading *Much Ado About Nothing*. The caption read, "8th Air Force Bombers."

Dickson was not aware that his face was so prominently displayed on *Life*'s cover all over America as he sat in his tent contemplating the coming battle. This low-level mission would be number 21 and he knew he would make his son proud his dad was on this one.

He was to fly with Lt. Enoch Porter on *Euroclydon*, a fitting name for a bomber carrying such a scholarly passenger. *Euroclydon*, a Greek word meaning "the storm," was no doubt the most cultured nose art name in the USAAF.

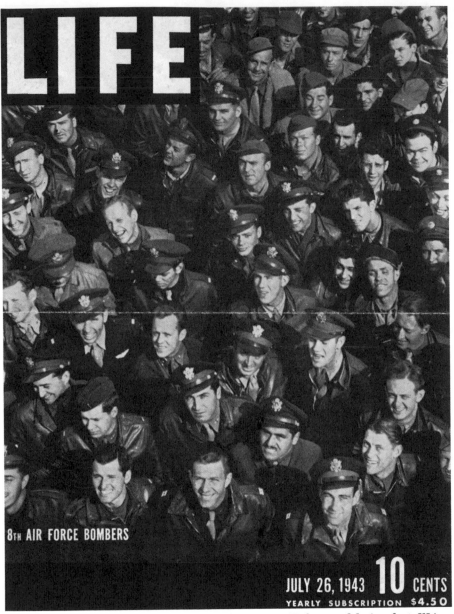

LIFE

8TH AIR FORCE BOMBERS

JULY 26, 1943 **10** CENTS
YEARLY SUBSCRIPTION **$4.50**

Ground officer Lt. Howard L. Dickson makes cover of Life *a week before he is KIA on a bombing mission to Ploesti. The lower right corner of the title block points to Dickson.*

Sgt. George Fulfer's plane had a name less appropriate to his role in life—*Fertile Myrtle*. Fulfer had an abiding faith in God and country, and had long wrestled with the thought of going into the ministry at war's end.

In early July the crew of *Fertile Myrtle* had finished its required 300 hours of combat (different rules than in the Eighth AF) and had been taken off

The B-24 Fertile Myrtle.

The B-24 Stinger *before the mission.*

combat duty. Fulfer was elated. He and his crew had survived the hell of those combat missions.

He gave heartfelt thanks to his God for his protection during those terrible months of stark fear and near panic on many occasions. He was overwhelmed with a feeling of deep pride and true patriotism that he had served honorably and courageously under the most adverse conditions imaginable. He had contributed to the cause of freedom and had seen the hated Nazis pushed farther and farther from the periphery of the extended war.

He asked himself, if he had had a choice would he have flown those 300 hours of aerial combat. His answer bothered him. He wasn't sure he would have. However, since he did do it he was glad for the opportunity to serve his country.

Then came the news. They would not be going home. The Air Forces had other plans for him. No more regular combat missions, but something else. About that time the low-level flying practice had begun.

Fulfer felt that his country had let him down and had reneged on its commitment to him. He was frustrated and angry. He recalled how unhappy he had been with God in the past for not fulfilling his promises as he perceived them.

He would understand years later that God, as well as his country, had a bigger picture of what was going on, and if they always gave in to his petty whims he would not be satisfied.

In mid-July Fulfer was selected as the radio operator for a cargo flight to Tel Aviv, Israel. On the way back, the loss of an engine forced them to land at Cairo, Egypt.

To the crew it seemed a simple request when they radioed back to Benghazi for a lift back to base. But they received no response; likewise on the second and third requests. They ran out of money and had no clothes except what was on their backs. Frustration and anger once more set in. Is the Air Force letting me down again? thought Fulfer.

The American Red Cross saved them from destitution.

They finally hitchhiked a ride back on another plane, and found out the reason for no response: Benghazi was on a radio blackout due to the practice missions on the desert Ploesti.

The nagging thought persisted that he had finished his tour of duty for his country unscathed, only to be held over to die at some place he had never heard of before. God and country, where are you when I need you? Are you listening? he thought, anxiously.

On the evening of July 19, the day the TIDAL WAVE flyers were taken off combat status in preparation for the big one, each flying enlisted man's tent received a bottle of whiskey. Sgt. Larry Yates was poured a cup of the contents and told to drink it right down. He said, "OK, for a price I'll do it," and collected two dollars in Egyptian money.

He awoke the next morning with dirt all over his hands and feet, and with a big head. He was told that after he chug-a-lugged the whiskey he wandered outside into the dark without a stitch of clothes on and finished digging a trench near the tent.

Later that morning they were all called in to operations and told they were to begin practicing low-level bombing. His plane, *The Lady Jane*, needed an engine change and other repairs. He spent the dead time taking his two machine guns out of his tail turret and cleaning them, and then helped change the spark plugs on the No. 3 engine.

The hot days and cool nights left the guns wet, and rust began to form. Yates cleaned his guns nearly every day because he knew all too well what good friends they were.

As they approached the mission day everyone's nerves were on edge, and tempers began to shorten. This reaction manifested itself in many ways. Yates's pilot, Lt. William E. Meehan, normally mild mannered, happened to notice a lot of dust on the gun frames. The pilot got overly upset, chewed out Yates and threatened to bust him to a buck private.

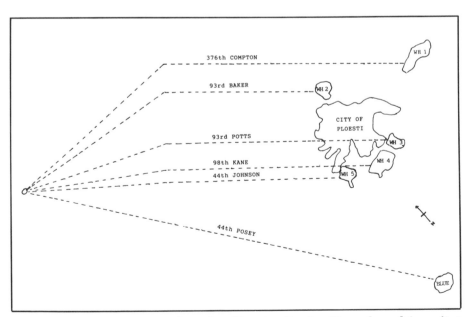

Planned TIDAL WAVE assault on key Ploesti refineries. Time elapsed from first bomb until last bomb was to be less than one minute. Each bomber within a group was assigned its own aiming point.

Yates attempted to explain how he had been cleaning the guns regularly, but the dust on the gun mounts could be cleaned off three times a day, and sand would begin collecting fifteen minutes later. He was in a no-win situation. Meehan was blowing off steam, and logic was no defense. Yates should have shut up.

Instead, Yates said, "You better get yourself a new tail gunner if you persist in threatening me. There is no sense in my being shot down as a private and my mother collecting $50 a month when I can be shot down just as easily as a sergeant and she gets $172."

He was wound up by now, and continued: "You know that crew whose tail gunner got shot in the neck by another B–24 by mistake? Well, they would love to have me. The day you bust me is the day I join their crew."

The pilot stomped out of the tent, leaving Yates to wonder where matters stood.

The night before the mission Meehan told Yates, "You are still a staff sergeant, and will remain so until we return."

In another tent at a nearby air base a more tranquil scene was transpiring. Andy Opsata, a twenty-two-year-old veteran of the bombing wars, sat on his bunk contemplating his life for the past ten years.

Opsata had grown up in the Depression days when a trip to the movies was an event. Aside from the cliff-hanging serials of the day, he was impressed with the "Movietone News" showing airplanes flying off America's first two aircraft carriers, the *Lexington* and *Saratoga*, and then landing back on their decks. Surely those pilots were supermen, he thought. He dreamed of one day being one of those supermen.

In those days of the early thirties any shots of a plane landing on a carrier had the lower half of the plane blacked out so the audience did not know how the plane got stopped. As a young twelve-year-old, Opsata had it figured out, though. He reasoned there had to be a hook on the tail of the plane that snagged a large rubber band of some sort. He was not familiar with the large elastic cables, such as were being used to do just that.

In June 1941 Opsata joined the newly formed United States Army Air Forces. After Pearl Harbor there was a demand for flight training candidates. Despite one of the requirements being two years of college, he managed to pass some special tests and was accepted and sent to Santa Ana, California, and his pay went from $21 a month to $75. I must be dreaming! he thought.

Opsata soon found himself at a flying school, sitting in the cockpit of a beautiful blue and yellow Stearman, goggles, helmet, parachute and all, trying to figure out what the instructor was trying to teach him. Could I too become a superman? he wondered. One day the instructor showed him his first pilot's license; it was signed by Wilbur Wright. The impressed cadet vowed to listen to everything this man had to say.

After graduation and the pinning on of his silver wings, Opsata was sent to four-engine school, and then to Davis-Monthan Field at Tucson where he was given a crew of nine other flyers. What are they thinking of? he murmured. Entrusting all these men and a quarter million dollar airplane to my hands?

He had this nagging feeling that he was not up to all of their confidence in him.

The USAAF in its inimitable way quickly solved Opsata's self-concerns. They sent him to Lincoln, Nebraska, where some people who had never before laid eyes on him issued the awed pilot a shiny new B–24 and told him to take it to England. Just like that. He was told to choose his own route and times, with no one there to correct any mistakes he might make. Were those superman carrier pilots treated like this? Opsata wondered.

None of the crew had ever been outside of their country, until they went to Newfoundland to await favorable weather to cross the cold, grey Atlantic.

When they arrived in England and landed at the air base of the 93rd Bomb Group and saw all the patched up bombers they knew they were in a war zone. This is for real, Opsata thought.

To top it all off, his first job was to begin flying all over the countryside at low level, every pilot's dream. I can't believe this, he thought excitedly.

Later they were assigned to the 389th Bomb Group which had just arrived from the States, and were on their way to North Africa for an unknown assignment, no doubt connected with the low-level flying.

Now the superman was winging across a land he had known only in geography books. To the north was the beautiful blue Mediterranean, disappearing into the summer haze as it blended into the sky. Somewhere just beyond were Italy, Sicily, the enemy and the war. To the south spread an endless desert, broiling in the African sun and empty of all signs of life. Obviously there is no war down there, Opsata concluded. Wrong!

The war *was* some 350 miles south, where lay the remains of a B–24 named *Lady Be Good*, the bodies of its crew twenty-five miles away. Nobody knew they were there. Two months earlier, returning from a mission to Naples, they had misread a nighttime radio signal and flew past their base and on into the desert until their gas ran out. They were reported Missing in Action (MIA), a status that would remain for sixteen years.

Finally, it was 389th's turn to enter the war. Their first four bombing missions to southern Europe were long ones: 8½, ten, fourteen and seventeen hours long. The seventeen-hour mission to Austria was too long for a return to the base, so they landed in Tunisia, slept in their plane, refueled and came on over to their base at Benghazi. Opsata and his crew learned about war in a hurry. On those four missions the Group shot down six enemy fighters, lost one bomber and had several men injured.

Opsata looked over at the three other flying officers of his crew, also sitting on cots, one writing a letter and the other two playing chess. They don't look like supermen, he reflected, but if I'm one they must be too. I wonder where those carrier pilots are now. Probably full colonels leading fighter groups somewhere in the world at war.

The reminiscing pilot also thought about how he had been a member of three bomb groups in the few weeks since he had left the States. He had just been discharged from a desert tent hospital, where he had been recuperating from an intestinal upset due to some African bugs. He was some twenty pounds lighter and a bit shaky, when he learned that he was on loan to the 98th Bomb Group for the big mission. His crew was needed to man a plane with no crew.

The plane they inherited was a beat-up old bomber named *Stinger*, and it appeared to be the oldest B–24 in the Middle East. It was the only B–24 in the five groups with the old needlepoint props instead of the broad paddle blades currently in use. It had another difference, as they would soon learn.

Two days before the mission the flying officers not yet privy to the destination and details of the mission were briefed on the target, with emphasis to the navigators and pilots on how to get to Ploesti, and to the bombardiers on how to locate specific targets once they got there.

Bombardiers spent all their free time studying assigned aiming points. This mission differed from high-level bombing in more than the altitude factor.

In high-level bombing only the few lead bombardiers actually used the bombsight. All other bombardiers merely toggled out their bombs when the bombs left the lead planes of their attack unit of some eighteen planes. If the leaders had good sightings and the pilots showed good formation integrity, an excellent bomb pattern would cover the aiming point. If those two ingredients were missing, all of the groups' bombs would miss the target by a wide margin.

On the coming low-level mission, *each* of the 178 bombardiers had his own aiming point. One would have the front door of a power plant, one the left side, and yet another the right side of the same building.

The bombers would not be in the orthodox six-plane box, as in high-level formations; rather, they would fly in up to ten waves. Each wave would have from three to ten bombers abreast. Truly a frightening sight to flak gunners or anyone still around a key building.

The planners of this mission were making it as easy as possible for the bombardiers to locate their assigned targets. Rather than have them learn the names of all the refineries, they gave logical code names to each one.

The five groups would be split into seven attack units when they reached the IPs.

Two of those units would bomb refineries located a distance from the ring of refineries around the periphery of the city. They were identified as Red target (twenty miles northwest of the city) and Blue target (five miles south of the city).

The other five refineries ringing the city were identified, as seen from the IP thirteen miles northwest of the city, generally from left to right, as White 1, 2, 3, 4 and 5.

Because all five White targets ringed the city, only White 3 and White 4 required the bombers to fly over the residential section of the city. Instructions were clear: no bombs were to be dropped on the residential area, and machine guns were not to be fired over the city, even in defense (try explaining that one to a gunner who sees an Me 109 coming at him, and he knows he is in the fighter's sights).

Six of the attack units' bomb runs would originate from the same IP, longest bomb run first. This plan would put all the bombers over the targets simultaneously, at least within a span of a few minutes.

The first waves at each target would drop bombs with a two- to six-hour delay, but the last wave over would drop bombs fused for only forty-five seconds, so all would be clear when they started going off. A few bombs were set to go off over the next few days, which no doubt would add some excitement for the cleanup crews.

The leading waves of bombers had fixed machine guns pointing forward, operated by the pilot so they could pour some additional firepower on the target.

The targets selected were boiler houses, power plants, cracking towers, distilling units and other key buildings. They were not after storage tanks, as the smoke and flames would make it difficult for succeeding waves if ignited by the first wave. Also, they were easy to repair. The prize in each refinery was the cracking tower that produced the high-grade aviation fuel so desperately needed by the Luftwaffe. Knock out the cracking tower and you stabbed a refinery in the heart.

If the mission went as planned the seven largest refineries would be totally destroyed, and would materially affect Germany's ability to wage the war as it had to in order to win. Nearly all of its aviation fuel came from Ploesti.

The day before the mission all crews were brought in for full briefing, and were forbidden to leave the base afterwards. At the briefing they were shown the forty-five-minute training film especially produced for this mission.

The crews learned the overall plan, which target they were going to and which wave they would be in:

Target	Target force CO	Group	Formation order
White 1	Colonel Compton	376th BG	Five waves of six
White 2	Colonel Baker	93rd BG	Three waves of six and one wave of three
White 3	Major Potts	93rd BG	Five waves of three
White 4	Colonel Kane	98th BG	Four waves of ten and one wave of six
White 5	Colonel Johnson	44th BG	Six waves of three
Blue	Colonel Posey	44th BG	Three waves of six
Red	Colonel Wood	389th BG	Ten waves of three

At a large wall map of the Balkans, a briefing officer pointed to the blue yarn stretched from Benghazi to Pitesti.

"Pitesti," he said "is the largest city in the general area west of Ploesti, and is our first IP. The lead navigator should be able to spot it there in the foothills.

"Due east is our second IP, Targoviste, which is in a direct line with the final IP, Floresti. Targoviste is a good checkpoint, as there is a monastery on top of a hill that will be visible at our low altitude.

"Floresti is little more than a crossroads, and isn't on many maps. That is why we have set up the first two IPs in a line to point to it."

The officer continued: "Floresti is an excellent final IP because it is located on a railroad that leads right into two refineries on the southwest edge of the city—a giant arrow pointing to Ploesti."

The briefing officer then showed the routes of the units attacking the five White targets, as well as Blue and Red targets.

General Brereton visited all five bases to give each briefing a little pep talk. It was a talk they would never forget. He told them that if they destroy all their targets the war could be over by Christmas. It would take a land force larger than the Eighth Army many months of fighting to accomplish what they could do in one attack. His words were impressive and over 1,700 men swelled with pride at the realization of their charge.

The general really got their attention when he told them that if they did destroy all assigned targets and none of them got back, the mission would be considered a success.

Lieutenant Opsata, seated on a bomb fin can off to the side of the main group, smiled grimly to himself, thinking, Seventeen hundred supermen.

Another officer strode to center stage with a second chilling announcement:

The B-24 Joisey Bounce.

To all friends of the United Nations. The bearer of this letter is in the service of the British and American Military Air Forces. Treat him well—guard him from harm—give him food and drink. Help him to return to the nearest place where there are British and American troops and you will be rewarded.

ROUMANIAN

Catre prietenu Naliunilor Unite : Purtatorul acestei scrisori este in serviciul Aviatiei militare Engleze (Americane). Pourta te bine cu el, apara-l de cei care ii doresc rau, dai de mancare si de baut, ajuta-l ca sa se inapoeze la cel mai aprcpiat post unde se afla trupe Engleze (Americane) si vei primi o recompensa.

USEFUL WORDS AND SENTENCES

English		*Roumanian*
Good day	—	BUNA ZIUA
Good evening	—	BUNA SEARA
Water	—	APA
Food	—	MANCARE
Bread	—	PAINE
Help	—	AJUTOR
I want to go to	—	VREAV SA MERG LA
Germans	—	NEMTI
Italians	—	ITALIENI
Enemy	—	INAMIC
Friend	—	AMIC or PRIETEN
How many Kilos to . . .	—	CATI KILOMETRII PANA LA

Reprint of actual "Escape Letter" issued to all participants in TIDAL WAVE. The top portion was to be read and memorized, then discarded. The lower portions were to be shown to any Rumanians in a quest for aid.

"Tonight we want each of you to write a last letter home and seal it. If you do not return from the mission it will be mailed uncensored. Tomorrow morning, place all items to be sent home on the left foot of your bed, with the letter on top. Items to be distributed among those remaining are to be on the right side of your bed."

Fred Anderson, a flight engineer on one of the 93rd's crews, was moved by what he heard and said to a companion on the way out, "There comes a time in every man's life when he hits something big and feels it all over. This is the biggest thing. The target must be destroyed to win the war. The idea is to take the bombs exactly to the aiming points. Coming back is secondary."

There was a lighter side to the exit from the briefing, and it spoke to the realistic, personal and human side of the undertaking. Another flyer emerging from the briefing tent was reading a mimeographed sheet given out at the briefing.

"There are some pretty good Rumanian phrases here," he said, "but I can't find 'where's the john?'"

"By the time you have to use that vocabulary sheet you won't need the john anymore," said his companion.

It was the night of July 31, 1943, and a mighty air armada slept, as it gathered strength for its daring assault on that taproot of German might.

Collectively it might have slept, but for most of the over 1,700 individuals in those dust-infested tents, sleep was slow to come. In the past many of them had often said that they loved to go on combat missions just to get a respite from that pesky red dust that even got in their teeth. It would be a safe bet that such a statement was not made by anyone this night.

It had been a beautiful purple twilight evening in Ploesti. The Grigorescu family all had taken their Saturday baths and were safe in bed as the North African warriors were wrestling with themselves and their God.

Ioan looked forward to attending a birthday party the following afternoon. He was to meet his best friend after church, have some ice cream at a local shop and then go on to the party.

General Brereton was a disappointed soldier as he sat with General Ent, Colonel Kane and Colonel Compton at a hastily called night meeting. That afternoon he had told the 1,700 men he would lead them into battle. It was to be the proudest moment of his military life. But just hours earlier General Arnold in Washington had ordered him not to go on the mission.

General Ent, who had planned to fly with Colonel Kane in the number four position in the group procession over the Balkans, was elevated to mission commander, and would fly with Colonel Compton's lead group. He would be a passenger on Compton's plane, which was a couple of planes back from the actual lead plane.

While they were meeting, all of the bombers were being loaded with either four 1,000 lb. or six 500 lb. bombs, extra cans of ammunition, and the two bomb bay tanks were each being filled with 400 gallons of extra gas. The 2,500 mile round trip would have been impossible without the extra fuel. At that, many were nervous about having enough fuel to get back.

The planes at each air strip were parked in a row, but cocked at forty-five-degree angles, so they could all be started at once and not eat each other's dust. Some of the air strips were wide enough for multiple takeoffs, which would get all planes into the air quicker and conserve gas.

That evening around the camps there were small clusters of men engaged in quiet conversations, whispered lest the enemy hear them. They understood tomorrow and what it might bring. Some of the crew members were giving away personal belongings in case they would not return. This was not a sign of lack of confidence, just reality.

Some of the men were more relaxed than others. Norman Adams, bombardier on Pilot Worthy A. Long's *Joisey Bounce*, had bought the premise of surprise and felt it would compensate for the expected risk of low-level bombing. He was no more apprehensive than for any other mission.

Adams was unaware of the real significance of his plane's name, soon to be revealed. He thought it was named after a popular song of the day.

Lyle Spencer, the pilot of *Fertile Myrtle*, was taking it all in stride. He hit the sack and slept like a baby.

J. L. Hinely, radio operator on *Li'l Abner*, piloted by Worden Weaver, walked out into the desert and looked up at the stars. He wondered how many there were, and whether there were people up there shooting at each other too. A desert sky at night, when the wind is down and the dust has settled, is a far brighter sky than is normally seen in a city environment. He thought he was alone as he spoke to his Lord. But he wasn't. Off to his left was another dark figure, head up to the heavens. To his right, another. None of these men, who felt this could be their last night on earth, were actually alone. They all took great strength from their little commune with the Almighty, who they knew *would* be with them.

While hundreds of men were spiritually engaged at the five air bases, one man was putting a more earthly plan into action to ensure his safety the next day. For several hours he had been quietly nibbling on the forbidden fruit he had stashed away. Now he was gorging himself on his unwashed ticket to dereliction of duty. By morning his diarrhea would be bad enough to require his replacement on the mission.

The scene and attitude in another tent were in direct contrast to the malingerer.

Lt. Jesse D. Franks, a red-headed bombardier on Lt. Enoch Porter's crew, sat on his cot finishing a letter to his father, pastor of the First Baptist Church of Columbus, Mississippi. He had been writing by candlelight, and when he finished he held it up to the light and read it:

"Dearest Dad:

"I want to write you a little note before our big raid tomorrow. It will be the biggest and toughest we've had yet. Our target is the refineries that supply Germany with three-quarters of her oil. We will get the target at any cost. We are going in at 50 feet so there will be no second trip to complete the job. We will destroy the refineries in one blow. Dad, if anything happens, don't feel bitter at all. Please stay the same. Take care of yourself, little Sis, and don't let this get you down, because I would never want it that way. Hope you don't get this letter, but one never knows what tomorrow will bring. My favorite chapter is the 91st Psalm.

"Your devoted son."

Part Two

TIDAL WAVE

Chapter 4

Low Road to Ploesti

Though a thousand fall at my side, though ten thousand are
dying around me, the evil will not touch me. . . .

—Psalm 91:7

August 1, 1943

The bomber's war, they say, is impersonal. Bomber crews do not see the face of the enemy. The enemy does not see the face of the bomber crews. Yet bombers with girls' names adorning their nose and flak guns with pet names suggest an attempt by both adversaries to try to personalize their encounters. The coming air-ground battle would be far more personal than any previous one.

At 0430 hours squadron orderlies began their morning ritual. They moved from tent to tent with a flashlight in one hand and a list of names in the other. As they entered each tent to awaken the men on their list they were generally met with wide-awake crewmen. Few had to be shaken and have a flashlight shoved in their eyes.

As the flyers went outside for their first stop of the morning—the urinal— they looked up at the red dusty sky that passed for dawn. Many thought, "Will this be my last look at this scene?"

A thousand miles north and a few hundred miles east of the red sky, a purple haze was disappearing into a clear blue Ploesti sky. The citizens down below had no reason to believe this day would be any different than any other day, but the men of Benghazi knew better. As these young men from America shaved in silence, inner thoughts crowded out any attempt at communication with others. Over half of those flying this day already had over twenty-five missions under their belts. They were well aware the law of averages was not in their favor.

Aside from the normal complement of combat crewmen there were a number of non-essential passengers coming along for an opportunity to par-

42

ticipate in what appeared to be a historical event: reporters, cooks, bomb loaders who wanted to see where the bombs they loaded each mission went, and assorted ground personnel. A strange mixture of individuals on a mission of destruction.

The 0500 hours breakfast was nothing special, just the usual pancakes with army spread, a yellow substance that looked like butter but refused to melt, and syrup.

When Lt. Jesse Franks returned to his tent he piled his personal belongings at the foot of his bunk and tossed the letter to his dad on top. Somehow, it looked kind of sloppy the way the letter landed, so he squared it with the otherwise neat pile of items. He had already disposed of the few items not to be sent home.

As he slipped into his parachute harness it occurred to him that it was almost pointless to bother with such equipment, as you can't use a parachute at 20 ft. There was no hesitation, however, about leaving his heavy flying suit behind. It was summer in Rumania, and his leather A-2 jacket would be warm enough for the short hop over the moderate-height mountains in Yugoslavia and Bulgaria.

The lieutenant's bright red hair formed an appropriate cushion for his grommetless hat, the hallmark of a combat flyer. No self-respecting air crewman would leave the steel grommet inside his hat. Only spit-and-polish groundpounders did that.

The parachute harness was buckled in the front, but the unbuckled leg straps jangled at his sides as the bombardier turned and reviewed his home, popped open the tent flap and slipped through to the awakening day. For the last time? he wondered.

No one ever fastened their leg straps until they entered the plane because properly fastened leg straps were so tight one could hardly stand upright. Loose leg harnesses during a parachute jump could make a soprano out of a man. Tight leg harnesses provide a seatlike arrangement that makes bailing out reasonably comfortable.

The day before, pilots had received special instructions, positions in the formation, and their group assembly area. They were reminded of possible barrage balloons, and were told to try to catch a cable with the thick part of the wing as it would probably cut the cable. The word probably did not induce a warm feeling among any of the flyers.

Bombardiers had received their target photos, and navigators their special maps, which were folded like auto maps, and showed distances, ETAs and magnetic headings—a remarkable navigational aid, never before used by the Air Forces.

Franks then joined others who boarded a truck heading out to the air strip where his B-24 named *Euroclydon* was parked. The olive drab color of his bomber identified it as being from one of the three Eighth Air Force groups on loan to the desert forces.

His 93rd Bomb Group, commanded by Col. Addison Baker, was assigned target White 2, the Concordia Vega refinery located on the north edge of the city. This third largest refinery at Ploesti produced high-octane cracked fuel and more lubricating oil than any other Ploesti refinery.

Franks's specific aiming point was the front door of the distilling plant, a building he had come to know like he had lived there. He had spent many hours at the model kept in the security tent. He knew the location of all of the other key structures in the vital twenty-two acres that also contained the cracking tower, power house, three boiler houses and numerous storage tanks. The three distinctive tall chimneys near the center of these buildings made beautiful checkpoints for the bombardier, but presented an obstacle course for the pilot.

While in the tent he had viewed the run in as filmed by the tricycle-mounted cameras. This helped to sharpen his perception as to where *his* aiming point was located.

By having a mental picture of all the targets in his refinery, he could head straight for his objective even though he was approaching at 250 mph and only 20 or 30 ft. off the ground. He also knew that if he placed his four 1,000 lb. bombs at the proper distance from the building they would scoot along the ground and crash through the front door of the distilling plant, and explode an hour or so later.

It was obvious that if every bombardier hit his aiming point they would destroy the seven largest refineries at Ploesti.

As Franks jumped off the truck, his mind 1,250 miles away from where he landed, he was greeted by Lt. Enoch Porter, the pilot of *Euroclydon*. "Jesse, are you ready?" Porter asked.

The big redhead just smiled and said, "Ready as I'll ever be. The Traveling Circus is gonna wow 'em in Ploesti today."

The previous period of self-centered reflections was quickly replaced by nervous chatter and small talk among the crew members. "Don't you ever shine your shoes?" had little relevance to the 2,500 mile bombing mission coming up.

As Lt. Howard Dickson walked up and kicked a tire, Porter asked, "Larry, you kick that tire like an old pro. How many missions for you?"

"This will be number 21," answered Dickson.

Porter just shook his head. "Will they send you home when you hit 25?"

"I doubt it," Dickson replied.

"What are you reading this trip?" asked Porter.

Dickson held up a book, "Shakespeare's *As You Like It*."

"Isn't that the one about some free spirited people in a forest living the way they 'like it'?" asked Porter.

"That's it," said Dickson.

"Well, don't get too deeply involved. We're going in on the first wave," instructed Porter.

"Should be interesting," Dickson said.

"Yeah, interesting," agreed Porter.

The other half of Baker's group would be led by Maj. Ramsey Potts with fifteen planes in an attack on White 3, Standard Petrol and Unirea Sperantza, a small refinery, but containing modern cracking and lubricating oil facilities.

Over at Col. Keith Compton's 376th Bomb Group, known as the "Liberandos," an unusual event took place.

Lt. John Palm alighted from his truck about 20 ft. from a bomber named *Brewery Wagon* and glared at it. This beat-up wreck was disliked by all who ever flew it. Always something wrong. Every time Palm had flown this bucket of bolts he got shot up. Mostly it was a gas hog, the worst reputation any plane could ever earn. Gas consumption was a subject dear to any pilot's heart. Gas got you home. A lack of gas got you in a parachute, in a cornfield or dead.

Amid some mumbling, Palm bent down and picked up three stones. As his amazed crew looked on he pitched them at the hexed bomber one at a time.

"Take that! And that! And that!" Palm said.

Somewhat satisfied, he went over and gave the right landing gear tire its perfunctory kick.

The enlisted men then started the customary trek, like an army of ants; each man carried the battle essentials from the squadron tent to the plane. They carried parachute chest packs, flak suits, Mae West life jackets and escape kits to outfit the entire crew. And of course, a case of K rations, that culinary highlight of World War II.

Each man made several trips. As the enlisted man doling out escape kits handed one to the navigator he said, "Lieutenant Wright, I know you will never get us lost, but just in case, here is your escape kit."

Wright just smiled and replied, "Thanks. I never figured I would ever need one of these so I've never looked inside one before." He opened the kit and peered in.

"Let's see what we have here: a hacksaw blade . . . I can saw my way out of prison. A map of the Balkans . . . looks more like a fancy hankie. A lot of U.S. dollar bills . . . I'll be a big spender. A metal button . . . this is the compass you hang by a thread. . . . Where are you gonna . . . ahhh, here's the thread . . . they think of everything, don't they!" He put the items back into the kit.

Palm walked up and said, "That may not look like much, but I know a guy who walked out of France and used every item in that kit . . . so be thankful. You may need it."

The flight engineer, however, was exempt from the pack rat detail as he worked with the pilot and co-pilot reviewing the checklist to prepare a B–24 for flight. With his head stuck out of the top hatch he vocally confirmed the movements of rudders, elevators and ailerons as activated by the pilots. He checked the gas gauges—just to be sure his plane wasn't forgotten.

Each gunner checked over his guns and made certain the ammo belts were properly positioned, and the ammo cans were full. Every plane carried extra boxes of ammo belts. In addition there were two Thompson submachine guns in the waist section for added strafing power, a show of poetic justice for the slogan of World War I German pilots —*Gott strafe England,* which meant "God punish England."

The bombardier checked the six 500 lb. bombs in the rear bomb bay, three on each side. He made certain they were properly attached to the bomb shackles, and the fuses had the safety pins in place. No one wanted an armed bomb aboard at takeoff. He also marveled at the two 400 gallon auxiliary gas tanks in the front bomb bay, thinking, What a prize for a German fighter pilot! We are indeed a flying time bomb.

He then crawled through the tunnel to the nose section, where he stashed his target photos and E6–B computer. He idly thought to himself, I hardly need this stuff. I know exactly where my aiming point is and where all the nearby checkpoints are.

Their target was the American-owned Romano Americana refinery (White 1), located three miles east of the city. It was the third most important refinery at the Ploesti complex, with a high cracking capacity; a third of its monthly capacity was aviation gasoline.

The left side of the cracking tower was his assigned aiming point. The cluster of six tall chimneys around the target bothered all of them, but it was decided they could lay their bombs in front of it and pull up in time to miss the chimneys. He had memorized the area and his line of attack so well it was ingrained in his mind.

The 98th Bomb Group, the "Pyramiders," commanded by Col. John R. "Killer" Kane, was abuzz with excitement. Their group would take the largest force to Ploesti—forty-four planes—to destroy the largest refinery in Europe. The modern Astra Romana refinery (White 4) had a monthly capacity of 167,000 tons, which included thirty-two percent of Ploesti's aviation gasoline production.

Located on the southern edge of the city and at the end of the railroad tracks coming from Floresti, it would be easy to find. The 200 storage tanks scattered throughout the premises would also help to identify it.

A bonus at this target would be the Phoenix-Orion refinery, completely surrounded by Astra Romana. While small, this refinery contained modern equipment and one of the few lubricating oil plants in the area.

The dozen smokestacks interspersed among the prime aiming points would add to the excitement of hitting this premium target.

Henry Lasco, pilot of *Sad Sack II* in Col. Leon Johnson's 44th Bomb Group, the "Eight Balls," watched the second hand of his watch creep to straight up at 0545 hours. When it reached 12 he would start his engines. Only one problem: his radioman had taken sick ten minutes earlier and had to be removed from the crew. A replacement was on his way. Just as the second hand reached its goal he felt a tap on his shoulder. It was a grinning radioman reporting for duty.

"Thought I was going to miss this one, sir."

The pilot's "Welcome aboard, sergeant" was drowned out by the blast of the first powerful Pratt & Whitney 1,250 hp engine starting up. The man standing behind the engine took his poised fire extinguisher to a position behind another engine and waited for its blast. This precaution was necessary when starting a B–24 engine, as they have been known to catch fire at start-up.

The 44th Bomb Group was split into two attack units; Johnson would lead eighteen planes into White 5, the Columbia Acquila refinery containing modern cracking facilities that mission planners wanted destroyed.

Deputy leader Col. James Posey would lead twenty-one planes into Blue target, Creditul Minier, located in Brazii some five miles south of Ploesti. Although a relatively small refinery, the prize here was the only high-octane gasoline plant at Ploesti.

Bombardier Al Romano was going to a target that almost had his last name. The Steaua Romana refinery was in Campina, twenty miles northwest of Ploesti. The others kidded him about going to bomb his cousins.

This third largest refinery in Europe boasted a large cracking facility for the important production of aviation gasoline. It was the only important paraffin plant in Rumania.

Romano's aiming point was the left front of the steam boiler plant. About 50 ft. to the left of the plant was one of two extremely tall chimneys which were like goal posts, only about 200 ft. apart. With luck, a B–24 could fly between them after dropping its bombs.

Flying between chimneys was a problem to be faced by many of the pilots in about five hours, but the immediate problem was to get all the overloaded bombers off the ground.

Wongo Wongo *at rest before the fatal mission.*

Wongo Wongo, *the first bomber to take off and mission lead, crashed into the sea.*

Each plane carried 3,100 gallons of gasoline and well over 4,000 lbs. of bullets, general purpose bombs and incendiary bombs (to be thrown out waist windows by the busy waist gunners).

Ground defenders would be facing a bullet-shooting, bomb-dropping demon like never faced before.

Designers of the B–24 would have been appalled at the extent of the weight overload this day. The entire force carried more firepower than B–24s were ever designed to carry.

As bombers lined up for takeoff, gasoline trucks topped off the gas tanks with about ten minutes of additional fuel.

A motorist may think of his gas tank as having so many gallons of gas remaining and be on the lookout for a service station, but there were no service stations in the unfriendly skies of the Balkans.

There is a camaraderie between the ground crew and the flying crew of each bomber. The flyers know their lives depend on the skill and care of the ground crew.

The ground crewmen love their plane and the men who they trust to bring it back each day. When the crew chief gives his stamp of approval on a plane the pilot trusts his opinion. He bets his life on it.

Obviously it is rougher out there being shot at by flak and fighters, but there is much to be said for the anguish the ground crews go through as they vicariously fly the mission from their home base. When the planes begin returning from a mission, the respective ground crews scan the skies for *their* plane. They wait anxiously at hardstands for their plane to land and pull up.

The first concern is for the wounded aboard; and then comes the pilot's report on known battle damage. When a plane fails to return, it is like a death in the family.

On this day there were tears in the eyes of crew chiefs as they waved what might be a final goodbye to the air crews.

One hundred seventy-eight fully loaded bombers were in various stages of readiness at five air strips; America's newest and most efficient bomber was preparing for its daring and unprecedented assignment: a mass assault on the principal source of Hitler's oil.

Lieutenant Lindley P. Hussey had revved up all four engines when suddenly No. 4 cut out. The distraught pilot, with a mental picture of the group taking off without him, frantically motioned to ground crew chief Sgt. Stuart L. Floyd to come up to the cockpit. When Floyd arrived he immediately saw the problem. The co-pilot had inadvertently knocked off the switch to that engine. Hussey felt like kissing the crew chief, but settled for a smile of thanks. Now he was going to Ploesti!

Mission leader 1st Lt. Brian W. Flavelle of the 376th was living on borrowed time, and wondered if he would ever see his four-month-old son. Four days earlier he had crash-landed his plane in Sicily, and returned by fishing boat to Malta, and then by air back to his base. This would be his twenty-ninth combat mission.

His navigator, Lt. Robert W. Wilson, had been given special briefing and special maps on how to find Ploesti after flying 1,250 miles, many at treetop level. The deputy lead navigator was the only other person to get this special briefing. All the other navigators received routine briefing.

At 0700 hours Flavelle shoved the four throttles forward to full power on a bomber named *Wongo Wongo*, and TIDAL WAVE was under way. All of his group made it off the ground without undue incident, but the mission was fraught with disaster from the outset.

Over at the 98th one of the last planes to take off, *Kickapoo*, lost an engine just as it left the ground. The pilot could not gain altitude with his overloaded bomber, and turned into a cloud of red dust for a blind emergency landing. His plane hit a telephone pole in the midst of the dust cloud, crashed and burned. Only two men survived the crash.

Another bomber of the 98th named *Northern Star* nearly suffered the same fate. On the last desert practice mission bombardier Bob Judy had invited two English flak gunners to go along for the ride.

They had the ride of their lives when the plane began to shake violently and pilot Glenn Underwood had difficulty maintaining control. The problem was caused by the elevator trim tab coming loose and flapping free.

When ground crewmen had fixed the trim they left it in the extended position, rather than setting it back to normal, and the omission went unnoticed in the preflight procedure.

This mis-positioned trim caused a horrendous takeoff for the overloaded bomber. They barely made it into the air at the end of the runway. Fortunately Underwood recognized the problem at once and instructed the co-pilot to reset the trim.

At the 389th base, waist gunner Earl Wescott was looking forward to his fourth mission. On his third mission, his plane had been shot up over the Straits of Messina, and pilot Melvin Neef had to crash-land on Malta.

They were given a replacement plane with an enviable name—*Boomerang*. There was just one problem with *Boomerang*. Its No. 4 engine would not start, and even a boomerang must be complete if it is to come back. Key people examined the engine and were ready to scrub the plane and crew in favor of one of the several standby planes with anxious crews aboard.

Neef finally got the reluctant engine going, and they were ordered to get in line with the others for the takeoff.

It was a busy sky over Benghazi that morning as each of the five individual bomb groups circled, their sizes increasing as succeeding planes joined them in formation.

Fully assembled, each group took its assigned place in the loose column for the route out. Dust at non-asphalt runways caused three groups to be late taking off. Within the groups the planes flew in loose formation because tight formation, so important for fighter protection, was too gas-consuming for this long flight.

The plan was to climb on course across the Mediterranean to an altitude of 2,000–4,000 ft. to a point about 125 miles south of Corfu, Greece, and then skirt the island so as to avoid the spotters expected to be there.

Northwest of Corfu they would begin a climb to 11,000 ft. to clear the mountains, and then head northeast across Yugoslavia and leave Bulgaria at Lom on the Danube.

When they reached the Danube they would descend on course to a low altitude and hold it until they neared the first Initial Point at Pitesti, in the foothills of the Transylvanian Alps where they blend with the Carpathians some fifty-eight miles west of Ploesti. They would stay low enough to avoid the mountain radar stations and still be high enough for pilotage navigation to Pitesti.

The planners were studiously trying to bypass the expected heavy flak battery concentration south of the city.

The 389th would be the last group to reach Pitesti, where it would take a northeasterly route to its final IP in the Carpathians about thirteen miles northwest of Campina, the home of Red target, located some twenty miles northwest of Ploesti. From the IP they would take a heading of 150 degrees and follow a well-defined valley right into Red target. As they say, You can't miss it.

As the other four groups reached Pitesti they would turn east toward *their* final IP, the Floresti Power Station, which was thirteen miles northwest of Ploesti. At their IP the White forces would spread out and take a heading of 127 degrees to their five targets and Blue force would take a 132 degree heading to Blue target, some five miles south of Ploesti.

The sixty miles to the final IP would be over relatively uninhabited mountainous wasteland, probably free of flak guns, and very supportive of the incursion's surprise.

Both elements would fly at a minimum altitude of 100 to 300 ft. over the foothills. Admittedly this low altitude would make navigation difficult, but the planners had stumbled onto a bit of luck when they noted the town of Targoviste, Rumania, lay midway between Pitesti and the Floresti Electric Power Station IP, the start of the bomb run.

Small as it was, the power station *could* be found by low-flying bombers with the help of this checkpoint, Targoviste, and its own unique landmark. On a hill just outside the city stood a centuries-old monastery.

The power station was about two thirds of a mile west of the Baicoiu Railway station on the Ploesti-Campina-Brasov Railway, and had a dozen or so houses in the area. This small, isolated power station stood all alone in the rich oil fields northwest of Ploesti, and would have been nearly impossible to find without the sixty-mile arrow pointing from Pitesti through Targoviste.

The attackers were blessed with a second giant arrow, thirteen miles long. This one was a railroad track pointing from the Floresti Power Station to the target.

When the attack forces made their turns at the IP to start the bomb run, they would change from route formation to their company fronts of three, six or ten planes for the run in.

Within each wave the bombers would fly wingtip to wingtip, with each wave close upon the preceding wave. The plan was to get all the bombers over the target in less than a minute.

All White forces were to continue on course after dropping their bombs until they crossed the railroad tracks running east and west. White 1, 2 and 3 forces would continue to hold for two minutes and fifteen seconds; White 4 for two minutes; White 5 for one minute and forty-five seconds. Then they would turn right to a heading of 233 degrees.

Blue and Red forces would turn right as soon as possible off the target, Blue taking a heading of 233 degrees and Red 220 degrees.

All forces would rendezvous at Rumania's Lake Balta Potelel, 120 miles southwest of Ploesti, to form up into protective formations and begin the climb on course to 10,000 ft. to Berkovista, Bulgaria, thence across the mountains to Corfu and on to Tocra, Libya, and home to Benghazi.

It was a great plan, and if carried out as scheduled the invading bombers would escape Ploesti and over a third of Hitler's oil products for his war machine would be destroyed.

After three hours of ocean flight, mission navigator Robert Wilson had brought the massive force of Liberators within sight of Corfu Island in the Ionian Sea, off the coast of Albania. From this point, halfway to the destination, he would give the pilot a new heading for the IP at Pitesti.

John Palm, in *Brewery Wagon,* was flying in the No. 3 spot off the left wing of *Wongo Wongo,* and wondering what on earth *Wongo Wongo* meant. (It was some kind of a bird.)

The official mission leader, Col. Keith Compton, flying in the No. 5 spot, just behind the plane flying off *Wongo Wongo's* right wing, gave the signal to begin the climb to 10,000 ft.

Wongo Wongo responded with a strange wobble of its wing, and a steep bank to the left as it went into an unexplained dive toward the sea. The plane began to pull out of the dive near the surface. Then it went into a tight spiral and plunged into the sea, sinking immediately.

The deputy lead plane in the No. 2 position broke the rules and dropped out of formation to look for survivors. Unable to get his overloaded plane back up into the formation, the pilot aborted, taking home the only other navigator to receive the special maps and briefing on how to find the little town of Pitesti, nestled in the foothills of the Transylvanian Alps.

The planners for the mission had not counted on this development, but the men flying the bombers were used to reacting to the unexpected. Lt. John Palm, the man who threw stones at his *Brewery Wagon* and believed in the motto, "Our job is to be successful under conditions as we find them," poured the power to his four Pratt & Whitneys and moved from his No. 3 position in the six-ship box on into the lead spot.

Colonel Compton, the group commander, flew left seat, and General Ent, the mission commander, sat on a makeshift seat between the pilots. Compton slid *Teggie Ann* from his No. 5 spot (right behind No. 2) to the No. 2, or deputy lead position. He was just off the right wing of Palm's *Brewery Wagon.* Now the box contained only four planes—in a diamond formation.

Palm became the mission lead pilot and young 2nd Lt. William M. Wright was instantly elevated to route navigator. Wright knew the responsibilities of a lead navigator. He suddenly appreciated a poster on the wall at navigation school. It showed several flyers in a yellow life raft pushing away another flyer

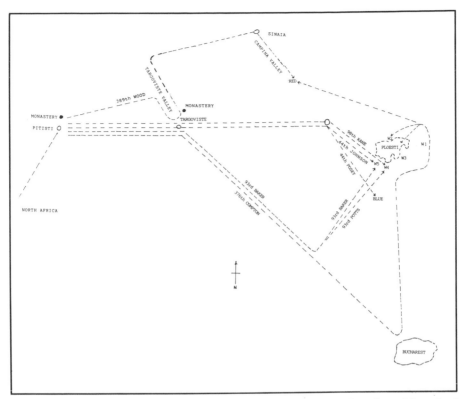

TIDAL WAVE targets as bombed. Compton and Baker turned early and bombed targets assigned to Kane and Johnson, causing confusion and chaos at White 4 and White 5. Wood also turned early, but recovered and bombed his assigned target.

still in the water. The captain read, "There's no room in a life raft for a navigator."

The job of finding Pitesti was *his*. Over 1,700 men were counting on him.

He had been plotting his position all along, as all navigators are supposed to do, and knew exactly where he was. After the shock of his new promotion wore off he gave his pilot the proper heading for Pitesti, still some 600 miles away.

A dual drama was taking place involving *Li'l Joe*, unbeknownst to pilot Hussey. As the old bomber, a veteran of fifty-three missions, was creaking its way toward its most significant target, its equally veteran crew chief for all its missions was deep into his customary long sweat. Sgt. Stuart Floyd had died a thousand times over from takeoff to landing on every mission *Li'l Joe* flew, and this one was no exception.

His vigilance was interrupted by a summons to report to the commanding officer's tent. There he was told that *Li'l Joe* and crew were to be sent back to the United States for a Bond Tour. As crew chief, Floyd was to go along.

As exciting as the new plans were, his main concern was simply to get his crew and plane home safely.

As news of *Li'l Joe*'s new assignment was being given to the crew chief, *Li'l Joe* was developing a serious problem that no one knew about. The fittings for the gas lines to the two bomb bay gas tanks had come loose, and all 800 gallons of extra fuel had leaked into the skies over the Mediterranean.

The flight engineer came up to Lieutenant Hussey with the first report of the problem. "Lieutenant, if we don't abort and return home right now we will not have enough gas to get back to base."

Hussey's reply was in keeping with the spirit of most of the men in the sky that morning: "They told us if none of us return from this mission, it will be well worth it if we hit the target. We are going to Ploesti!"

The climb on course took its toll of bombers unable to take the extra strain on the engines. *What's Cooking, Doc?*, piloted by 1st Lt. Hoover Edwards, was scheduled for the right-hand end of the first wave of ten planes of the 98th.

The navigator, Lt. John Fontenrose, was curious as to how smoothly the wave replacement plan would work in actual practice. For example, if No. 4 of the first wave fell out of formation for any reason, No. 4 of the second wave would move up. The same for the next three waves. The waves of course did not yet exist, as all planes were in the normal stagger formation of boxes containing six or less planes for the trip to the IP. As the formation turned onto the bomb run it would break up into the specified waves for the run in.

Fontenrose would never know how the wave replacement plan would work. No. 1 engine began acting up, and despite the efforts of the pilot, co-pilot and engineer they could not get it to function properly, and were forced to shut it down.

It was impossible for the overloaded bomber to continue the climb on three engines, so they reluctantly dropped out of formation and returned to the base.

Eleven other planes were forced to abort while still over water and go home. As the returning planes flew under the Ploesti-bound bombers, many flyers exchanged waves. Most of the returning flyers were embarrassed in that situation, and would gladly have exchanged places with the men heading north.

As much as most of the men still heading north were glad and proud to be on this historic, and possibly one-way, mission, many were envious of the ones heading home who were reasonably assured of being alive when the sun came up the next morning.

When the formation reached land, Compton was dismayed to see huge cumulus clouds reaching from below the 9,000 ft. peaks up to 17,000 ft. He could not break radio silence to discuss the matter with the other leaders so he waggled his wings and began a steeper climb. Col. Edward Baker of the 93rd fired a signal flare and followed the mission leader over the top.

The three trailing groups had lost visual contact with Compton and Baker and when they reached the towering cumulus they did not know how the others had circumvented it.

This cloud situation was the second serious disruption not accounted for in the meticulous planning of this mission.

The USAAF standard procedure here is called frontal penetration. In this method, a shrinking formation flies in a giant circle in front of the clouds as three-element flights, in turn, peel off, spread out and fly right through the clouds.

Once on the other side, the three-element flights grow to a full formation in a new giant circle and resume an on-course heading.

Colonel Kane chose to use the penetration method, at 12,000 ft. so as to avoid the hidden peaks, and was followed by the other two groups.

After Kane's group reformed on the other side of the clouds, Kane saw a group trailing behind. Being too far away for identification, he wrongly guessed it was the No. 2 formation, Baker's 93rd, and began circling his group over the Danube to allow the other group to pass it and move into its assigned No. 2 spot. By the time they got things sorted out, without the use of radio, the trailing group turned out to be Col. Leon Johnson's 44th, which joined them for a three-group element that was now far behind the first two groups.

Mission planners were assured the bombers would have enough gas for the long trip. Several days before the mission, they had loaded one plane from each group with a full complement of gas, ammo, bombs and crew, and sent them on a 2,500 mile round trip over the desert, complete with the climb over a simulated mountain and the dropping of the bombs at the other end of the trip. All five planes returned to the base with a comfortable gas supply.

Murphy's law may not yet have been invented, but its principle certainly was in effect, for the second time: the two lead planes with the highly briefed navigators aboard *did* leave the formation; the cloud debacle *did* happen, depleting the attack force's gas supply beyond the tester's findings.

Perhaps a more devastating result of the bout with the clouds was the separation of the force into two elements. The 376th and 93rd were now sixty miles ahead of the other three groups, and neither element knew where the other was. Each went on its relentless way to their common objective, without the benefit of radio communication.

As they cleared the mountains the two lead groups were reduced to fifty-eight planes due to early returns and the loss of *Wongo Wongo*. Navigator William Wright brought them to the small town of Lom just south of the famous Danube that serves as the border between Bulgaria and Rumania. Fifteen minutes behind them were the 105 planes remaining from the other three groups.

Soon over 1,600 American youngsters, representing all forty-eight states, received a surprise geography lesson. The blue Danube of musical fame was in reality a muddy brown, just like the Monongahela in Pittsburgh.

The 163 giant metal birds swooped across the same Wallachian plain that Michael the Brave had crossed some 345 years earlier, and headed for the former campsite of the great Rumanian warrior. In addition to some other obvious differences between the two invaders, the aerial warriors knew what they were going after—the black gold that had made the historic campsite famous.

The contrast of the green pastures, tilled land, healthy looking trees, and flowing streams with the barren desert and its red dust provided a dramatic lift to the men of destiny.

As they passed low over hamlets too small for the maps, many parents and children, dressed in their Sunday best, smiled and exchanged waves with the bomber crews.

All encounters, however, were not met with smiles. As the bombers approached a man and girl on a buggy, the man shook his fist and the girl pulled her skirt up over her head, much to the delight of the men in the sky.

The flyers speculated on what the people on the ground thought was going on. Did they realize these were Americans on their way to war, or did they think they were out joy riding? The visitors in their low-flying planes were for the most part enjoying the scenery, at the opposite end of the beauty scale from that observed over the African desert.

The young flyers, most in their twenties or younger, were an extension of America's march to freedom that began at Concord on Apr. 19, 1775. They, too, were pursuing the cause of human dignity and freedom, a cause that goes to the heart of our national character and defines our national purpose. Less loftily stated, they were out to lick Hitler and all he stood for.

As the modern freedom fighters sped low across the plains the forced joshing and wisecracks tapered off, to be replaced by quiet reflections of similar pastoral or family scenes back home. A pretty girl waving to a young-ster with a sweetheart or wife back home made a lonely heart skip a beat.

Two armies were about to be joined in this personalized air-ground battle of individuals: tense young flyers with their hands on machine guns, airplane controls, a bombsight, or a pencil poised over a navigator's log; equally tense young men awaiting them with hands on their flak gun controls, or ramming an 88 mm shell into the gun chamber. Machine against machine? Or, man against man?

Even the machines represented individuals: Rosie the Riveter built the bombers in Ft. Worth; ordinary men and women at the Krupp works built the guns.

Though crews fought and died together as a team, they were individuals. In one blinding instant of a single bomber's explosion, ten young Americans would disappear from this earth; ten mothers, far apart, would soon each grieve for her son.

As determined as the some 1,650 individuals were to get to the target and make their contribution to shortening the war, they were to a man more scared than they had ever been en route to a target. Most of them were veterans of many flak-filled skies over Europe. They understood air war at 20,000 ft. They didn't *like* it, they just understood it, as bad as the odds were.

Now, as they flew into this new kind of battle, with its lurking, hungry barrage balloons and ensnaring cables waiting to gobble them up, light artillery and pointblank 88 shells, some engraved with their names, and 100 ft. chimneys towering above their bombing altitude, their souls filled with terror.

Sgt. George Fulfer, riding in the top turret of *Fertile Myrtle*, was as frightened as anyone as he surveyed the pleasant countryside, and contem-plated his possibly short future. The previous evening during his prayer for survival he also asked for guidance on his long-range contemplation of a ministerial life after the war.

Suddenly, Fulfer *thought* he heard the voice of God asking him to do what he wanted him to do—to be a Christian minister. Fulfer was startled by this occurrence, and looked all around. Was it a joke? Someone on the interphone?

Finally, he responded with, "God, you know I cannot do that."

God's answer was, "If you will not fulfill the purpose I have for your life, then there is not any reason for you to continue living. Today, you will die!"

God had used a very compelling argument, so Fulfer looked up and answered, "OK, God, you win!"

With that, an inner calm came over him and he knew all would be well for him this day. Fulfer was now the only man in the mighty armada who was no longer apprehensive.

From Lom, Bulgaria, the aerial tidal wave roared across the flat green plain to Bals, an even smaller town of 6,000 located on the Ottetul River at the very roots of the foothills that led to the Carpathians, and eventually to the Transylvanian Alps.

The green flatlands were replaced by deciduous treetopped ridges running northwest to southeast. About forty miles north, and out of sight, was the timberline marking the beginning of the evergreen trees of the alps.

En route from Bals to Pitesti, at about 200 ft. above the ridges, they passed over five rivers flowing through their respective valleys. Along their path an occasional small town would dot a river. Pitesti would lie in a valley containing the fifth river; another town on another river in another valley. Unknown to the planners, Pitesti like Targoviste also had a monastery on a hill just outside of town.

Navigator Wright proved his worth that day, however, as he unerringly brought his charges to their first IP. He was said to be "dead nuts on," a compliment coveted by navigators.

The first mass of bombers made their turn and headed due east toward the Floresti Power Station. At the turn they met the first of several rain squalls they would encounter that day.

The valleys continued to pass under the bombers as they headed east. By the time they reached the valley containing Targoviste, their second IP, the valleys had all begun to look alike from the low-flying, speeding vantage point. But this valley had two important features: a railroad track and river ran southeast. In the mist the monastery landmark would be difficult to see. Had anyone seen the monastery at Pitesti? A valley? A river? A railroad track? All running southeast? These were all features included in the description of the final IP at the Floresti Power Station and its cluster of houses that might pass for a small town.

When Colonel Compton and General Ent, flying in *Teggie Ann* just off *Brewery Wagon*'s right wing, looked through the mist and saw the anticipated landmarks spread out below them, they were convinced Palm's navigator had missed the final IP.

They ordered the co-pilot at the controls to turn right and take a heading of 127 degrees down the railroad tracks. In so doing they pre-empted Palm's lead responsibility.

Ent and Compton were conspicuously in the minority in their selection of the turn onto the bomb run. Compton's navigator, Capt. Harold Wicklund, one of three HALPRO veterans on TIDAL WAVE, knew they had turned early and reported this to the cockpit. The general and colonel ignored his advice.

The other planes in Compton's 376th followed a chain reaction conformity so as to avoid mid-air collisions. They turned in behind their new leader, the silent world of muted earphones shattered by cries of "Wrong turn!" and "Not here!" from trailing, unbelieving, incredulous pilots.

Colonel Baker, despite the radio outbursts, instinctively followed military discipline and made the turn that would lead fifty-eight B–24s to the city of Bucharest, where the Air Defense Command for all Rumania was located.

Mission leader Palm, in his left seat, was unaware of Compton's abrupt move until his tail gunner reported that everyone else was turning sharp right. Palm turned with them. Navigator Wright called and told him they should not be turning at that point. Palm's confidence in his navigator, reinforced by all the cries of "Wrong turn" and "Not here" in his earphone, was enough to heed Wright's recommendation for a course change that would bring them to the target they were ordered to destroy. Palm and Hussey thought alike. They came to bomb Ploesti and that was where they were going.

Chapter 5

Rape of White 4

On a misty, hazy first day of August, fifty-seven errant bombers, some 1,200 miles from home on a mission to shorten the war, lowered en masse into the Targoviste valley.

They planned to maintain a minimum 100 ft. altitude to perform elementary pilotage navigation southeasterly—along the railroad tracks that would lead to their target, Ploesti.

The railroad tracks, however, led them *away* from their objective, to Bucharest some thirty-five miles south of Ploesti.

Pilots in fifty-six of the planes were dutifully playing the follow-the-leader role required by military discipline.

Fifty-six bombardiers and navigators, brains crammed with weeks of intensive memorization of target identification and route landmarks, were puzzled, frustrated and trapped as they crouched in their cramped nose compartments.

Powerless to do anything else, they peered forlornly ahead into the haze for the chimneys and high-profile cracking towers that would reveal an oil refinery. Perhaps I am wrong, each man was probably thinking.

When the Byzantine spires of Bucharest churches came into focus through the haze, General Ent and Colonel Compton finally realized the radio alarmists were indeed correct. Ent then broke radio silence and acknowledged his error to his followers.

Compton waggled his wings and started as sharp a left turn as he dared with a formation of planes behind him, and headed toward where Ploesti should be, some thirty-five miles north.

His twenty-five bombers fell in behind, with all the crew members wondering what would happen next. As the formation neared the southern edge of Ploesti, they were met by the heavy flak defenses the planners had hoped to avoid when they chose the Floresti Power Station to start the bomb run.

Rather than face that unplanned-for gunfire, Ent ordered Compton to veer right and skirt around the eastern edge of the city so as to come in from the north. The general then went on the air again, to release all pilots from the planned discipline and permit them to bomb "targets of opportunity," a tacit admission of the total collapse of the 376th's part in the assault on Ploesti.

Compton's formation came apart and scattered all over eastern Ploesti. A few planes managed to form small three- to six-plane elements. One such element made a successful run on White 2, the Concordia Vega refinery on the north edge of the city; a target assigned to the 93rd.

Another small formation headed west and dropped a few bombs on Red target at Campina.

Some of Compton's fractured group meandered across the city at twenty or so feet above the rooftops and headed south where they would converge over the city with Maj. Ramsey Potts and Col. John Kane coming off White 4.

This particular deviation from the original plan resulted in an incongruous scene: low-flying bombers roaming the streets of Ploesti; civilians on the sidewalks waving to the air crews as machine gunners on rooftops were firing at the flyers. The aerial gunners, forbidden from firing their guns over the city, could only wave back. A gunner on the odyssey observed they had run ten red lights on one street.

While his 376th was taking the scenic tour of Rumania Lt. John Palm, the man who had thrown stones at his plane, aborted the Bucharest run and took aim for where he thought Ploesti was located.

He ploughed through a heavy rain squall, hoping for enlightenment when and if he broke out of it. Emergence into sunlight soon revealed the profile of a refinery on the horizon, and he headed for it.

Low-level bombing has its merits, but a few power lines and tall trees en route make such an attack mode dangerous to one's health. He managed to hurdle all of these obstacles as he instructed the bombardier to open the bomb bay doors. They were on the bomb run. Where to, nobody knew. Hopefully, a target would soon show up.

Another dubious indication that they had lucked out was the heavy ground fire they began to encounter; not just ordinary light artillery and machine guns, but anti-aircraft 88s firing pointblank at them. A fighter plane was circling overhead, ready for the kill. The crew assumed they must be near the target.

Disaster was imminent: they were alone; a surprise attack was now impossible, the defenders by now alerted. The hexed *Brewery Wagon* was stranded 20 ft. above the ground, 1,250 miles from home, without escort, engines at full power pulling it along at 250 mph into the snarling teeth of Gerstenberg's brutal defense.

An 88 shell exploded in the nose compartment, killing the bombardier and the navigator that had brought the entire armada to its objective. One engine was knocked out, and two others set afire. Palm and co-pilot William F. Love fought to keep the plane from going in. Palm thought his right foot pedal was a little mushy; he looked down and discovered his right leg had been partially blown off below his knee. In one last effort to make his statement at Ploesti he pulled the pilot's emergency salvo lever and jettisoned the bombs on a refinery.

German ace Willie Stahman spotted the dying bomber, nose and one engine blown away and two others trailing smoke; he dived on the cripple for the coup de grace, as Palm and Love made a spectacular crash-landing in a field. (Note: A personal letter from Palm, in the possession of the author, uses this spelling for the German ace's name. Another book on the subject spelled Willie's last name *Steinman;* and he was credited with a B-24 kill for Palm's already crashing bomber.)

All of the survivors escaped the burning plane and hid in a cornfield. As Sgt. Alexander P. Rockinson was applying a makeshift tourniquet to Palm's leg, a German soldier cut Palm's watch off his wrist and departed. They were captured and taken to a POW camp, where the pilot was given medical treatment.

Col. Addison Baker, CO of the trailing 93rd hurtling down the wrong tracks, apparently decided discretion was not always the better part of valor.

Realizing the folly of following a misguided leader to failure, he abandoned the 127 degree heading and racked *Hell's Wench* into a tight turn toward the north, where *he* knew Ploesti was located.

This sudden maneuver without warning caused a traffic jam for the other thirty-one planes in his formation. Capt. Ed Baker (no relation), flying *Little Lady* off the left wing of his element leader located farther back in the pack, had an experience typical of the situation.

As the plane in front turned left, it was like a car cutting in front of a driver on a busy highway. All he can do is hit the brakes.

Captain Baker had no brakes and couldn't drop down, as he was only a few feet away from the ground. All he could do was pull off power. Even that option was limited, as too much of a reduction in power would put him on the ground. He feared his momentum would cause his propellers to chew the tail off his leader's plane. After the group somehow made its turn, Captain Baker had to increase power to keep up with the other planes.

En route to the target area they passed over a little lake where the beaches were loaded with bathers. It must have been a military facility as some of the ground people began firing rifles at the planes. A few rounds from the waist gunners soon put an end to that sport. A little farther on the bombers raked a machine gun tower and blew it up.

As Baker buzzed a small town, he was so low he had to raise a wing to avoid hitting a church steeple. Human minds work strangely under such conditions; he noticed the time on the steeple clock read five minutes to three.

The 93rd split into the two attack forces as planned, except they were heading north for someone else's targets, instead of southeast for their two assigned targets.

Col. Addison Baker led his twenty-two remaining planes, with Lt. Col. George Brown off his right wing in the deputy lead, to attack what turned out to be White 5 (Columbia Acquila).

Maj. Ramsey Potts led the 93rd's other force of some ten planes for a devastating unauthorized assault on White 4.

Each of the two attack forces had reformed into company fronts: Baker's in four waves of five or six, Potts's in three waves of three or four.

In the meantime, and unaware of the reception he would soon meet at his target, Colonel Kane was blissfully leading the 98th down the railroad tracks from the IP at Floresti to his target at White 4, the largest refinery in all of Europe.

As Colonel Baker led his force north into the heavy flak concentration, about eight miles from the target, he came face to face with the first barrage balloon of his career. As instructed at the briefing he plowed right into the tether cable, and it separated (as promised), sending the freed balloon on an unplanned trip to somewhere.

That was easy, but there was far more in store for the invaders.

The flak batteries located south of White 4 and White 5 had been alerted an attack was imminent and the observers were looking up into the sky with binoculars for the customary vapor trails that would point accusing fingers at a bomber formation some 20,000 ft. above them.

As the gun crews in each battery looked skyward in anticipation of some welcome duck shooting, they were startled to hear shouts and see arms pointed out to the adjoining cornfields—cornfields alive with four-engine bombers.

German flak battery fires pointblank at bombers.

B-24 waist section in action.

The unique shape of the B-24 added to the spectacle: the high wing and underslung fuselage permitted the main body of the plane to be *in* the cornfield, with the wing riding a few feet above the tall stalks. The four propellers were picking ears of corn in a manner never envisioned by farmers, as the open bomb bays in turn prematurely detassled the stalks in a likewise foreign manner.

The furniture vans, as the German gunners and fighter pilots called the B-24s, flying six abreast and wingtip to wingtip in their several waves, with all machine guns blazing, bore down on the flak gunners.

The surprised gunners frantically turned their cranks to bring the gun muzzles parallel to the ground.

The first full-scale air-ground battle in military history was thus joined: German 88 mm cannons firing pointblank at oncoming bombers who were firing .50 caliber machine guns back at the flak gun crews—David and Goliath.

Colonel Baker soon learned what Palm already knew. The nose compartment of a B-24 is no match for an 88 shell.

Baker's *Hell's Wench* took an 88 in the nose and three more hits from lighter guns, setting the bomb bay on fire, the flames fed by punctured bomb bay fuel tanks. The bomber by now was trailing flames and smoke. Baker, a true leader to the end, eschewing a possible wheels-up belly-landing in a cornfield, jettisoned his bombs from the cockpit so as to keep the crippled bomber airborne and lead his formation over the target, even without a payload on board.

One man bailed out, but his chute did not open. He had no chance, as they were less than 20 ft. off the ground.

As they neared the target *Hell's Wench* took another hit, setting the cockpit on fire. Baker, knowing he could not save the plane, hauled back on the controls to put his stricken plane into a steep climb, so others might bail out. The climb was so steep it was obvious to others that co-pilot Maj. John Jerstad was adding muscle power to the death climb. When the plane reached about 300 ft. four men were given a short reprieve on life as they dived out available openings. It was not to be; none of the chutes opened in time to save any of them.

The flaming coffin reached its apex, fell away and crashed to earth where it exploded, just missing Brown's plane by 6 ft. on the way by.

Baker and Jerstad were later awarded the Medal of Honor, posthumously, for their courageous acts of dropping their bombs early so as to lead their men to the target, when they could have tried a life-saving crash-landing, and for putting their plane into a steep climb so a few others would have a chance to be saved.

Lt. Col. Brown calmly assumed the main lead as the relentless waves of four-engine bombers pressed on to White 5.

Lieutenant Meehan flew his *Lady Jane* into the full force of the ground fire, which included 37 mm and 20 mm guns, not as powerful as the 88s but more effective because of their maneuverability and sheer force of numbers. His plane, too, was mortally hit by several shots and quickly engulfed in flames, which were fed by the leaking bomb bay fuel tanks.

Tail gunner Larry Yates, with his precarious sergeant's stripes still on his sleeves, sat in his little cubby hole that he had affectionately named *Dolores*, his little world of metal armor plating and bulletproof glass that protected him from some of the enemy flak and bullets. He knew from interphone reports that the plane was on fire.

When he climbed out of his protective lair to ponder his next move, he could not see beyond the canvas partition that was intended to cut down on some of the draft from the loose-fitting airplane parts. He fumbled with the fastener, but finally zipped open the canvas, expecting to see the three gunners somehow fighting the fire he had heard about.

Yates was not prepared for the frightening sight before him: the entire waist section was a roaring furnace. His parachute was someplace in that inferno. A thought raced through his mind: What good is my parachute just 20 ft. off the ground?

The sight became more than frightening when he witnessed a pinnacle of human emotion and action. In the midst of the fiery scene were three of his buddies with whom he had shared many grueling combat missions over Europe.

The left waist gunner was standing in the middle of the fire with a terrible look of despair on his contorted face. Suddenly he found a solution. He leaped out the large side window, without his parachute, to the welcome relief of the hard ground below.

The other waist gunner was a crumpled, burning, undulating heap on the floor, body in a fetal position and hands clutched to his face.

A human torch stumbled toward Yates in a vain effort to reach safety. Yates instinctively reached for his friend and grabbed his arm. The arm came off in his hands. Yates fainted.

When he awoke all was still. No engine noise. No wind whistling through the leaky fuselage. No more war. Just the incessant flames. Even *Dolores* was gone.

Where *Dolores* had been moments ago was now a large opening through which he could see the cornstalks outside. *Dolores*, in being torn off in the rough crash-landing, had saved his life in a way he had never anticipated. Instead of going through the wall of flames in front of him he weakly staggered out onto the welcome ground, the only crew member to escape the pyre of twisted metal, gasoline, bombs, bullets and condemned bodies.

His immediate thought was of the others as he went around the left wing to the front of the plane. The pilot had made a wheels-up crash-landing, but the careening bomber hit a tree as it slowed down, crushing in the nose compartment. The navigator and bombardier probably did not survive the crash.

The distraught tail gunner saw Meehan halfway out of his little window, just hanging there. Whether the pilot was still alive he could not tell. The flames were reaching for the pilot and for the No. 2 engine. Before he could take more than three steps to help, the wing tanks blew up, knocking the would-be rescuer to the ground.

As Yates picked himself up, the plane was engulfed in flames. Only then did he realize that the man who would take away his stripes for some dust on his guns had given his life for him.

Realizing that no one else was alive, the lone survivor fled into the cornfield to hide from expected captors. As he peeled off his flying boots and helmet he realized how badly burned his hands were. After a short rest on the ground Yates tried to get up, but found his shoulder pained so much he could hardly move it. He could still use his arm, so he assumed his shoulder probably was not broken.

Low-level B-24 flies through fire and smoke to bomb a refinery at Ploesti.

When Yates found a road and began walking toward a nearby house, some peasant women motioned for him to get back into the cornfield and hide. He was so weak he didn't care what happened to him at that point.

A German squad car drove up and several soldiers leaped out and ran toward Yates, with bayonets drawn. The defenseless American threw up his hands, painfully, and walked toward them.

The leader asked in English if he was a Russian, to which he replied, "No, American."

"Do you speak English?" asked the German.

Yates resisted commenting on the stupidity of the question and replied, "Yes."

"Who are you, and where did you come from?"

"My name is Larry Yates, sergeant, United States Army Air Forces, Serial Number. . . ."

"I said, 'Where did you come from?'" cut in the German.

"Sorry, sir. I cannot give you that information."

"We'll see about that."

After a search for non-existent weapons the leader found a small first-aid kit in Yates's leg pocket of his flying suit, and put some bandages on his head. It was the first he realized his face was badly burned. After a day or so at a first-aid station, he was sent by ambulance to a German military hospital in Bucharest, where he joined some other Americans. There he received daily treatment for the burns, but no food. One of the men traded his watch for six packs of ten-to-a-pack cigarettes. Yates had lost his watch to the first German soldiers he had met.

Later he was moved via a Red Cross train on the king's private railway to the Rumanian Red Cross hospital in Sinaia, north of Ploesti. He was now a Rumanian POW.

Yates shared a room with six other POWs, all seven of which had serious deficiencies, but which were complemented by the working parts of the others.

He was going blind from his swollen face and could not use his hands, but he could walk. The others could not walk.

When Yates wanted to go to the latrine or call a nurse to minister to the needs of the others, one of them would direct him to the door. Even when he summoned a nurse a problem would not be solved, as she could not speak English.

The others all knew each other and talked about the good times they had had in England or the States. Excluded from all that happy talk, and blind, Yates's morale began to sink.

As his sight started coming back he saw his horrible-looking face, covered with Vaseline instead of skin. During one delirious spell he was heard to say, "You know, I used to be good looking before, and look at me now." (He would rue the day he said that. When his face eventually healed the others kidded him about what happened to his good looks.)

He had seen other men who were badly burned and knew how terrible they looked. The fear of such a fate weighed so on his mind he slipped out onto a balcony with intentions of leaping off. A new nurse caught him in time, and since she spoke excellent English she persuaded him that he would recover and look like new. As a precaution, however, they moved him down to the second floor, where she helped to boost his morale.

The other patient in his room had taken a bullet in his mouth and had to hold a can under his chin all the time, so his two good hands were of little help with his roommate.

They finally exchanged his roommate for a fellow named John English who, despite a bad back, waited on Yates the best he could. English would help Yates smoke by putting the cigarette between his puffy lips and removing it as he puffed. They talked of families and former good times. English's father had died just before he went overseas, and his mother died soon after he started combat. He had no one to go home to.

About a week after Yates arrived he was told to go down and meet with a German captain. He was so weak from lack of food he could hardly walk, so two nurses escorted him to the meeting, or interrogation as it turned out to be.

The fat, smiling, polite captain asked him for his name, rank and serial number, which Yates gave. He saw nothing wrong with revealing his home address and an overview of his schooling and where he was born.

Then it started. "What group were you in, sergeant?" asked the captain.

"I'm afraid I can't give you that, sir. All I have to give you is my name, rank and serial number," Yates replied.

"Do you want a cigarette?" the German continued.

"Sure, but you'll have to put it in my mouth for me," returned Yates.

The officer smiled and lit a cigarette, then held it to Yates's mouth.

"Thank you very much."

"Here, take some more and put them in your pocket," the officer said, as he handed Yates ten cigarettes, adding, "By the way, Sergeant Yates, what was your pilot's name?"

"I'm afraid I don't know, sir. I was a new man on the ship and didn't know any of the others."

The interrogator read off some names, some of which were the first six men he bunked with, to which the prisoner replied, "I don't recognize any of them, sir."

"Do you know the letter and last three numbers of your plane? Or the name of it?"

"No, sir."

"Then how did you know where it was and what plane you were flying in?"

"Oh, they always park it in the same place and all I ever did was walk out to where it was." He knew he wasn't making much sense, but he kept on. "The radio operator and pilot were the only ones that needed to know where the plane was parked and what the number was."

The swastika on the German's white coat had fascinated the American all during the interview. He had been struck with the contradiction of that symbol of hate associated with this nice man who was helping him to enjoy a cigarette.

Suddenly the Nazi stopped smiling. His polite demeanor faded as he snarled, "You sure are a dumb fellow." Now the swastika fit the fat man in the picture.

"Go back to your room," demanded the German.

When the flyer got up to leave, the captain called him back, snatched the cigarette from his mouth, and took the cigarettes out of his hand, saying, "You don't need these cigarettes now."

Later a Rumanian colonel came by and asked for the names of his crew members so they could put their names over the correct graves, but Yates refused to comply. After several days of pestering he decided the man might be on the level, so he told him the names of each man and where they would have been in the plane. It's the least I can do for my buddies, thought Yates; now they can notify the families that the men are dead.

About the middle of September his face cleared up, and a look in the mirror showed that he would not be scarred. It took a week of painful exercise and hours of practice writing to get his hands working well enough to write his first postcard home.

Early in December Yates was released from the hospital and sent to a POW camp where he joined hundreds of other invaders from Africa.

During the Ploesti mission Lt. Enoch Porter also faced the devastating ground fire from the ambushing flak batteries, as *Euroclydon* took a direct hit in the bomb bay with its extra cargo of 100 octane gasoline. Fire poured out of the bomber and formed a trail of flames that stretched for some six plane lengths.

Flak from a near miss tore up navigator Jack Warner's shoulder, and before bombardier Jesse "Red" Franks could do anything to help his buddy, Porter rang the bail-out alarm and hauled back on the controls in a desperate bid for more altitude so some of his crew could escape. He knew he could not.

Franks pulled the emergency handle that snapped open the nose wheel door yet permitted the nose wheel to stay in the stored position. This left room for a man wearing a parachute to dive out of the plane.

Helping the injured man out through the opening wasn't as simple as diving out. The plane was in a steep climb, so the escape hole was like a wall window near the floor. The navigator's table became the floor. Franks struggled to lift the injured man and push and stuff him through the small opening, instructing him to pull the rip cord as soon as he got outside the plane.

He then snapped on his own chute and climbed out the hole just as the plane reached its peak and fell to earth.

The injured man's chute opened just seconds before he slammed onto the soft bank of a stream. He survived to become a POW.

Red Franks's chute did not open. His last letter, written to his dad, was mailed the next day and would later be entered into the *Congressional Record*.

Howard Dickson, also on *Euroclydon*, would never see his baby son again.

The determination of these young men from all parts of America, all types of backgrounds, all kinds of hopes and dreams, to perform the task assigned that day—destroy oil production at Ploesti—was demonstrated hundreds of times in the action-filled short time the battle lasted.

The pilot of *Jose Carioca* was a young man of Greek descent, Nicholas Stampolis; his nineteen-year-old co-pilot, Ivan Canfield, was called Junior by the enlisted men.

The final moments of this their first bombing mission are a tribute to all who have ever tasted battle. Five miles from the target the plane was hit in the bomb bay gas tanks, spewing flames far behind. They flew over flak gunners who knew the big bird was going to explode at any moment and, possibly out of respect, did not even fire on it.

The flaming bomber, still under control, flew into the black smoke at the refinery they had chosen for their target, not knowing what was beyond. Emerging, and spotting a building with a flak gun on the roof, Stampolis steered his plane, machine guns blazing, right into the middle of the structure.

When *Jose Carioca* emerged from the other side it had left its wings inside. The momentum carried the fuselage a short distance across a corridor and into another building, which it destroyed with a mighty explosion.

Like the other warriors, Stampolis came to bomb Ploesti.

After taking a time check at the church clock, Capt. Ed Baker headed for a row of eucalyptus trees only to learn they were harboring several pointblank-shooting flak guns. Baker's mind was working off beat again. Though they were traveling over 250 mph, the frequency and immediacy of the 88 shells coming at him made him think he was standing still in the air. *A sitting duck.* He was right. A shell caught the No. 3 engine, setting it on fire. Quick action with the internal fire extinguisher put out the fire, and a tap on the feathering button feathered the propeller.

Extinguishing the fire so quickly was a lucky move, as the bomb bay tanks had been hit and were spilling gas out the open bomb bays.

Bombardier Joel M. Silverman had opened the bomb bays and dropped his bombs, so when Baker opened his side window he got some fresh air to offset the gas fumes from the bomb bay.

When Silverman called out, "Bomb bay doors closed" and closed them, Baker began choking again and called for the doors to be reopened. At that moment the plane flew over a storage tank that had just blown up, and as they barely skirted the flaming mess the heat was nearly unbearable. Had the bomb bay doors been open for those few seconds, the escaping gasoline would no doubt have been ignited.

Once past the fire zone the doors were reopened for a welcome relief for the pilots.

About a dozen of Brown's bombers hit their target of opportunity, Columbia Acquila, doing little damage to any key structures, but setting fire to many storage tanks, evidenced by voluminous columns of black smoke.

Col. Leon Johnson's 44th would have this unplanned obstacle to face when it would arrive at its White 5 target in a few minutes.

Maj. Ramsey Potts had barely a dozen planes at his command as he too faced the full fury of the German flak batteries, now aware that their prey was down at ground level with them.

While Colonel Baker and Major Brown had picked on Colonel Johnson's target at White 5, Major Potts headed for Astra Romana, Colonel Kane's White 4, to unload his bombs.

Flying off Potts's wing was *Joisey Bounce*, piloted by Worthy A. Long, speeding northbound into Kane's White 4 target. Dead ahead Long could see the distinctive profile of an oil refinery in the background, bracketed by two flak towers.

The flak gunners were doing their job, pumping 88s pointblank at the dozen target-poaching bombers, as other gunners fired rapid-fire four-barreled 20 mm armor-piercing and incendiary shells.

The devastating firepower was effective. *Joisey Bounce* was hit in the No. 3 engine, forcing Long to feather it at once. They pressed on in the face of the oncoming wall of flying steel. A second engine was hit and caught fire as they zoomed past the flak towers and on into the target area.

Suddenly a tall cooling tower loomed ahead, and it took all of the two pilots' strength to haul back on the controls to avoid hitting it.

By now all intra-plane communication was shut down and the pilot did not know if anyone in the nose was still alive. Bombardier Norman C. Adams and navigator David Lipton, however, were alive but wounded. Lipton continued firing his nose machine gun, as Adams tried unsuccessfully to release his bombs.

The herculean effort by the pilots averted impact with the structure, but the weakened condition of the plane's engines meant they could not maintain aerial flight. Long lowered the nose so as to avoid the impending stall from the leap over the towers, and dropped *Joisey Bounce* into a cornfield for a wheels-up crash-landing.

The impact of striking the ground at a steep angle and the succeeding jolts as the defeated bomber bounced along in a cornfield not only complemented its name in a manner not intended by the writer of its namesake popular song, but the landing tore off the entire nose section.

It must have been a remarkable sight for the flak gunners to watch the bull's-eye of their marksmanship partially disintegrate before their eyes, the nose section tumbling along in front of the fiery furniture van as it plowed to a halt.

Even more remarkable must have been the sight of a figure staggering out of the nose section some 30 ft. from the burning plane. Norman Adams had somehow survived the ordeal of tumbling along in his little prison. David Lipton did not.

Adams went back into the burning plane to pull out an injured mate, and then returned to help others. Four crew members died in the crash and one died soon after from injuries and burns.

The dazed bombardier was taken to a nearby flak battery where he was held captive, later to be hauled away by other German soldiers. While in the flak battery, Adams was treated to a unique experience. He watched in horror as the flak gunners shot down several oncoming B–24s. More horrifying was the hail of .50 caliber machine gun fire from the attacking bombers.

My buddies are shooting at me! was Adams's reaction.

The bewildered bombardier was pulled down by one of the Germans to join them behind a barricade of sandbags—side by side with the enemy, hiding from American bullets. Strange bedfellows.

The man who earlier had bought into the concept of a surprise advantage, and therefore was not apprehensive about the mission, had now learned firsthand that the roles of the surpriser and surprised had been cruelly reversed.

Pudgy, named after the bombardier and piloted by Milton Telster and his co-pilot Wilmer "Bill" Bassett, took a hit in the No. 2 engine, but it could not be feathered due to a lack of feathering oil. *Pudgy* was able to unload its bombs on a convenient building, and the plane escaped the target area.

Bassett had psyched himself up to concentrate on his job and not dwell on the negative aspects of what he would be doing on the mission. Up to this point he had done very well. In fact, his attention to duty had enabled him to trim the wings quickly to compensate for the windmilling No. 2 propeller.

Their main concern now was to vacate the area and find one or two other cripples to join for the long trip home. As a lone straggler they would be sitting ducks for even the reportedly poor quality Rumanian fighter pilots. It must be noted that it was a poor-quality Rumanian pilot in a second-rate IAR 81 Rumanian plane that had disabled No. 2.

Most of Potts's flight made it through the flak trap, though they all suffered light to heavy battle damage. Several of the planes, however, were claimed by the flak gunners, and never made it to their goal.

The ones that did make it arrived at the Astra Romana refinery in time to face an unexpected sight. As they stormed in ragged company fronts across the largest refinery in all of Europe, below chimney level and with no idea which refinery they were attacking or where the choice targets were located, they saw low-flying Liberators coming at them from the one o'clock direction. The rape of White 4 was on.

The well-conceived plan was crumbling before their very eyes. Pilots from both errant forces made skillful moves to avoid mid-air collisions, as they unloaded their bombs mostly on storage tanks and doing very little damage to the key buildings, although flaming and smoking tanks made it appear a success.

This misdirection of attacking forces posed a new problem beyond the obvious one of not ramming into each other. The forty-five-second-delay fused bombs were being dropped by planes that were no longer in the getaway last wave as planned. Other bombers soon would be flying low over the short-fused bombs, as they lay sleeping out in the open, soon to awaken with a roar.

The blazing, smoking storage tanks caused relatively little target damage, which was not only a waste of bombs, planes, lives and effort, but would make it difficult for Kane's 98th to locate their assigned aiming points on the key structures within the compound.

One of the errant bombers dropped its bombs on the target and was trying to make its escape as it passed low over the city proper. A Rumanian fighter plane stormed in and riddled it with machine gun fire, causing it to go partially out of control.

The stricken bomber was too low for the men to bail out, and there was no open field for a crash-landing. The men inside were imprisoned in what was now a flaming projectile hurtling down a boulevard that ended at a three-story building—the Ploesti Women's Prison.

In a cruel metaphor of fate the two prisons collided with a sickening crash. When the airborne prison and its ten inmates slammed into the ground prison, gasoline from the auxiliary fuel tanks spread throughout the rooms and cells. Most of the women prisoners were trapped in their quarters and died.

Thirteen-year-old Ioan Grigorescu and his friend were leaving church when they noticed the sausages were up all around the city. This was unusual, as they had never seen more than one or two in the air at one time for occasional tests. As Ioan was counting the barrage balloons he heard a loud roar.

Suddenly several monstrous four-engined bombers, flying side by side, appeared over the top of the nearby houses. As the planes skimmed low overhead, their bomb-filled bellies just a few feet above the houses, the flimsy roofs were no match for the prop wash from the powerful propellers. The roofs simply lifted off the houses, shattered into many pieces and fell to earth.

The bomb bay doors were open, so the young boys were treated to a target's-eye view of undropped 1,000 lb. American bombs, as the four-engine bomb carriers zoomed overhead on the way to a nearby refinery.

The boys didn't even say goodbye to each other as they parted and raced off for home. Ioan was so frightened, he ran into some woods and got lost.

As he ran along a river bank, a burning bomber crashed into the chemical-saturated water and set it on fire. *A river on fire!* This heightened his fear and confusion.

Farther along he came across another crashed bomber. Nearby was a uniformed flyer lying on his back, blue eyes open as if he were looking into the sky. Ioan went up to offer him aid, only to discover his legs were shattered and he was indeed dead. Ioan had never seen a freshly dead person before, but he knew the man was dead and had come from the airplane. By now he was bewildered and well into a state of shock and did not realize what he was doing, but managed to find his way out of the woods and ran for home to tell his mother of his frightening experience.

Ioan had heard about the women's prison being hit by a bomber and the resulting fire. The news alarmed the young man, as a friend of his was an innocent inmate who was being held improperly by the authorities.

The distraught youngster later ran to the prison site and watched them bring out the bodies, most of which were charred beyond recognition. He counted ninety bodies.

The press, however, reported only fifty deaths. They had chosen not to report the deaths of the forty women being held illegally.

Chapter 6

"I sent my Soul through the Invisible"

As the drama of TIDAL WAVE unfolded, the small sector of the world stage known as Ploesti's Astra Romana and Columbia Acquila was in chaos: undisciplined players entering the wrong scenes and nearly bumping into each other; disorganized players stepping on each other's lines, as it were, and departing by the first convenient exit. Meanwhile, the main players were waiting in the wings for their cue.

The cue for Col. John Kane's 98th and Col. Leon Johnson's 44th to enter the opening scene of the final act was the power station at Floresti. The well-rehearsed players responded to their cue as they broke out into company fronts to face the opening curtain, unaware that the scene had already started without them.

Kane, leading his 98th Bomb Group to its assigned White 4 target at Astra Romana, formed his remaining thirty-eight planes into three waves of ten planes abreast, and one wave of nine planes. Eight of his forty-six scheduled planes were no longer with them, due to the takeoff crash and seven aborts.

Kane's majestic formation flanked the north side of the railroad tracks that were expected to lead four bomb groups to Ploesti. The tracks, however, would lead only two groups to their targets.

Johnson, leading his 44th Bomb Group, split into two formations. He led sixteen planes in four waves of three and one wave of four in a parallel route along the south flank of the tracks that would serve as the pathfinder to his assigned target at Columbia Acquila.

Col. James Posey led the 44th's other formation of twenty-one planes at a slight angle from Johnson, to its Blue target at Creditul Minier at Brazii, five miles south of Ploesti. His company front consisted of three waves of five and one wave of six planes.

The American attack force, thundering across miles of oil fields on the outskirts of Ploesti on their under 100 ft. bomb run, showed an unprecedented mile-wide company front of B–24 Liberator bombers, armed to the hilt and carrying the potential destructive power to wipe out over a third of the production capacity at this bastion of oil production for Hitler's war machine.

The time lapse between the first and last bombs dropped at each target would be under thirty seconds.

As the 750 players raced along the giant arrow leading to the entry to their battle scene, they encountered three ad libs not in the script—surprises.

The bombers began overtaking a seemingly innocent freight train heading toward Ploesti, and the crews gave it a scant thought.

69

Then came surprise number one. The German defense command, with over an hour's warning, had quickly moved in a flak train to patrol the railroad tracks that had been unwittingly chosen by the planners as a static pathfinder to the targets. The unheard-of flak train was a self-contained mobile unit consisting of crew quarters, kitchen and mess facilities in several cars, along with the main purpose of the ensemble: several box cars containing flak guns.

The sides of these box cars folded away, revealing the first flak guns any of the Americans had ever seen. The big 88s were pointing right at the bombers on either side of the tracks. The bright red flashes from the mouths of the guns were quickly followed by the wrenching sound of the projectile ripping through a $\frac{1}{64}$ in. thick fuselage side and out the other—heard only, of course, by the occupants of that bomber. If they were lucky, the fuses were not timed to explode the shell during its trip through or near the plane.

If it hit a vital component such as an engine or control surface it need not explode to damage the plane, perhaps fatally. Picture a 3½ in. hole in a bomb bay tank full of gasoline.

Several of the bombers suffered battle damage ranging from minor to destructive. Bombers were seen to explode in mid-air, while others burst into flames, forcing the pilot to crash-land in a field. Some crash-landed, skidded along the ground and ended in a burning heap.

The aerial gunners were exacting some revenge as they poured their bullets, thirteen per second, per gun, at the flak gunners.

Here was another version of a land-air battle pitting .50 caliber machine guns against 88 mm cannons. The top gunner on one of the planes called the pilot on interphone and requested the wing be "dropped a little." The obliging pilot dipped the wing as the gunner fired a fusillade from his twin fifties over the wingtip at a gun crew. Bodies came tumbling from the gun mount and the gun was silenced.

Their speed, some five times the speed of the ambush train, soon took them out of the face-to-face confrontation, but the flak guns kept after them as they sped away toward their destination, and more flak reception in a new guise.

The second surprise in Gerstenberg's arsenal was the scattered, innocent looking haystacks in front of them, their sides falling away to reveal more flak guns. So the air-ground battle was on again. This time the flyers were meeting the big guns head on, and the flak gunner's job of aiming became easier, as the deflection factor was reduced to nil.

The head-on exchange likewise was a boon to the airmen firing the machine guns, especially the first wave on either side of the tracks equipped with the fixed machine guns, fighter style. Most bomber pilots secretly yearn to be fighter pilots, so all of the frustrated fighter pilots now manning the lead bombers were in their glory, thinking, I am controlling the triggers of my strafing guns.

The apprehensive crews in the low-flying Liberators were by now convinced that their ace in the hole, surprise, had been exposed.

The third surprise for the onrushing bomber crews that had survived the double ambush added further to their concern that all was not well with the attack plan. The general feeling was, Why are there dark clouds over our targets on this relatively sunny day?

This new surprise was not one of Gerstenberg's creations, rather, it was unknowingly set up by the two errant groups vying for bombing rights at White 4 and White 5.

70

One clue to the black cloud mystery came in the form of a B-24 approaching the bombers from the target area. A second clue was an Me 109 in hot pursuit.

The attack force, to a man, thought they were coming in at minimum altitude, but they soon learned that low is a relative term. The escaping bomber and pursuing fighter flew under the attacking bombers. A few seconds later, as they peered ahead at the strangely developing target, several more escaping B-24s flew under them. What's going on here? the troops wondered.

It finally dawned on both Kane and Johnson that someone had been bombing their targets; the curtain of black clouds between them and their entry into the unfolding drama called TIDAL WAVE was smoke from burning oil storage tanks.

Johnson's company front of only three planes proved to be a stroke of luck as the seemingly impenetrable black wall of smoke parted like the Red Sea and provided a slim hole for the narrow waves to slip through. A huge explosion had literally sucked the smoke from that spot for the brief moment required for their entry into battle.

Like a quick opener in an NFL line the miraculous hole stayed open only long enough for two waves to go through, both of which hit their assigned aiming points.

Worden Weaver, flying a weakened *Li'l Abner*, was leading the third wave, his No. 2 engine losing power from an earlier hit. As he approached the quick opening hole that had allowed entry to the first two waves, he found the hole could close just as quickly. As the door slammed in his face he had no choice but to crash through.

He led his wave into the billowing black smoke mixed with raging fire, with no idea what lay on the other side: A chimney? A building? An approaching bomber? When they came out of the inferno the bombardier located his target, steered his pilot to his aiming point and unleashed his payload as previously rehearsed; then the pilot turned his plane to head for home. Routine, except by then No. 2 had quit, two other engines were on fire, the hydraulic system had been hit and some of the controls had been damaged.

Radioman Jesse Hinely, who the night before had prayed out in the desert and peered into the sky to wonder if people out there were shooting at each other, now wondered how much more he could take and still expect to be saved. He didn't know about the other planets, but he knew people were shooting at him on this one. He was finally able to take his mind off his worries when he responded to a call from the tail gunner and went back to give him first aid for a flak wound.

Others, as they headed south, knew the flaming *Li'l Abner* was doomed.

When the last two waves followed Weaver into this hell on earth more of the planes caught fire, probably from leaking gas tanks.

Lt. Henry Lasco, flying *Sad Sack II*, saw the first three waves plunge into the inferno. If they can do it so can I, he pledged.

So in he went, and joined the others as he too sent his "Soul through the Invisible," as Omar Khayyám, some nine centuries earlier in the *Rubáiyát*, had aptly described their situation.

He also learned about heaven and hell in those few seconds in the flames and smoke before emerging on the other side, just as the *Rubáiyát*, said he would. *Sad Sack II* was surrounded by flames, and as ground fire raked his plane upon emerging, the No. 2 engine was destroyed, several crewmen were injured and the tail gunner was killed.

Lasco had led a flight of three planes into hell and his was the only one to come out. Other planes were crashing and burning all around him. An Me 109 swooped down on his tail, and with no response from the dead tail gunner was able to cut off the right vertical stabilizer with a hail of bullets from his guns. In that sweep he killed the replacement radioman and navigator, and mortally wounded the top gunner.

The pilot knew he could not make it back to the base so he decided to head for Turkey, but with his navigator dead he could only guess the right direction for his neutral haven.

It didn't really matter where Turkey was, because the plane was so difficult to control with the missing rudder it was all they could do to stay airborne.

The two pilots had to hold full right rudder and aileron just to *skid* straight and level. As they departed the target area they went down on the deck to reduce the sphere of fighter attack.

Another Me 109 pilot saw this crippled straggler, licked his chops and dived down to his prey's level. A short burst of guns hit Lasco in the face, knocking him out.

The co-pilot did not have the strength to hold the plane aloft without help. It snapped to the left, a wing caught the ground and it cartwheeled into a crumpled heap.

Lasco awoke in the center of the disintegrated plane; the fire around him was burning his leg. Still in his seat he managed to unlatch his seatbelt and pull himself and the unconscious co-pilot from the plane. Both of the co-pilot's ankles were broken or dislocated.

The pilot managed to do all of this despite his mouth and teeth being shot away. The two waist gunners and top turret gunner managed to crawl out of the plane, but the top gunner was so badly wounded he soon died. The four wretched survivors gathered in a cornfield and watched the flames consume *Sad Sack II* and its dead occupants.

Overhead, the Luftwaffe pilot circled in a victory dance; on the ground, local peasants ripped watches and rings off the defenseless, wounded men. In a final show of contempt, as they ran away, the looters threw stones at the Americans.

Colonel Johnson led sixteen planes into his seething target and lost nine in the battle. While the losses were overwhelming the bombing results were spectacular; the Columbia Acquila refinery, known as target White 5, was put out of production for eleven months.

Despite all of the confusion and misdirection of the wandering bomb groups, Blue target, located at Brazii, escaped the attention of Colonel Baker's 93rd, as it flew by it on the way to Astra Romana. It remained a virgin target for Colonel Posey's detachment of twenty-one planes of the 44th, the right flank of the mile-wide company front of invading bombers.

The Creditul Minier refinery at Brazii was the most modern high-octane gasoline producer in Europe; this coveted prize of the TIDAL WAVE planners was assigned to Posey because his experienced attack force was considered equal to the assignment of destroying specific buildings by specific bombers at this key target.

Flak tower gunners near the refinery had already tasted the blood of Baker's fly-by formation and were lusting for more as Posey bore down on them. This time, however, the attack came from the northwest.

The defenders no doubt were reacting, as were many others, to the seemingly clever American plan of attacking from several directions simultaneously; the disorganized bomber force was receiving quiet accolades from both ground personnel and fighter pilots.

Blood-thirsty flak gunners were not to be disappointed, however, as several waves of five abreast bombers came into range of their 37 mm automatic guns. Posey's plane, *V For Victory*, piloted by Capt. John Diehl, had part of the tail assembly cut off by ground fire. A waist gunner was killed in the attack.

The bombardiers bearing down on the target were thrilled to see their assigned aiming points show up just as they saw them in the training movie, and as indicated in the photos they held in their hands. At last TIDAL WAVE was proceeding as planned.

As *V For Victory* roared into the final minutes of its bomb run, two men in the nose section were performing diverse jobs: Bombardier Howard Klekar was peering into his bombsight and calling for minor course corrections by the pilot. Navigator Robert Stine was not navigating, he was firing his twin fifties at the oncoming flak towers.

Between Stine and the other gunners in wave one they cleaned out several flak towers, bodies falling off the towers as all eight guns fell silent. This combined effort of the first wave preserved the integrity of the formation and allowed all of the trailing planes to reach their assigned targets.

From that point on it was a textbook bomb run. Klekar nailed his aiming point at the base of a key building. The second wave slid several 1,000 lb. bombs into a boiler house and a US-built Dubbs still, both key elements in the production of aviation fuel.

The bombs were not destined to go off for a half hour to six hours. Subsequent waves skipped their big bombs into the power house and cracking plant. The last wave's bombs were fused for just forty-five seconds, so the fireworks would be starting soon after the tailend planes made their getaway.

Not a plane was lost on the run in to Blue. Every aiming point was hit by the bombardiers and the refinery was totally destroyed, never to reopen—further testimony to the soundness of TIDAL WAVE planning.

Two of their planes were lost in the general mess of bombers rallying off the three southwest targets and being hit by flak and fighters.

When Colonel Kane saw the black clouds far in front of him, he remarked to his co-pilot to the effect that it was too bad it had to be raining over their target.

After he ran the gauntlet of flak trains, flak-belching haystacks and B–24s coming at him and under him, it dawned on the crusty commander that the backdrop of black clouds was in reality black smoke from burning oil storage tanks.

This was not in the plan, flying a few feet off the ground through thick black smoke. Neither was turning back in the makeup of Col. "Killer" Kane; he didn't know what had happened, but he came to bomb Ploesti, and obviously that was Ploesti dead ahead.

Thirty-eight bombers, in waves of six to ten abreast, flew into the billowing black smoke, none of the occupants knowing what was on the other side.

Behind their curtain on the war was an obstacle course to test the mettle of every pilot: 100 ft. chimneys, tall cracking towers, and three-story buildings laying in wait for low-flying Liberators.

One of the early formations left three planes in the fire and smoke caused by others.

In addition to flying through their own private hell, Kane's crews had their first experience with barrage balloons, something not found at the customary 20,000 ft.

Merle Bolen, a waist gunner on *The Sandman*, was on his maiden combat mission so he didn't even *know* about 20,000 ft.

On the way to the target he was convinced they would just go out, bomb the target and come home. In his naiveté he wasn't overly concerned. Going into this target, however, he soon changed that belief.

As his plane approached a barrage balloon, dead ahead with its tether reaching to the ground, he tried a little body English, so unsuccessfully used by bowlers, to swerve the plane; *The Sandman*, however, was hemmed in between two B–24s so his pilot could not avoid the inevitable, and had to plod straight ahead.

The propeller on the No. 3 engine cut the cable and the balloon soared away. *The Sandman* shuddered and pressed on to the target.

The balloon, fire, smoke and general chaos at the target made a believer out of Bolen; once in the target area he wondered if he would ever get out. Only forty-nine to go! (Bolen did make it home, and went on to fly forty-eight more combat missions before being shot down in Austria, where he evaded capture for sixty-three days and walked back to Italy.)

When *Li'l Joe* lost its reserve fuel out over the ocean it was doomed not to make it back to Africa, but there was hope to get partway home or to Turkey before running out of gas. The loss of the precious fuel, however, savaged them in a more direct manner. A fume-filled empty fuel tank, when exposed to flak and fighters, is far more dangerous than a full tank. One little spark inside will explode the tank and destroy the plane. Conversely, a red-hot piece of flak or an incendiary bullet entering a full tank will be extinguished by the liquid.

Hussey's ill-fated bomber was hit in one of the empty bomb bay tanks and the bomber burst into flames. The pilot, who earlier had shunned a chance to abort with honor, now knew it was over for him. He hauled back on

Tail gunner's view of Ploesti—low level.

the controls for a short-lived climb from their 20 ft. altitude, and rang the bail-out alarm so others might get out. Eight bailed out but only three survived their jump, each of them seriously injured.

The plane reached its apex of about 75 ft. and fell back to earth. Hussey and another crewman miraculously survived the crash, and Hussey was unconscious for two days. Both men, badly burned and injured, were taken to a POW camp for the remainder of the war. Later in civilian life Hussey underwent many plastic surgery operations as a result of his burns and injuries.

The opportunity for Lieutenant Hussey and his crew to take a triumphant War Bond tour of the United States ended in the crash of *Li'l Joe* at Ploesti.

Lt. Wesley Pettigrew, piloting a plane named *Little Joe,* has tasted crowd adulation on the way to the target; he enjoyed seeing people on the ground wave to him en route, but did not view this unexpected show of affection as a forerunner of things to come for his soon-to-be-historic bomber.

Pettigrew's trip through hell was no different than that of the others; it took both pilots to control the plane in the violent updrafts and downdrafts as they skimmed just a few feet above the flaming tanks. The sight of bombers and fighters flying around in all different directions, swerving to miss each other and the tall structures, was mind-boggling. Of particular impact was the sight of a bomber striking a barrage balloon cable and climbing up the cable until it hit a contact bomb. The explosion blew the entire wing off the plane.

He was appalled at the sight of his sister planes being blown up by bombs on the ground. How did they get there? The last wave, with the forty-five-second delayed-fuse bombs, is behind us, Pettigrew reasoned.

As Pettigrew rallied off the target and headed south, Colonel Kane came on the air and announced he had lost an engine and was heading for Cyprus. Any other damaged planes could join him.

A straggler was easy pickings for a fighter plane, and certain to be shot down. Two or three cripples, limping along in a pathetic formation, at least had the advantage of multiple firepower and therefore a reasonable chance of survival. The radio was busy with other crews frantically trying to reform for the escape to Africa. The beautiful route back plan, which called for reforming groups south of Ploesti, was as shattered as the attack plan.

Lieutenant Pettigrew, with little battle damage to *Little Joe,* and no injured aboard, found some formation mates and headed for home. (In 1945 Pettigrew, who survived the mission, was at Pueblo Army Air Field checking out in B–29s when he saw his old friend *Little Joe* parked there—stripped of all its engines and instruments. It had been on a bond selling tour ever since its Ploesti days.)

The drastic updrafts and downdrafts over raging tanks caused some strange antics. Lt. Dwight Patch was airplane commander of a bomber named *Black Magic.* Patch flew *Black Magic* into the mass of seething, flaming, smoking cauldrons as a member of the second wave. A friend of Patch's entered as part of a later wave. Patch's friend emerged *ahead* of Patch. Black magic?

As *Black Magic* broke out into the clear the bombardier lined up his aiming point, but back in the waist section Sgt. John Ditullio was already dropping his bombs. The big camera hatch on the floor was open and the junior bombardier stood in front of it throwing out incendiary bomb clusters.

This is no Fourth of July firecracker throwing. The bomb in your hand is

The B-24 Black Magic *before the mission.*

Black Magic *after the mission.*

armed, which means it will explode on impact (don't ever drop one on the floor).

At the height of Ditullio's bombing the plane suffered a direct hit, pitching him backward between the waist gunners. Had he pitched forward he would have joined his bombs on the ground. The blast that tore away a large section of the rear fuselage also severely injured Ditullio in the face, legs and under the arms. The two waist gunners were also hit. Navigator Philip Papish, a veterinarian in civilian life, was pressed into service ministering first aid and morphine to the three badly injured men.

At the height of the deadly ground fire and general confusion Andy Opsata took his old-style *Stinger* into the thick of the fray, and was horrified to see a formation of B-24s flying directly over his plane, bomb bay doors open. It was his first view of the bottom of a 1,000 lb. bomb.

Opsata dropped his bombs and rallied off the target, all alone. He never again saw any of his group's forty-six planes that had left Africa with him some seven hours earlier. He slid up to another straggler and within a few minutes there were ten wretched B-24s snuggling up to each other for comfort and protection on the long, long trip home.

Sgt. George Fulfer was the only one of the over 1,600 Americans flying into the hell of Ploesti that *knew* he would not die that day. The others on *Fertile Myrtle* may have gained some rub-off effect from his deal with God, but they did not know it at the time.

Fertile Myrtle was the object of an Me 109 attack as they rolled into the target, and Fulfer's faith was so strong that he faced the attack with the calm assurance that all would be well with him that day. Even when a machine gun bullet came through the plane, hit the turret in which he was sitting and tore into his leg, he had a deep and abiding inner peace. After the war, George Fulfer kept his promise and was ordained a minister.

Lt. Harold "Harry" Korger, the bombardier on Colonel Kane's *Hail Columbia*, needed only three more missions for his ticket home, and had determined that if he was shot down on this one there would be no way out, because of the extremely low altitude. On that assumption he decided to make himself comfortable for perhaps his last moments on earth.

The nose section of the B–24Ds and Es was fronted with plexiglass, which created a greenhouse effect. The sun's heat rays would enter the compartment but could not get out. The result was a build-up to a high temperature inside, especially on an early August day just a few feet off the ground.

As they neared the IP, Korger stripped for comfort. He removed his shirt, put his parachute harness over his T-shirt, stashed his chest chute pack nearby and placed his flak vest under him—To protect my family jewels, he no doubt was thinking. He then opened the small nose ventilation hatch to get some air moving in the small, stuffy compartment that was his home this day. I'm in your hands now, God, reckoned Korger.

Korger's flight through hell was a nightmare. When his plane plunged into the unexpected smoke-covered flames at White 4, Korger saw his wife's face in his mind's eye: "Bunny, don't worry. I'm going to make it," he whispered.

As his plane emerged from fire and smoke, an approaching renegade flight of five sand-colored Liberators confirmed the nagging feeling that something was wrong with the picture. Snafu! What's the 376th doing *here?* he panicked. A terrifying scene: B–24s dropping like flies on either side; bombs at rest on the ground exploding, and blasting B–24s out of the air. (Six bombers were lost this way.) Those bastards have been dropping their short-fused bombs on *my* target! Korger thought angrily. Here were pilots who came to bomb Ploesti, trapped 20 ft. off the ground in flaming coffins, making the final course correction of their lives; fiery projectiles, each with their cargo of bombs and ten young Americans, some of whom a year or two earlier may have been pumping the gas they came to destroy, were thus steered into a powerhouse or cracking tower in one final effort to do the job they had been asked to do—destroy the oil production at Ploesti.

The intensity of the shocking scene drove every thought out of his mind, despite the continuing images being sent from disbelieving eyes; the words of Tennyson, drilled into memory during school days, swarmed in to fill the void and occupy every corner of his consciousness:

> Forward the Light Brigade!
> Was there a man dismayed?
> Not though the soldier knew
> Someone had blundered.

The nightmare went on: Colonel Kane ravaging the landscape with tracers from his fixed guns; flak gunners toppling off flak towers; bombers hitting barrage balloon cables, some getting through and some not; fighter planes raking bombers on the bomb run; a fighter plane ramming a bomber, the pilot parachuting to safety, ten bomber crewmen perishing; American bombers swerving to avoid American bombers; a man on the ground running for cover. Few were safe in this bi-level battlefield.

Relentlessly, unmercifully the words pervaded his mind:

> Theirs not to make reply,
> Theirs not to reason why,
> Theirs but to do or die;
> Into the Valley of death
> Rode the six hundred.

(Alfred, Lord Tennyson, "The Charge of the Light Brigade")

It never occured to the bombardier, as those words gushed through his head, that the likewise ill-fated charge of *his* brigade was only ninety minutes' flying time due west of the blunder at the famed battle of Balaklava.

One engine was shut down and another sustained hits that weakened it, so they could barely hold enough speed to avoid stalling. Kane's wingmen stayed with their leader, and two other cripples tagged along to shepherd them to Cyprus.

General Gerstenberg was standing with some other officers at a command post within the city as American bombers flew directly overhead in several directions. His thoughts must have echoed the words of the Luftwaffe pilot who looked down at the same sight and said, "Damned clever, these Americans."

The last plane over White 4 was *Chug-a-Lug*, piloted by LeRoy Morgan, and the defenders made sure he would remember the occasion. The plane cut a barrage balloon cable on the way in and while at the target suffered five direct flak hits. One destroyed the top turret and killed the gunner instantly. Another hit just below Morgan's seat and wounded the navigator. Other hits produced 250 holes in the fuselage and knocked out the radio, the oxygen and the hydraulic system. The hydraulic system operates the landing gear, bomb bay doors, brakes, flaps, nose wheel, tail turret and other components. Morgan showed he had the right stuff even before the term was coined, as did all of the men of Ploesti. He nursed the crippled *Chug-a-Lug* back to Africa.

When Morgan left the target the largest refinery in Europe was in flames, and half of its production capacity had been destroyed. Had White 4 not been obscured by smoke, it would no doubt have been shut down for good. The price for Kane's half victory was twenty-one planes lost out of the thirty-eight making the bomb run, with many dead and wounded brought home by lucky survivors. At that, only nine made it home; the rest of the battle-damaged planes managed to limp to a neutral or friendly country. Several TIDAL WAVE planes crash-landed at those welcome havens. Others ditched their plane in the sea. Of those ditching, some men survived but several sank with their plane.

Col. Jack Wood's 389th Bomb Group fielded the latest version of the B–24. These B–24s had greater range and were equipped with ball turrets, two improvements that suited his group's planes for Red target, located at Campina, twenty miles northwest of Ploesti. The Steaua Romana refinery was farther than Ploesti, and the drag induced by the ball turrets would have made it difficult for Wood's formation to keep up with the other bombers for the precise timing required by the wave-by-wave assault on the Ploesti targets.

The plan called for the 389th with its two attack units, twelve in the first and seventeen in the second, to leave the others at Pitesti, the first Initial Point, and head northeast across several valleys between the first and third IPs—at best a difficult navigational feat while flying a few hundred feet above the many ridges, under misty conditions. Several of the valleys had a river flowing through them. Some had a railroad, a key landmark for locating Floresti, the Ploesti IP.

Floresti and Red target's IPs were approximately fifty miles from Pitesti, so the seven attack forces would be starting their bomb runs at approximately the same time.

Wood's briefed turning point, a valley running northwest to southeast, was the one just prior to the valley containing Campina. This was akin to being told when lost in a strange city, "Go to the next-to-last traffic light and turn left."

They were to proceed northwest up this valley and turn east over the

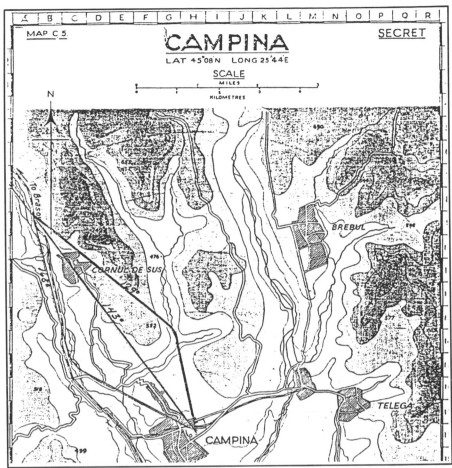

MAP C 5.

CAMPINA

LAT 45°08'N   LONG 25°44'E

SCALE

About 4½ miles from Red target, Col. Jack Wood's group split into three attack units of three-plane elements: one veered 15 degrees to the left, one veered 25 degrees to the right and one went straight for the target. The two staggered flanking units converged onto the target a few seconds behind the lead unit, ensuring maximum spillover damage to the uniquely diamond shaped refinery complex. The refinery was out of business until December.

intervening ridge at a point between Sinaia (which, unknown to the fliers housed a POW camp) and Campina; then turn southeast down the attack valley to Campina. This bomb run heading would take them on toward Ploesti where they were to rally south, short of the city, and join the other groups for the flight home.

The meticulous plan of TIDAL WAVE had been violated at Targoviste some fifteen minutes earlier, and now it was to be torn asunder again. Confronting the same misty conditions that befell Colonel Compton, Colonel Wood thought he had gone past the penultimate valley and turned southeast down the valley where he should have turned northwest.

About halfway down the valley, on what he thought was the bomb run, Wood realized he was in the penultimate valley and executed a 180 degree full-formation turn to head northwest to the proper point and hop over the ridge to the Campina valley.

At last, twenty-nine bombers were heading southeast for the target, a tight, diamond-shaped configuration of buildings and structures that included a power station, boiler house, cracking plant and two Dubbs stills. This concise target was only 400 ft. at its widest point, as seen by the attackers. A dream target.

The run in was like a wild-west movie: machine gunners and flak gunners along the hillside firing *down* at the bombers; a million bullets pouring into the hillside, and moments later into the target area, as over 400 American machine guns spoke back to the ambushers.

Red target was one of only three virgin (one slightly tainted) targets to bear witness to the validity of the battle plan. The bombers bore down on their assigned targets in three-plane waves, several waves moving to the left and several to the right. The flanking waves would then converge at an angle on the diamond-shaped target area. The idea was to gain maximum value from any spillover bombs.

It was a bloody entry for the 389th. The ubiquitous flak towers belched pointblank 88s, fused to explode just after leaving the barrels, and spewed small cannon fire from twin Bofors automatic AA guns.

The hail of death cascaded into the unprotected bombers; wide-eyed pilots stared intently back through the lethal shower, looking for assigned targets. Unflinching bombardiers peered into bombsights, as they homed in on briefed aiming points: the front door of a power station; the base of a Dubbs still; the right side or left side of a boiler house; the center of a cracking plant. It never was like this at 20,000 ft.

Only the aerial gunners could avoid the frustration that faced the other members of the crew, who were powerless to retaliate. The busy gunners picked off flak tower crews where they could, but not before the defenders had collected their price of admission.

Shoot, Fritz, You're Faded was too good an offer for the ground marksmen to refuse. Capt. Bob O'Reilly took his cockily named Liberator to the shooters and they responded with the full force of their guns. As the tracers headed their way, and homed in on their target, thuds could be heard as the bullets bit into the plane; the occupants now knew they had arrived. Thoughts of, Where are we hit? When will I get it? went through their minds.

A particularly loud thud signaled trouble. A few seconds later Sgt. Clell Riffle climbed out of his top turret and said he had been hit in the leg, and No. 1 was on fire. Co-pilot Ernie Poulson glanced at the instrument panel and received confirmation that the outboard port engine was indeed dead. He hit the feathering button and prayed it would respond. His prayers were answered. How bad are we damaged? How bad is the fire? Will we be able to stay with the formation for the trip home, with only three engines? he brooded.

During the ferocious interlude Al Romano stayed with his sighting and landed his bombs on the left front of the boiler plant, as instructed. All but one, that is, because one bomb hung up in the bomb rack.

No one wants an extra 1,000 lb. bomb hanging around while trying to escape from a target, so Romano went back to the bomb bay, after telling the co-pilot to give him a high sign when they went over a bridge or something worth destroying, and waited with hand poised on the bomb shackle.

The pilots had more on their minds than blowing up some bridge or building. They had just learned the rudder and aileron controls were shot out and knew the trip to Africa was out of the question. Their only concern was to try to crash-land the burning, helpless plane. Poulson called on interphone and told everyone to prepare for a crash-landing, and signaled the bombardier to jettison the bomb.

By now they were at 200 ft., so the pilots were surprised when Lt. Kenneth H. Matson's plane flew under them and made his turn off the target.

O'Reilly, unaware of the bomb-drop signaling between co-pilot and bombardier, called the bombardier on interphone to tell him to dump the last bomb. No answer. Will we have time to get rid of it before our crash-landing? O'Reilly wondered.

During this unrehearsed predicament, reactions by the pilots were measured in milliseconds. They had lost altitude and suddenly the looming power line posed an immediate problem. Pilot O'Reilly did not see the new menace, but Poulson did and reacted by hauling back on the elevator controls, not knowing if they even worked. They skimmed over the lines but by now the left wing was down, nearly touching the ground.

Knowing it would be suicide to land in that mode O'Reilly did a wonderful bit of thinking: he cut the power on the two starboard engines and gave full throttle to the still operating No. 2. This instinctive maneuver pulled up the left wing and permitted him to try for a successful crash-landing.

Poulson lowered the landing flaps, thinking, Is the nose compartment cleared? I know Romano made it out. Did Britt?

The only thing resembling a landing area was a dry river bed, fortunately pointing in the same direction they were locked into. O'Reilly, despite his limited resources, skillfully dropped his faltering bomber to the ground in a rough, wheels-up belly-landing on the makeshift landing strip. This is it! he thought.

The initial impact crushed in the nose compartment, but momentum moved the crumbling hulk across the dry surface. As the horrible sound of metal scraping and screeching subsided the burning engine was ripped from its moorings and the wounded battlewagon ground to a halt, the tail pointing into the air toward whence it had come.

Unusual for a crashed B–24, there was relatively little fire; just a few flames where the engine had been, but the fire hazard was in everybody's minds as they knew a burning B–24 rarely lasted over ten seconds before blowing up.

The smell of raw gas spurred them all on to scurry out of the plane as fast as possible. In the deathly silence following the crash, and before Poulson could unbuckle himself from his safety belt and parachute, he was trampled by crewmen climbing over him to escape through a gaping hole in the cockpit above his head. The pilots followed them out. Others jumped out the waist windows.

A quick check among the survivors outside revealed that navigator Britt and engineer Frank Kees were still inside, but dead.

Some of the gasoline ignited, and hastened their decision to get away from the crash area, splitting up into three groups as they crawled through a cornfield to questionable safety.

The namer of Lt. Melvin Neef's *Boomerang* tried, but his ploy did not work. *Boomerang* did not return from Ploesti.

Waist gunner Earl Wescott, who had felt a kinship with the desert farmers and their wheat threshing because of his interest in history and geography, had another brush with the bygone days. As *Boomerang* flew into the target at tree level, people on a horse-drawn buggy smiled and waved at him. He felt bad that he could not wave back; both hands were busy at the time wielding his machine gun, looking for ground gunners.

Boomerang led the flight of three into the waiting refinery, as guns blazed and the bombardier lined up his aiming point. All three planes felt the full force of the defenders' wrath. Flak bursts knocked out a starboard engine, and the pilots could not feather it, but the wingman's plane was in worse shape. Both wings were on fire, trailing flames fifty yards behind, as it roared past *Boomerang*.

The top gunner of the flaming plane, his twin fifties blazing, searched out and found the crew of a flak gun atop a flak tower. Even though the fiery bomber's wings burned off as pilot Robert Horton attempted a crash-landing, Sgt. Zerrill Steen's guns continued to rake the flak tower as the plane bounded to a stop. Bomber crews on the way by were dumbfounded to see the top turret still firing out of the blazing hulk until the ammunition ran out.

More startling was the scene a few seconds later after the guns stopped firing: a human torch emerged from the plane, stripping off its burning clothes and running naked for shelter—the only man to survive the crash.

Boomerang's unfeathered engine was a problem at that low altitude, so the pilot boosted the mercury pressure above the redline for makeup power on the other engines to offset the drag from the windmilling engine. They were barely clearing a cluster of trees. In the near background was a ridge of low hills to climb in order to escape Rumania. Many of the crew were not aware the plane had been hit that severely until instructed to begin throwing out every available item not bolted down. An excited major, riding as an observer, told everyone to get ready to bail out. Cooler heads prevailed and he was reminded that a bail-out at 30 ft. wasn't a good idea. A crash-landing seemed more appropriate.

The ensuing crash-landing in a cornfield was successful, except for the fixed machine gun under the nose section catching the lip of a ditch, and pulling the bomber head on into the ditch while it was still skidding along at a high rate of speed. The nose wheel was shoved up under the flight deck, raising the floor up to the roof. When the top turret fell onto the flight deck, it pinned four men in a veritable prison. The top gunner and navigator had their feet jammed under the rung of the turret.

Bombardier Charles Wallace was wedged between the turret and the armor plate behind the pilot's seat, and with a seat cushion crammed into his face he could barely breathe and could not cry out. The strong fumes from 100 octane gasoline permeated the prison as Wallace drifted in and out of consciousness. He prayed and thought fearful thoughts: Will we blow up? Where is help? Will these fumes kill me? Oh, God, I am going to die in a strange country and my folks will never know what happened to me.

James Sedlack, the radioman, was the fourth captive, and he too was immobile, but was able to yell for help. The only ones within earshot of his cries were the looters, busy taking anything of value from the plane.

The others escaped from the bomber that surprisingly did not catch fire. They were unable to extract the four, and scattered for some mechanical help. Some came back with a little old man, a woodcutter complete with axe, who chopped a hole in the side of the fuselage. Four and a half hours later Wallace and the radioman were pulled out. It required heavier equipment and a couple more hours to get the others out. The entire crew spent the rest of the war as POWs.

A delayed-action bomb from one of the front waves had bulldozed its way into an active steam boiler, and as a trailing bomber passed overhead the boiler exploded, destroying the plane.

The bravery of these young men who came to bomb Ploesti perhaps is best exemplified by the actions of Lt. Lloyd "Pete" Hughes, when his ship was hit by flak that ruptured the left bomb bay fuel tank. Gasoline poured out of the open bomb bay in a stream as thick as the heavy end of a baseball bat. The stream spread and obliterated the waist gunner from the view of air crews flying off their left wing.

They watched in silent horror, for they knew that Hughes's target was aflame from released gases sparked into raging fire. Hughes did not falter. The cool, dedicated pilot, who had come to bomb Ploesti, held his altitude below the top of the flames, eschewing the option of climbing above the holocaust for a safer but less accurate bomb release, and pressed on without wavering.

The bombardier dropped his bombs on target, but as they sped into the flames the exposed fuel was ignited, and set the left wing aflame. Only then did the pilot take action to save the plane and the crew. He brought the nose up and mushed toward the ground. The game pilot appeared to be winning the battle, but just as he was about to touch down the left wing burned off, and the stricken bomber cartwheeled into a blinding explosion. (Hughes was later awarded the Medal of Honor, posthumously, for his bravery in staying in the bombing formation to drop his bombs on the target, fully aware that the escaping gas would destroy his plane.)

The bombardiers of the 389th were all doing a superb job of hitting aiming points for which they had been so thoroughly briefed. The entire group was executing the plan as developed by the planners.

The only blemish on this target was the surprise formation of sand-colored B–24s that showed up about three miles away, coming at right angles toward the departing bombers. Fortunately they were too late to foul the target and were forced to drop their bombs on a refinery that had just been neutralized, and would be out of production for about five months. They simply supplied a few dozen more delayed-action bombs for the exciting fireworks that would be starting in a few hours, keeping cleanup crews on their toes.

The delayed-action bombs had a feature that would strike fear into the hearts of cleanup crews watching the first crew try to disarm one of the sleeping bombs. The first crew soon learned that a slight unscrewing of the delayed-action nose fuse would detonate the bomb. The next few days of exploding bombs would no doubt add to their job concerns.

The successful bomb run was not without penalty. Six of the twenty-nine planes were lost this day at Campina, or on the way home.

The time elapsed from the first plane over a Ploesti target to the last one was twenty-seven minutes, but in that historic air-land battle more firepower was exchanged than at two Gettysburgs. More men were lost in the air than on the ground.

Happenings were so hectic and confusing over some of the refineries that participants later could not recall the chronology of events: bombers and fighters flying in all directions swerving to avoid each other or tall structures; airplanes streaking smoke and fire, some striking the ground and breaking into many pieces or simply into a ball of flames and smoke; parachutists at 30 to 80 ft., playing the only long shot available to them. A few won, but most lost. (The Duke of Wellington once likened a battle to a ball: you could later recall the identity of your partners but never the order in which you danced with them. It seems war, like social events, never really changes.)

In those few minutes 1,650 brave young Americans had sent their souls through the invisible, that fine line between life and death; seeking some message of that afterlife, to learn its meaning. A staring match with death. If death blinks, the soul returns. If not, there is no return.

None of the participants was prepared for that electric few moments in hell: seasoned veterans of high-level bombing missions over heavily defended German targets were astounded at the spectacle; rookies on their first combat mission were shocked (this was like no combat horror story they had ever heard). Each reacted in his own way. Some returned to base with no memory of the target experience, those terrifying moments erased from their consciousness forever. Some did recall the event after the shock wore off. Many tucked it away in their memory for an occasional recall years later.

As *Penelope* came off the target, seeking a traveling companion for the trip home, its crew encountered more barns and haystacks firing at them. The gunners, still in a state of shock, instinctively fired back.

Navigator Lt. Robert Stephens spied something that did not seem to fit the picture of the past few minutes. They had come across a swimming hole and a small beach filled with bathers who probably thought the exploding bombs in the distance was thunder. When the ground-hugging bomber appeared, many of the beach people ran off in all directions.

One particular well-endowed young lady in a two-piece red swimsuit caught his eye.

"Look there!" he said to the bombardier as he tapped him on the shoulder. With that the bombardier, still shell-shocked from the target debacle, swung his machine gun around and began firing at the hapless girl.

Stephens tackled what proved to be a poor marksman, shouting, "I said *look* at her, not *shoot* her!"

The beautiful rally plan was a shambles. Instead of five neat groups of bombers gathering in protective formations for the trip home, the sky ten to twenty miles south of Ploesti was filled with individual bombers and small flights of three to six planes. There were some larger, luckier assemblages to be seen. Some of the bombers trailed smoke. Many had obvious battle damage: one rudder shot away; a top turret or tail turret missing; the plexiglass nose section demolished; a section of the main wing missing; a propeller or two feathered. Unseen, but there, were the wounded and the dead being brought home for repairs or burial.

Several pilots faced a dilemma no youngster should have to face: what to do about a badly wounded crew member who needs medical attention in a matter of an hour or two or he will die, and you are seven hours from home.

Do you fly back to Ploesti or Bucharest, to crash-land and try to get him to a hospital—facing more flak and fighters, and risking the lives of nine men? Or, do you sacrifice him to save nine others, and watch him die as you fly home?

Chapter 7

"I Myself am Heav'n and Hell"

Ernie Poulson, Al Romano and aerial gunner Louie Medieros crept through the cornfields and away from the crumpled heap named *Shoot, Fritz, You're Faded;*, the rumbling and black smoke of war continued in the background and the roar of fighter planes circling overhead reminded them they were still in the war. Soon, voices could be heard, along with a more fearful sound— nearby gunfire. What now? they thought.

After a short conference they all stood up, hands held high, trying to be noticed among the cornstalks, all the while hoping they would not be shot.

Poulson was the only one armed, so the soldiers and peasants quickly stripped him of his .45 and knife, and tied them all up. One young boy then tore Poulson's pilot's wings from his shirt (bombardiers never wore their wings on combat missions as they were not very popular with civilians whose homes have just been bombed), and stood poised with the knife held to the pilot's chest. Several held cocked pistols or rifles, all pointed at the captives. I've seen this scene in movies hundred of times. Read it in books. This time it's for real, thought Poulson.

The captors may have been speaking a different language, but the captives knew a shaky voice when they heard one; the shaky strange words worried them even more. Especially when the gun hands were shaking too. It later developed they were afraid their prisoners were Russians, who they both feared and loathed.

Poulson tried out a Rumanian phrase he had learned, "Yo sunt Aviator, Amerikan." They seemed to understand, but still remained fearful of the three likewise fearful men. They continued to argue among themselves, apparently about what to do with the aviators. Finally, they led, pushed and prodded their prisoners back to the crash site, where they were placed on their stomachs, to receive a few kicks and other forms of physical abuse. The three men were learning firsthand what it is like to lose the freedom they were fighting for; a bit of knowledge gained only through experience.

From their prone position all they could see was the remains of their proud warbird: a broken heap, all four engines torn off and scattered behind in the landing area; the nose section partially gone; the cockpit, what was left of it, a mass of wrecked and twisted metal, lying practically on the ground, and with the top exposed. Halfway back to the tail the fuselage was broken in half.

Medieros, flat on his stomach and legs and arms tied behind him, looked over at his similarly attired co-pilot and said, "How in hell did you get out of that cockpit alive, lieutenant?" The best Poulson could do was offer a puzzled sigh, as he contemplated the twisted and mangled bodies of the two men still in the wreckage.

Their presence by now had attracted several hundred townspeople—some of who, curious by nature, attempted to talk to the three. Gruff guards pushed them back.

The horse-drawn cart trip to a nearby town was not a comfortable one for Poulson, who had flak wounds in his left leg and under his left armpit, a broken left wrist and a damaged shoulder. The others, with minor injuries and a mild case of shock, found it rather quaint, considering the mode of transportation they had been using the past seven hours.

At the Rumanian village of Nadalia they were herded into a cold, dank basement and on two occasions were treated to some water, but no food.

Shortly after they left on their buggy trip a nicely dressed, pleasant looking lady of fifty drove up in her 1939 Plymouth to see who had crashed on her property. This lady was no peasant, for she owned a thousand-acre estate that included the village of Nadalia. She was Princess Caterina Caradja, whose grandfather had built the world's first oil-producing well on that property, a move that helped launch Ploesti onto the world stage.

A few minutes earlier she had seen Col. James Posey's neat formation of bombers flying overhead, heading north. Then, along came Col. Jack Wood's contrasting ragged formation, with several planes missing, and others trailing smoke or with feathered engines, heading south. She had been certain they were Russian bombers.

When she read *Shoot, Fritz, You're Faded* on the crumpled side of the crushed fuselage she knew better. She knew they were Americans, and she wondered if anyone might still be inside.

A young boy came up and told the princess that one of the Russians was moving, so she rushed up to the crushed nose section to find navigator Dick Britt jammed in there, just opening his eyes. She asked, in English, if he was an American. His Texan accent confirmed her assumption; the words weren't needed. When she turned and told the crowd he was an American aviator smiles broke out and men ran to get tools to pry the man out.

They tried to rescue engineer Sgt. Frank Kees, but he lay dead beneath the heavy top turret.

Possibly the reason everyone thought the bomber was Russian was the red field surrounding the white star in the plane's main insignia. (Later in the war the red was removed from the US insignia.)

The ongoing bad feelings between the Rumanians and their German allies was evident in the squabble over the injured navigator. Two German soldiers began dragging Britt away, but the little princess grabbed him by the feet and dug in her heels. The ensuing international tug of war would have been comical to a disinterested spectator, but it was a deadly serious point of order for the combatants: the Germans and the Rumanian seemingly trying to pull apart an unconscious American in their efforts to establish ownership.

The diminutive, scrappy, determined lady won. Royal position and ownership of the land no doubt had a larger bearing on her victory than physical strength.

The victor hid the navigator in her Plymouth and drove to her town. When she arrived at the house where the three men were held captive, their living conditions changed abruptly. Bread, milk, tomatoes and assorted fruits were brought to them, and they saw their first smiles since visiting Rumania.

The princess told them she had Lieutenant Britt hidden in her car, and was taking him to a doctor friend in a nearby village to be treated for the skin irritation from high-octane gasoline dripping on his face while he lay unconscious in the wrecked bomber.

The fortunes of war are unpredictable, and never more so than that evening when pilot Bob O'Reilly, Poulson, Romano and Medieros ended up at Princess Caradja's manor house for a festive evening and the best meal they had eaten since leaving the United States. Later, they joined the other crew members, who had missed the free meal, for the more normal prisoner experience of interrogation and internment as POWs.

(Princess Caradja helped many American flyers downed at Ploesti, and personally saw that they were given the best possible treatment at a special Rumanian POW facility set up just for the men of TIDAL WAVE. After the war she came to America to live, and has attended many combat unit reunions, has given numerous speeches and has been a guest in the homes of many of her "boys.")

Earlier that morning 178 bomber crews tentatively ate what many believed would be their last breakfast, silently contemplating the coming event as their forks pushed around the sections of pancakes smeared with the army spread that the army cooks laughingly called butter.

Some nine hours later only about 125 of those crews had reached and survived hell at Ploesti. Now they were scattered all over one section of the Wallachian plains in a mad scramble to get away, and back to where they served pancakes and that wonderful army spread.

Ploesti was now behind them; the battle wasn't. The sky was alive with fighter planes bent on cleaning up on the stragglers, the cripples that had to go it alone because they could not keep up with the others that had their systems and components still functioning.

It was a pathetic sight to see a bomber with a portion of a wing or rudder shot away sidle up to a brother with one engine feathered; neither was a match for two or three fighters who might come upon them, but together they just might dissuade an attack. Some such twosomes were lucky enough to be joined by a compassionate pilot who had to drop flaps to slow down his full-powered plane in order to stay with them. A flight of three would show enough firepower to increase their chances of making it to neutral Turkey or possibly to friendly Cyprus.

The planes trailing smoke and those with two engines feathered or with fuel leaks had little chance to escape enemy territory. Some crews by now had determined their options: crash-land, bail out, try for Turkey or Cyprus or take the long shot and go for Africa. A remarkably few planes were unscathed. All they had to fear if they were alone was a flight of fighters.

One common denominator among nearly all of the escaping B–24s was an effort to get down on the deck and skim across the plain at treetop level. The exceptions were those with impaired powerplants that needed all the altitude they could muster in order to stretch out their range and put as many miles as possible between their bombs and where they might be forced to end their flight. The tradeoff was deadly: a distance gain for a higher likelihood of being shot down by a fighter.

There wasn't much humor in the helter-skelter flight for life, but Colonel Posey's crew got a chuckle out of a man who ran out of his house clad in his red long johns, waving and firing a shotgun. As low as they were the man would have been an easy mark for any of the gunners, but they were all laughing so at the spectacle they couldn't have hit him if they had tried. The men of course were forbidden to shoot at civilians under any conditions.

Bob Judy's *Northern Star* threw a fright into some field workers just after leaving the target. As the bomber hugged the earth, in the pilot's own expression of fear, some of the workers knelt as if in prayer for their fears of these monsters that caused the loud rumbling explosions in the background. When Judy and the navigator waved to the people, they then waved back with big smiles on their faces. What a relief! The greeters were so close the missing tooth in one man's smile could be seen.

When they passed over a horse and wagon a few minutes later a pretty girl threw a kiss to the airmen, much to the delight of the crew, and the two men waved. A few miles farther on they waved to a group of children swimming in a shallow river, but the children were too frightened to wave back. The nun in charge did give them a look of recognition.

It was difficult to reconcile this friendly joy riding with what they had just been doing. The two activities didn't jibe. The pilot, however, knew that as a straggler he was fair game to any wandering band of fighters, so when he saw some other stragglers off to the left he slid over and joined them to form a small protective formation. They climbed to a higher altitude and into some scattered clouds for added protection.

Li'l Abner did not fare as well as *Northern Star*. After rallying off White 5, radioman Jesse Hinely went back to the tail position to render first aid to the tail gunner, who had been hit by flak.

Just after bombardier Lloyd Reese and navigator Walter Sorenson had vacated the nose section, because of the three damaged engines and other battle damage, the nose took a hit by an explosive shell and showered bits of metal into the cockpit. Worden Weaver and co-pilot Robert Snyder managed to milk the no longer burning, but now smoking outboard engines. It was this or go in, as a B–24 can't hold altitude on one engine. Only No. 2 was at full power.

The pilot struck a southwesterly heading and hoped the engines would somehow get better. In the meantime, he fell prey to some fighter planes. They made several passes but *Li'l Abner*'s guns drove them off each time. Then it happened. The smoldering engine fires blossomed into full-fledged fires, the nemesis of all B–24s.

Weaver had no choice but to cut both No. 1 and No. 4, and feather them before they exploded—a difficult decision at about 200 ft. altitude. Now he was confronted with several major roadblocks to survival for his crew: only one operating engine, which dictated an immediate landing; no way to lower the landing gear and flaps without the hydraulic system; and a large hole in the right wing prevented the use of the ailerons, a normal requirement for a landing.

The harried pilot somehow found time to notify the crew that they were going in for a crash-landing, and to hang on. With only one operating engine he had difficulty missing a tree in his landing path. The cornstalks somewhat cushioned the landing as they bounced along the flat field, but as the plane came to rest a fire began raging through the flight deck behind the pilots' armor plating.

The nose section buckled on impact and popped most of the rivets in the pilot's windshield, enabling Weaver, who was burned by the fire, to push the window open and squeeze through. As he emerged outside one foot became entangled in his parachute harness and left him dangling upside down. The bombardier, waiting in line, cut the pilot free.

The navigator followed the pilot out and became jammed in the window by his parachute harness. The obliging bombardier freed him too, and after doffing his harness went out himself. Co-pilot Bob Snyder was the last to escape through the busy windshield opening. Snyder had burned his hands when he touched the hot armor plating, and was in severe pain as they gathered outside. Sgt. William Schettler was killed by his falling top turret. The five men in the rear of the plane, while shaken up, had no difficulty getting out the waist windows.

The crew walked into the nearby village of Visnia-Dombovitsa, Rumania, where they were given water, milk and kindness. One Rumanian soldier used a feather to apply what appeared to be fish oil to the men's burns. Then they were led away to a small hospital as prisoners of war.

As *Pudgy* left the target area, the No. 1 engine dead and its propeller windmilling, the prospects for making Turkey were grim. A dead engine means a twenty-five percent loss of power even if the propeller can be feathered to reduce its drag to zero. As a result, airspeed is reduced. If the propeller cannot be feathered and windmills in the onrushing air, airspeed is reduced by another 12 mph.

While limping along at under 200 ft., the crew began throwing out everything not bolted down in an effort to increase the margin between stalling speed and airspeed. In the midst of this last-ditch effort to remain aloft and make it to neutral Turkey, they were jumped by fighters.

One wave of Me 109s challenged the storm of machine gun bullets from the bomber's defensive team and blasted the No. 1 engine, but not before one fighter burst into flames.

The loss of a second port engine dropped the plane to near ground level, with the left wing down, and the pilot had no recourse but to try and control the inevitable crash. The left wing caught the ground and nearly cartwheeled the plane, but luckily the wing ripped partially away from the fuselage and they made a bumpy, semi-controlled belly-landing—a remarkable effort by the pilot.

At the time of the fighter attack the engineer was transferring fuel from the bomb bay tanks to the main tanks. At impact, gasoline fumes were ignited and the bomb bay burst into flames, threatening the occupants of the flight deck and cockpit.

Milton Telster blacked out and had no idea how he got out of the plane. Co-pilot Bill Bassett later told him that when the left wing ripped away from the fuselage it left a large hole through which he staggered to safety. The dazed co-pilot then followed him out. A few seconds later the plane blew up. Five of the eleven-man crew survived.

The reception committee consisted of angry and frightened farmers brandishing pitchforks.

"Ruskee?" asked one of them.

"Ya Sam American," replied Telster, as he had been briefed.

Later, in a hospital, Telster, head covered with bandages for his facial burns and only his eyes showing, was interrogated by a German Gestapo captain, decked out in leather riding boots, riding crop, leather straps across his chest, flared riding pants, mustache, monocle and medals on his chest and speaking in a clipped British accent.

Telster had little to laugh about at this point, but all he could think about was the real life stereotype Hollywood creation standing in front of him. The mental picture of this bit player talking to a pair of eyes in among a ball of bandages struck him as funny, and he had difficulty controlling the convulsive shuddering from suppressed giggles. The bandages negated the need to keep a straight face, but his eyes must have been laughing throughout the imperious questioning.

"Name?"

"Milton Telster."

"Religion?"

"Jewish."

"Squadron?"

"I don't know."

"Group?"

"I don't know."

"Don't lie to me. You are with the 333rd Squadron, 93rd Group."

The frustrated questioner stomped away, saying, "Your kind is not liked around here."

The bandaged head could take it no longer and shook with uncontrolled laughter.

In a plane called *The Witch*, pilot Julian Darlington's bombardier had been assigned the powerhouse at White 4. He had paid attention at briefing and studied his target photos until he knew every door and window in the building.

The Witch hit its target and was now winging its way south in search for company on the way home. Darlington remembered the advice of the briefing officer, "If you're going to fly low, fly very low." He hit the deck and found several others heeding the same advice.

A bomber to his left, with flames streaming out of both waist windows, skidded into a field and burst into flames. Scattered all around him were other planes in various stages of disarray: engines feathered; sections of control surfaces shot away; smoke or fire streaming from engines. He spied his old buddy James Gunn flying *Prince Charming*, at ten o'clock, slid up to him and waggled his wings, "Hello!"

The Witch *before meeting up with* Prince Charming *and* Daisy Mae.

The Witch *after crash-landing in Yugoslavia. Photo smuggled out by Partisan resistance fighter.*

Neither plane had any visible damage, so in his naiveté, this being his first combat mission, he thought they had it made. The two planes soon became four, with *Daisy Mae*, piloted by Lt. Lewis Ellis, in the lead of the diamond formation.

It was an interesting group of escapees from hell: *Prince Charming, The Witch,* and *Daisy Mae*; the one cartoon character needed to round out the foursome was *Li'l Abner*, a burning heap left miles behind. The attacking German fighter pilots probably saw no significance in the names.

Darlington, concerned that he did not have enough gas to cross the Mediterranean, had called the navigator for a reading on their fuel supply and location, in case Turkey or Cyprus should be determined as their destination.

During their confab the No. 4 engine began to overspeed, soon emitting a high-pitch whine—the sign of a runaway prop. He quickly reduced power, but the rpm needle continued to climb. Then he hit the feathering button. All the while the shudder of twin fifties firing from his top turret told him they had more trouble in the form of attacking Me 109s.

The co-pilot added to the aerial meleé with the announcement that No. 3 was losing oil. The pilot, knowing if the rapidly dropping oil pressure got too low the engine could not be feathered, hit the No. 3 feathering button, and rang the abandon ship alarm.

Prince Charming dropped back to help *The Witch* but was hit by an Me 109 and was set afire. Only one man safely parachuted.

Another fighter attacked *The Witch* from nine o'clock and raked it from just behind the flight deck to the tail, injuring five men. One of the injured was the engineer on the flight deck, unconscious and bleeding profusely from a bad leg wound.

When No. 2 began losing power the plane fell behind their two other companions. Darlington couldn't trim the ship but kept control with full left rudder. A bail-out was out of the question for the pilot, with so many wounded aboard, but a B–24 with one good engine, one at reduced power and two feathered would not long remain airborne. They obviously would have to land at once.

The bombardier and navigator had come up from the front and were on the lower flight deck, contemplating a bail-out through the bomb bay. From the waist door at the rear of the bomb bay came the wounded members, chutes in place, with the same thought in mind.

Darlington began a steep descent, turning into the good outboard port engine, and searching for a suitable landing spot. The would-be chutists somehow got the message to stay with the plane, and well they did because by now they were too low for a successful jump. The busy pilot managed to pick out a suitable level area and bring his plane in for an excellent wheels-up landing in a wheat field. They were lucky, there was no fire.

The engineer was lifted out through the top escape hatch and given what little first aid they could offer. He had lost a lot of blood, and they were afraid he would soon die.

The crew split up. The engineer ended up in a hospital at Skopje, Yugoslavia, where German surgeons amputated his leg above the knee. Four of the crew joined the Partisans. The others became POWs.

Fertile Myrtle and its crew, who thought the war was over on July 11 when they had completed their tour of duty, turned off the target and headed for home on their reprise last mission. Aside from Sergeant Fulfer's leg injury, everyone had survived their little piece of hell known as White 4.

Daisy Mae *left* Li'l Abner *behind in a Rumanian cornfield, and snuggled up to* Prince Charming *in the unfriendly skies of the Balkans.*

The B-24 Li'l Jughaid *made it home, but went down in the Mediterranean two weeks later.*

On the way back pilot Lyle Spencer was concerned about their gas supply because of the time lost in the cloud mess on the way to the target, so he was cruising very slowly across the Balkans. Suddenly he thought he had been transported back in time to World War I. A biplane fighter made an aborted pass at the slow-moving bomber. Spencer, who had never seen a biplane in combat, felt more like a spectator than a target. The biplane pilot could not reduce his speed enough to match that of the creeping B-24, which no doubt was lucky for him as there were hundreds of .50 caliber bullets awaiting his charge.

At the coast of Greece they fought off an attack by a real fighter plane, but suffered a big gash in the leading edge of a wing from an aerial cannon hit. They made it back to Africa.

Li'l Jughaid, piloted by Robert Nichelson, lost both wing aircraft flying through the holocaust at White 4. The bombardier and navigator were injured, and on the way home they had several encounters with fighters.

By the time they reached Africa the problems were many: it was dark; the plane was down to two engines and was full of holes; the hydraulic lines were gone; the pilot was overcome with exhaustion.

After fourteen grueling hours and Ploesti survival almost in their grasp, the crew had two big jobs remaining: lower the landing gear by hand cranking and land the plane with the pilot incapacitated. The former was relatively easy. The co-pilot then took over and landed the plane, with assistant engineer Sgt. Manny Rangel acting as co-pilot and calling out airspeeds during the landing.

Hadley's Harem, piloted by Lt. Gilbert Hadley and co-pilot Lt. James Lindsey, was hit on the run in to White 4 when flak ripped off half the nose plexiglass, killed the bombardier and wounded the navigator. Engineer Russell Page salvoed the bombs from the cockpit. No. 2 engine took a hit and began burning. Hadley feathered the prop and the fire went out. The hydraulics were gone, and No. 1 began leaking gas as they left the target area for their attempt to get home.

As they passed over an excursion train the passengers leaned out of the windows and waved. The shaken crew were glad to respond in kind as a change of pace from their past few moments of terror.

They latched on to some other cripples and wended their way south for Africa or possibly a neutral country. As they got out over the ocean and were holding about 5,000 ft., No. 3 began losing oil pressure and had to be feathered. With only two good engines left and one in trouble Hadley told the crew to prepare to bail out. Soon the supercharger on No. 4 caught fire, endangering its engine.

Hadley decided to try for British-controlled Cyprus, but while still off the Turkish coast No. 1 began losing oil along with its gas. It was now beginning to get dark.

The pilot told the crew he was going to try for land (neutral Turkey) because "one and four may go out soon." He offered the crew a choice of bailing out or sticking with the plane. It was unanimous: "We'll stick!" Anything was better than floating all night in the ocean. Also, a Turkish beach was in sight.

From the steep descent it was clear they would ditch, so the men removed shoes and clothing. Engineer Page opened the top hatch, for a quick exit after landing.

Landing a B–24 in water is difficult and dangerous. Hitting water on a wheels-up landing has far more impact than on land. On land the plane bounces along in a rough manner, but when the plane hits water it stops for a split second, bounces and settles a second time. A person not properly braced will be badly injured and probably knocked out in a water landing.

Hadley saw the beach approaching and used all his powers of body English to will the rate of descent to be shallower than it was. It was clear that he would be about a half mile short. But that wasn't too bad, if they could survive the ditching. Both operating engines quit as he nursed the bomber across the waves and he had to drop it in for the premature ditching.

Hadley's Harem hit the water, and the impact slammed the top hatch shut. Page had braced himself, so he survived the landing and was able to try and reopen the top hatch, but could not do so. My God, am I going to die like this? he panicked. Water gushed in to the flight deck through the open nose, and several flak holes in the fuselage. Hadley and Lindsey unbuckled their safety belts and splashed through the rapidly rising water to help open the hatch. They could not budge it, and by now they were all under water.

Page swam up to the top of the top gun turret and could not get through the plexiglass bubble, but he did manage to gulp a fresh supply of air trapped in the bubble. A lighted area off to one side attracted his attention and he struggled toward it. The fuselage had broken off at the rear of the bomb bay and the light he saw was daylight through the water. The passageway was so narrow he could not swim so he made his way hand over hand through the bomb bay, using the bomb racks as a horizontal ladder.

Others made it out through flak holes or other openings. The seven floating survivors, six in Mae Wests and one clutching an oxygen bottle, watched in horror as their plane sank from sight, taking along their pilot and co-pilot.

The seven exhausted, half-naked flyers finally stumbled onto the Turkish beach and were met by peasants with pointed guns, who quickly saw they were defenseless and not a threat. They gave them clothing and built a fire for

TELEGRAM RECEIVED

NMC   Ankara

This telegram must be
closely paraphrased be- FROM Dated August 8, 1943
fore being communicated
to anyone. (SE)   Rec'd 9:30 p.m., 9th.

Secretary of State,

Washington.

1388, August 8, 11 p.m.

MOST SECRET

I discussed with the Minister for Foreign Affairs
yesterday the status of the various American
aviators interned in Turkey after the Ploesti raid.
I suggested to him that the survivors of the crew
of the LIBERATOR which crashed off the coast and
who were rescued by the Turkish coast guard be
regarded as "shipwrecked mariners" and be released,
and that all of the wounded aviators (some of
whose wounds are very light) be regarded as unfit for
further military service and be released and that
subsequently the Turkish General Staff be instructed not
to interpose too many barriers in the path of attempted
escapes by others. Numan replied that he would give
serious consideration to the release of the "shipwrecked
mariners" and the wounded, and that he would suggest
to the General Staff that they should not take

"exceptional

---

them. After awhile some Turkish soldiers arrived and they were given cigarettes and made as comfortable as possible.

The next day a power launch arrived from Cyprus containing some RAF Air & Sea Rescue people with much needed medication for the badly wounded members. One man had a compound fracture of his leg.

Just like in Rumania, a jurisdictional dispute arose over ownership of the American captives. If the Turks won, the men would be interned for the rest of the war. If the RAF won the men would be taken back to Cyprus, and then on to Africa.

The RAF people mounted a unique argument. They claimed the men were shipwrecked mariners whose ship sank at sea, not belligerents. After much discussion they convinced the Turks, bundled up the happy flyers and took them to Cyprus.

Col. John Kane's *Hail Columbia* was also heading for Cyprus, with a small band of two cripples and a couple of healthy brothers for protection. They flew on the deck across the Wallachian plain and barely stayed airborne at minimum airspeed, just above stalling. Crew members resorted to what so many others were doing, throwing out everything that was not bolted down. They were aerial litterbugs, even though the term may not yet have been invented.

As they crossed the Danube for the second time that day they were treated to some bathing beauties sunning themselves on the beach. Some insisted (or hoped) they were nude.

Two daring pilots in obsolete biplanes dived on them, but one failed to pull up and crashed into the ground. The biggest concern, aside from real fighters, was the Bulgarian mountains they had to cross after they left Rumania.

After things simmered down bombardier Harold Korger looked at his little finger and noticed it was badly gashed. He had no idea how and when it happened. Ah ha, he jested, now I get me a Purple Heart! An unceremonial affixing of a Band-Aid would have to suffice for the time being.

In the meantime the unsung hero of the flight, navigator Lt. Norman "The Baron" Whalen, was earning his keep by taking LOP (Line of Position) sightings on Polaris with his sextant to determine exactly where they were and establish the compass heading for Cyprus. Once over Cyprus, Korger helped The Baron locate the airdrome.

The Baron brought the weakened bomber dead nuts on to the airdrome, but Kane was unable to make the end of the runway, hitting short and tripping on a ditch at the near end. The plane bounced and came down on the left wing.

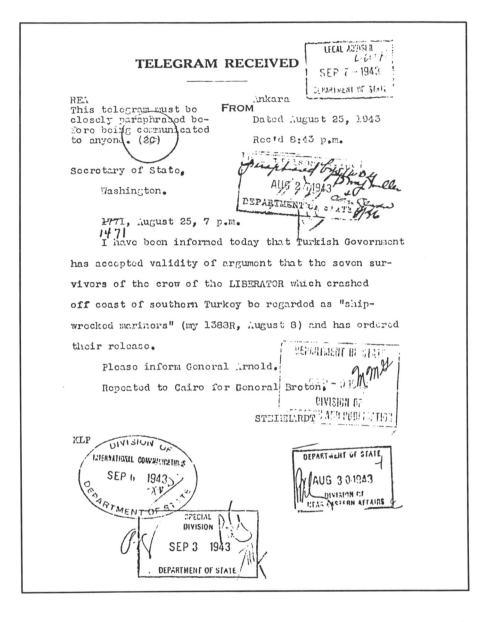

REA   Ankara
This telegram must be   **FROM**
closely paraphrased be-   Dated August 25, 1943
fore being communicated
to anyone. (SC)   Rec'd 8:43 p.m.

Secretary of State,

Washington.

AUG 27 1943
DEPARTMENT OF STATE

1771, August 25, 7 p.m.
1471
I have been informed today that Turkish Government

has accepted validity of argument that the seven sur-

vivors of the crew of the LIBERATOR which crashed

off coast of southern Turkey be regarded as "ship-

wrecked mariners" (my 1383R, August 8) and has ordered

their release.

Please inform General Arnold.

Repeated to Cairo for General Broton.

STEINHARDT

KLP

DIVISION OF
INTERNATIONAL COMMUNICATIONS
SEP 6 1943
XV
DEPARTMENT OF STATE

SPECIAL
DIVISION
SEP 3 1943
DEPARTMENT OF STATE

DEPARTMENT OF STATE
AUG 30 1943
DIVISION OF
NEAR EASTERN AFFAIRS

Korger, in his haste to open the top hatch, pulled it down on the engineer's head, inflicting a big gash and nearly knocking him out. Time was so important at that moment, because of the fear of fire in a crashed B-24, that an apology was neither expected nor given.

The plane did not burn and all got out unscathed except, of course, the engineer.

The Officer's Club bars did a brisk business with the many American visitors that evening.

It wasn't your ordinary flight of bombers; it just grew from a starter of two or three, and picked up other singles looking for support. Soon it was a rag-tag formation of ten bombers containing 100 escapees from hell.

Lt. Andy Opsata was happy to add *Stinger* to the force of fleeing bombers, boosting the total firepower to some eighty machine guns to confront any attacking fighters.

All of his crew was in a mild state of shock so he tried a little humor, addressing them over the interphone with a comment he had heard back in England: "So far, we've been working for the government. Now, we are in business for ourselves." It was apropos, self-evident and did relieve the tension.

Despite the formidable face of the very tight formation several waves of fighters did dare to challenge them, but were warded off. What the last attack wave did not know was that most of the planes were running out of ammunition.

Once out to sea, however, and with the fighters gone for good, Opsata heard an alarming forecast by the engineer: "We are low on gas, and I don't think we can make land."

The aerial litterbugs went at it, strewing the ocean with machine guns, flak suits, the bombsight, a few rounds of ammo and even the radio.

Opsata throttled back his engines to conserve gas, and the reduced speed caused them to drop out of formation. It was discouraging to see their buddies, whoever they were, dwindle into the horizon, but they weren't actually needed any longer. What they needed was gas.

The engineer came up to the pilot and told him that the four gas valves were set so the fuel was equally directed to all engines; when one ran dry the others would follow quickly.

The plan was to fly until that happened, then ditch.

The inevitable finally happened. All of the fuel gauges registered zero, and then No. 1 cut out. No. 4 followed.

The weary pilot shook his head grimly, throttled back all four engines, flicked off all four engine switches, punched all four feathering buttons to feather all four engines, and shoved the control full forward to set up a steep power-off glide for his seventeen-ton hunk of metal, flesh, bones and souls. Thus they sped toward the water, far below.

Gravity, once his enemy and the force his four engines had been holding at bay for over ten hours, was now his only source of power. The steep dive

The B-24 Hadley's Harem, *home of the "shipwrecked mariners."*

would enable the momentarily inert mass to be converted to controlled flight, as air began passing over and under the Davis-designed wing to provide lift, just as it does in ordinary powered flight, the big difference being the plane must continue its descent in order to maintain control over the newfound friend.

It was strangely quiet for being in an airborne B–24; the only sound was the whistle of air coming through the many small cracks and open windows. The annoying ear pounding of four Pratt & Whitneys would have been welcome indeed.

As Opsata stared ahead he reviewed in his mind all he had been taught about ditching. Like parachuting, they never made pilots practice this procedure. It was all books, lectures and on-the-job training.

Now I finally get to be Superman, Opsata thought to himself. But I'm not landing on the *Lexington*, I'm landing on water. I wish I were Jesus. I wish those carrier pilots could see *me* now. Could *they* do this? Well, they trusted me with this quarter million dollar plane and ten men. *I can do it!* Please, God.

The co-pilot was calling out the airspeed.

"160–160–155–155–155–155."

They were so near the water he could see the waves clearly. As the waves grew in size, Opsata slowly eased back on the elevator control so as to glide nearly parallel to the surface. This delicate move had him flirting with the bad side of his new friend gravity, and the airspeed dropped accordingly.

"145–140–135."

Opsata rehashed his flight training instructions: Try and land along the length of the wave, they said. In the valley between waves. Not on top. Not at right angles. Well, that's what I'm doing. How high are those waves? Three feet? Thirty feet? I've never seen a wave in the middle of an ocean. Oh, God.

"Andy! Andy," the engineer shouted into the pilot's ear, "Unfeather them. We have some gas. Try No. 3."

The uncomprehending pilot didn't ask for any explanation. He unfeathered No. 3 to get it windmilling, flipped on the engine switch, hit the throttle full forward and thanks to a good battery got the engine started. The equally busy engineer, who had been switching valves, gave No. 3 its transfusion of life-saving gas.

The waves were just a few feet below them as the right inboard engine roared to life.

"Try No. 2!" shouted the engineer, and it too burst into full power. By now gravity was no longer needed to keep them airborne, but the other two engines were put back on line so they could climb and increase their chances of making their base at Benina Main in Benghazi.

"Sorry about the scare, skipper, but this old tin lizzie has a different fuel transfer system than the newer ones we have been flying," was the only explanation offered by the embarrassed and now vindicated engineer, who went from goat to hero within a few minutes' time.

A couple of hours later the navigator, who had been doing an excellent job of celestial and dead-reckoning navigation, announced with pride the coast should be dead ahead. In the pitch blackness all they could do is take his word for it. A dim row of lights, however, seemed to justify his claim, and Opsata headed for this lighthouse beacon that would lead his weary ship to a safe haven.

The lights turned out to be a row of flare pots on the runway at Benina Main. Dead nuts on. *Stinger* would be the last bomber to return to home base that day.

The landing was routine; Opsata coasted off the runway, taxied up to near his parking spot and ran out of gas. He and the co-pilot had not been out of their seats for fourteen hours, but they took time to bow their heads in prayer before touching the welcome terra firma.

Just standing on the ground was not enough; they scooped up the loose dirt and threw it on each other. Several crewmen knelt and kissed the earth.

Stinger's ground crew had been keeping vigil for hours, their beloved plane and crew not being among the few bombers that had been straggling in, one here, two there.

Their minds and hearts were filled with questions: Will *Stinger* make it home? Will they all be OK? How much blood and vomit will we face? Will we have to flush one of our friends out of a turret with a hose, as was done on one of the earlier returnees? How many bullet and flak holes will we count this time? These men are family, God.

As the elated flyers emerged from within *Stinger* the relieved ground crew was waiting there, gaunt faces and tear-lined eyes of just a few moments ago replaced by wide grins and unabashed free-flowing tears of joy.

Andy Opsata climbed into an awaiting jeep, turned and took a long look at his prison for the past fourteen hours. He saw for the first time a manhole size gap in its side, and the countless other fresh flak and bullet holes.

Those moments in hell, with death all around, and the hectic near ditching crowded everything else from his mind except, How did we ever get home?

As he peered skyward, he knew it had little or nothing to do with the ability of himself or the air crew.

In the adjoining parking space several dark figures could be seen huddled together watching the joyous scene: the ground crew of a bomber yet to return.

The small red glows near the tops of the figures would soon drop to the ground to join other cigarette butts that lay there, stamped out by frustrated feet—hundreds of silent tributes to the hours of faithful waiting.

It was like a widow's watch of bygone seafaring days: a forsaken ground crew, vainly waiting for their flying crew, long dead:

> And by and by my Soul return'd to me,
> And answer'd "I Myself am Heav'n and Hell."

(translated by Edward Fitzgerald, *The Rubáiyát of Omar Khayyám*)

The assault on Ploesti was costly. One hundred seventy-eight B-24s were crashed dispatched: one crashed on takeoff; two were lost en route; thirteen aborted; twenty-two landed at other Allied bases; fifty-one were lost in battle or on the way home; eighty-nine made it back to home base—of which only thirty-one were flyable for the next day's mission.

One hundred ten of the Americans became prisoners of war. Over 300 were missing in action, many presumed dead. Several of the returning planes brought back dead comrades for a decent burial. They also brought back many wounded men, some of whom died shortly thereafter.

Colonels Kane and Johnson had faced a terrible decision as they learned their assigned targets were under attack. To continue the bomb run into smoke and fire, with its hidden barrage cables and tall chimneys and not knowing how many forty-five-second bombs would be under them, boded sure death for many of their charges. Weighed against this certainty was the realization they would not get a second chance to be so close to destroying this crucial target located beyond normal bombing range.

Both would have been fully justified to abort the bomb run, but neither leader even considered turning away from his assignment.

The two courageous group commanders were awarded the Medal of Honor for their decision to press on against such incredible odds.

The United States is famed for its Monday Morning Quarterbacks, and they were out in full force in the days following TIDAL WAVE: should have gone high level; should not have even tried such a wild scheme. A monumental flop.

The British view was that the mission's major defect was the lack of experience by USAAF personnel in this type of operation at this stage of the war. This attitude, they said, was fostered by the stubborn American belief in the self-defending bomber, which, despite ample evidence to the contrary, would persist until the second disastrous attack on Schweinfurt later that fall. They had, however, the utmost respect for the bravery of the men of TIDAL WAVE.

The criticism was for the most part unfair. The planning was superb. Over 1,700 brave men did their best under terrible conditions. It could have worked.

The three refineries that were hit as briefed were shut down tight on August 1. Creditul Minier (Blue) never reopened. Columbia Acquila (White 5) was shut down for ten months and never peaked beyond fifty percent of pre-attack production. Steaua Romana (Red) was shut down for five months and never peaked beyond sixty-five percent of pre-attack production.

Concordia Vega (White 2) lost fifty-nine percent of its July production rate in the attack, but was back in one month to 133 percent of pre-attack production. Astra Romana (White 4) lost fifty-eight percent of its pre-attack production but was back in one month to 106 percent of production, and in two months, 132 percent.

Romano Americana (White 1) was not touched, and in one month was at 180 percent of pre-attack production. Standard Petrol was not touched and in one month was at 267 percent of pre-attack production.

What the Allied intelligence did not know about Ploesti was that the entire complex of some twelve refineries was operating at under sixty percent of total capacity. The destruction that day has been calculated at forty-two percent of capacity, which means all that was accomplished, beyond a few months' slowdown, was the elimination of surplus production. It was clear the USAAF had to go back to Ploesti—but not at low level.

Reaction to the attack by the German and Rumanian military at Ploesti was one of sheer admiration for the audacity and daring of the Americans. At General Gerstenberg's direction the American dead at the attack site were given funerals with full military honors.

The Rumanian women held wakes for the Americans, and on the caskets they placed special thin cakes baked for such occasions. On each cake was a small American flag made of colored candies. When some German officers entered the room they hastily put paper doilies over the flags and placed a candle on top.

A German officer asked why the women were crying for the Americans. One lady replied, "We cry, because we know American mothers soon will be crying for their sons."

Seven hundred and fifty miles northwest of Ploesti, Berlin Sally, who American GIs got to know as well as Amos and Andy, put it succinctly on her radio broadcast the next day.

"Fine job at Ploesti, Brereton, but you lost too many."

Indeed, the losses were too many, but the gallant men of TIDAL WAVE had come to bomb Ploesti, and they had set a precedent that would be maintained throughout this war and those to follow: no United States Army Air Forces unit has ever been turned back by enemy action.

1943 Ploesti oil production
(metric tons per month in thousands)

Target	Refinery	Capacity	Production			
			July	Aug.	Sept.	Oct.
Targets hit as briefed						
White 5	Columbia Acquila	45	34	Reopened July 1944		
Red	Steaua Romana	125	44	Reopened Dec. 1943		
Blue	Creditul Minier	45	35	Never reopened		
Targets hit by others						
White 4	Astra Romana and					
	Phoenix-Orion	211	155	65	165	205
White 2	Concordia Vega	110	58	24	77	80
Briefed targets not hit						
White 1	Romano Americana	92	60	108	77	80
White 3	Standard Petrol and	69	15	40	65	45
	Unirea Sperantza					
Targets not briefed						
	Dacia Romana	15	2	7	7	6
	Xenia	22	0	15	22	22
	Redeventza	22	0	0	0	0
		756	403	259	413	438*
Percent of capacity		—	53%	34%	55%	58%

*Peak post-attack production.

Sources: Impact, December 1944, and Air Objective Folder No. 69.1 Ploesti Area, Oct. 15, 1942.

Part Three

High-Level Meeting

Chapter 8

A Gathering of Groups

> *. . . an aerial conflict, the like of which will never be seen again.*
> —Steve Birdsall, foreword to *Target Ploesti: View from a Bombsight*

Aug. 2, 1943, Victorville Army Air Field

It had been a long, hot, grueling ordeal in the nose section of the AT–11 bombing training plane, the two bombardier cadets taking turns making five bomb runs each on the desert targets. The sun's rays treated training planes no differently than B–24s. It was all in and no out for the hot rays. Sweat splashed onto the bombsight eyepiece and made sighting difficult. The cadets felt put upon, having to endure such daily punishment.

Both cadets sported a big black ring around their right eye, the proud mark of a working bombardier. The sponge rubber eyepiece, heated by the sun, oozed a black substance onto the face which they hated to wash off.

The AT–11 landed, and it was Cadet Newby's turn to check in the Norden bombsight for overnight storage. He unhooked the sight from its mounting, placed it in a canvas carrying case that looked like a gym bag and started out to circle the engine and head in toward the orderly room.

It takes a bombsight gyroscope about five minutes to wind down, so when Newby made the turn the seemingly alive bag squirmed and almost wiggled out of his grasp as the still-spinning gyroscope resisted the directional change.

(Everyone has held a toy gyroscope by one axis and been amused by the way it tends to move in a direction other than intended for it to move. The reason for this action is that a gyroscope precesses ninety degrees from the point of pressure, in the direction of rotation. This, the cadets learn, is the Law of Precession. For example, if your gyroscope is spinning clockwise and you push the top of the spin axis toward the three o'clock position, the gyroscope will tilt toward the six o'clock position.)

Newby wasn't amused by the recalcitrant bag; he had a far greater concern regarding the bombsight.

"I'm worried about that last thousand footer I dropped. That will kill my CE (Circular Error) average. I had it synchronized all the way! Bubbles were level. Had to be a sight malfunction," the distraught cadet lamented.

Bill McMahon spoke up: "You're lucky it was the last bomb out of the plane. If it had been bracketed by two good bombs your malfunction claim wouldn't hold up. I think they'll allow it. So, knock off the long face."

Newby, with his stubborn bombsight finally under control, smiled and said, "Well, I'll give it a try."

McMahon, changing the subject, said, "I'll be glad to get into a bigger plane that flies at 20,000 feet, where it's a little cooler."

"Yeah, a heavy bomber up there in combat can't be as hot as these things," Newby returned.

As the sweaty cadets entered the ready-room to file their bombing results and the hoped for reprieve for Newby's bad last bomb, they ran into a lot of excited would-be bombardiers.

"Where is Po-les-tee?" No one could pronounce the new name correctly.

"Did you hear the news? They sent a bunch of B–24s into a refinery at *low level.*"

"Lost fifty-four," someone stated.

Newby whistled, "Low level? What goes? Here we are learning to bomb at high level, and now this!"

The two grimy, black-eyed cadets who had been grumbling about the hot greenhouse in their AT–11 didn't know what hot was—like the men at Ploesti knew.

Both cadets kept their CE under 230 ft. and passed all ground school courses. On September 11 they were handed the silver wings of a bombardier,

Bombardier Newby's official 460th BG photo.

commissioned second lieutenants, given shipping orders for Davis-Monthan Field in Tucson and sent home for a two-week leave.

Ted Newby arrived in Tucson late at night and checked in to a downtown hotel. The next morning the brand-new self-conscious second lieutenant sat down at the coffee shop counter to order breakfast. A major sat down beside him, and for the first time he was about to engage in a conversation on an officer-to-officer basis. Since his eating companion was a major he did slip in a few "sirs," but it came off fairly comfortably.

After some small talk the major said, "How would you like to do me a favor?"

"Be glad to, major," Newby said enthusiastically.

"I have a date this evening and I received orders to ship out this morning and wondered if you would mind taking my place. With the girl, that is."

Newby, who could not believe officer's life would be this good so soon, replied, "I'll make the sacrifice, major. What do I have to do?".

"Her name is Bernice Gaunt and she is staying at the Arizona Inn. Here's the number. Give her a call later in the day and explain matters. I can't reach her this morning, and I'm leaving in a few minutes for the airport."

After checking in at the base Newby called the girl and explained the substitution. She was very pleasant and asked if he could bring along a friend for her friend.

That evening, Newby and the first person he contacted taxied to the Arizona Inn, and found it to be a very deluxe resort, with trees and a high, vine-covered brick wall around the premises. Apprehensively they entered the front door, to an evening the bombardier would long remember.

In a rustic, lounge-type room there were several small tables, at which some diners were still finishing their meals. Two nice-looking girls in their mid to late twenties occupied a booth, so the two awed adventurers decided, or hoped, they were the dates.

They were, and the two bombardiers sat down to join them in a cup of coffee.

It was a fun evening: dancing to the juke box, enjoying scintillating conversation, finally topping off with Bernice at a piano playing and singing all of the popular show tunes of the day.

How can I be so lucky? Newby asked himself.

A civilian asked Newby, later in the rest room, "Do you know who that girl is, playing the piano?"

"Why, sure, she's my date, Bernice Gaunt," he answered.

"No, she is Shirley Ross, the movie actress," said the civilian.

Newby turned white, and said, "You mean the gal who sang 'Thanks for the memories' to Bob Hope in *The Big Broadcast of 1938*?"

"That's her," he assured Newby.

"I feel like a fool, not recognizing her."

He decided to play it *cool,* a new word he had picked up from his buddy Bill McMahon, a former Zoot Suiter from Boston. He went on as usual, calling her Bernice the rest of the evening.

The next day, he finally got up enough nerve to phone Shirley and admit he knew who she was . . . and "How about a date tonight?"

Shirley had a good-natured laugh over it and told him she really enjoyed the evening because he seemed to like her for herself, and not who she was. She gave him her Hollywood address and unlisted phone number, and asked him to write her from overseas, and phone if he ever got to Hollywood. She was leaving that afternoon for home.

This officer's life was starting out OK!

The month of October was significant for the formation of not only many dozens of new bomber crews at this and several other bases, but of a new powerhouse to be known as the Fifteenth Air Force. As crews were being gathered to man the bombers, bomb groups were being gathered at numerous air bases to accommodate the planes and crews.

The nucleus of the new Strategic Air Force was six bomb groups of the Ninth Air Force based in Tunis, Tunisia, two of them veterans of the Ploesti low-level mission. A dozen more groups would be added by early spring. The planners' eyes were focused on Ploesti.

The bombardier met his crew on his second day at Davis-Monthan and they began training together to become a team. Except for pilot Charlie Hammett and co-pilot Ed "Dusty" Rhodes, some had never been inside a B–24. Navigator Sherman Wood, the old man of the crew at twenty-six, liked to party every night, but was wide awake when he entered the plane for his navigational duties.

Flight engineer Dominic Minitti was an experienced B–24 man, and manned the top turret. Tail gunner Sid Woods and waist gunner John Woodland served together on B–24 sub patrol duty off the South American coast. Howard Thornton, the youngest at nineteen, was a rarity; he was a radioman who also rode the ball turret. Assistant engineer Danny Smith was the top turret gunner; Bob Kaiser, another assistant engineer, wrote songs, which he sang over the interphone without invitation.

The fledgling crews got a taste of combat when some of the old relics they were flying would go off on a training flight and never return. The old pink, sand-colored D and E models with the plexiglass nose were mostly battle weary veterans of the North African campaign, perhaps even Ploesti. Some were blowing up on takeoff. One day as Hammett's crew was attending a ground school gunnery class, a B–24 crashed on takeoff and landed among some trees right outside their schoolroom window. The horrified students could hear the screams of the men in the burning plane, and wanted to run to the rescue.

The instructor, however, commanded them to sit down and not look at the spectacle just outside their window. They learned it was Air Force policy for flying personnel to stay away from crashes. Trained men with proper equipment were at the scene in a matter of minutes.

Later in the month Bill McMahon rushed up to Ted Newby and said, "Hey, Newb, I'm shipping out in half an hour as a replacement and I'm broke. How much can you loan me?"

Newby checked his wallet and pulled out $30. "This is all I have 'til pay day."

"Thanks, pal. Give me your home address and I'll send it to your home," McMahon promised.

Newby complied, and Mac ran off for his new assignment.

On November 1 the Fifteenth Air Force started off under its own colors when it struck its first of thirty-six blows that month: it sent the 5th Bomb Wing, consisting of four B–17 Bomb Groups, into Italy to bomb the naval base at La Spezia and a railroad bridge at Vezzano.

That was just a warmup for the next day's 1,600 mile round trip attack on the Messerschmitt fighter plane factory at Wiener Neustadt, Austria. Of the 114 bombers making it to the target, eleven were shot down by flak and fighters. Between the seventy-two escorting P–38s and the bombers' own gunners they fought a forty-five-minute running battle with 160 German fighters, who were voicing their objection to the bombing. Our forces claimed fifty-six enemy aircraft destroyed, twenty-seven probably destroyed and eight damaged.

While the new combat force was getting off to a rough start building up a mission count (same targets they had been bombing all along) under its new management, the Training Command in Tucson was easing up on its casualties. A new order went into effect prohibiting smoking on takeoff or landing, and the bomb bays were to be cracked about six inches at those critical moments in the life of a B–24D.

Hammett's fun-loving crew had been conducting a mission count of its own each time it went up in a bomber, an early manifestation of the black humor that would become its trademark in months to come. They had amassed fourteen "combat" missions by the time the Fifteenth flew its first two.

In early November the crew was put on a troop train for Chatham Field in Savannah, Georgia, happy to be alive. Combat can't be much worse than this. Can it? Newby wondered.

The cocky crew had not yet heard of the Fifteenth Air Force, and its stated objectives:

1. To destroy the German Air Force in the air (by making it come up and fight) and on the ground, wherever it might be located within range of the Fifteenth planes.

2. To participate in POINTBLANK (the Combined Bomber Offensive), which called for the destruction of German fighter aircraft plants, ball bearing plants, oil refineries, rubber plants, munition factories, sub pens and bases and other strategic targets.

3. To support the battle of the Italian mainland (mainly by attacking communications targets—in Italy, along the Brenner Pass route and also in neighboring Austria).

4. To weaken the German position in the Balkans.

Later, more targets would be added in preparation for the coming (August 15) invasion of southern France.

Some observed that a key incentive for the Fifteenth Air Force was its opportunity to destroy the Luftwaffe *in the womb, in the nest* and *on the wing.*

At Chatham Field the wide-eyed Hammett crew, veterans of the Arizona war, were dumbfounded to see sixty-two brand-new B–24H models lined up in a row. No more pink, sand-colored hand-me-downs from the African desert. These were *airplanes!* The overall dark, olive-drab paint job highlighted the distinctive emblem located on the nose section just in front of the pilot's window.

A black-bordered white square framed a ferocious-looking black panther with its red open mouth, white teeth and green eyes, crouched to spring at you. It was the emblem of the 460th Bomb Group, one of fifteen new bomb groups being formed originally for the Eighth Air Force, but to be diverted to the new Fifteenth Air Force over the next several months.

Now the crew knew why they were ten. Songbird Kaiser would ride in the nose turret that replaced the plexiglass nose on the D models, his own broadcasting studio.

Bombardier Newby looked at the new addition with mixed emotions. It did place more protective metal and bulletproof glass in front of him, but it cut down his field of vision. All that was left for him to try to locate his target twenty miles away was a relatively small window at a forty-five-degree angle.

It was when Newby went up and peeked into his window on the war that he got the real shocker. Instead of seeing a Norden bombsight mounted in there he saw a large black box with an eyepiece sticking up like a chimney. It must be a Sperry, he concluded.

He soon learned he was one of only a few bombardiers there trained on a Norden, and would have to take special training to learn how to use the Sperry. After a few days' training on a "hangar bomber" he learned the fundamentals of establishing course and determining the rate (of approach) on a bomb run. The principle of synchronizing the cross hairs was no different, but the initial pickup of the target some twenty miles away was far more difficult.

With the Norden you can physically pivot the sighthead, and aim it at the target, before putting your eye to the eyepiece and engaging the sight. The box-like Sperry just sat there. You had to look into the eyepiece and search for the target through the sight telescope; much more difficult.

November and December were spent honing the crews' skills of aerial gunnery, takeoffs, landings, formation flying, aerial engineering duties, radio communications, bombing and navigation.

It was the latter two skills, while on a long-range 20,000 ft. formation flight to bomb Richmond, Virginia, that nearly were the undoing of Hammett's crew. Col. Bertram C. Harrison, deputy commanding officer, had heard reports of the raunchy Hammett crew and chose to ride with them on the Richmond mission.

Everything went wrong. Savannah was having its first snow in history, and the crew's enlisted men were up on the wing of the plane sweeping off the snow when Harrison arrived. He wasn't pleased to be showered with snow as he alighted from his Jeep. No one saluted him, and the enlisted men were calling the officers by first name. This was too much for the West Point graduate.

When he asked why the engines weren't running, he was told that on an earlier run-up attempt one of the men failed to start the internal auxiliary engine (putt putt) and it drained the batteries. An external auxiliary engine was on its way.

The colonel's own engine was revved up by then, and nothing could have pleased him from that point on. En route to Richmond the formation ran into scattered clouds and was split up. Only three planes pressed on to Richmond, one of which was Hammett's plane. What pilot would have the guts to turn back with the irate colonel aboard?

Navigator Wood had difficulty finding Richmond, eliciting some choice comments from the colonel, including the ominous words, "buck private." Bombardier Newby likewise had difficulty with the clouds between his bombsight and the capitol, his aiming point for this dry run, and could not line up his target in the bombsight. The dreaded words, "buck private," filled his interphone too.

On the way home, Sgt. Bob Kaiser could not resist singing his newest song, "Baby, It Is You," on the interphone, as was his normal habit. That had the colonel sputtering and fuming as he added the crew's songbird to his diatribe.

The crew continued to accrue negative points, despite warnings from Maj. Charles Ward, 763rd Squadron CO, for Hammett and his crew to "shape up, or ship out." He also reminded Hammett that he would not likely be one of the sixty-two crews to be assigned a plane. If he was still around when they left for overseas, his crew would be split up and go over as passengers.

The crew may have been undisciplined, but they worked together in the air, and were very competent on their respective jobs, Richmond to the contrary. This very looseness would stand them in good stead later in combat.

Typical of the enlisted men's camaraderie, they were all the time having fun with Bob Kaiser, who had never been out of Brooklyn before the army. When Durham-raised Howard Thornton learned Kaiser had never seen a tobacco plant he told him there was one just outside the tent. He took Kaiser out to a magnolia tree and told him it was an overgrown tobacco plant, and the leaves near the top were tender and good for chewing. As gullible Kaiser climbed up to the top to get his tender leaves Major Ward walked by and said, "Soldier, what are you doing in that tree?"

"It's not a tree, it's a tobacco plant. I'm up here getting some of the tender leaves for chewing."

The major, keeping a straight face, ordered Kaiser down.

"Buy your tobacco at the PX like everyone else does. Who is your airplane commander?" demanded Ward.

"Lieutenant Hammett," answered Kaiser.

"I might have known," said Ward.

The reputation the crew had acquired was hard to shed. Chuck Stevenson, another pilot in Ward's squadron, had several talks with the major trying to save Hammett, who he felt was one of the best pilots in the group.

Finally the day arrived when the lucky sixty-two airplane commanders' names were posted on a bulletin board, and Hammett's name was missing.

Thornton and Smith read the bad news together, and then a friend from another crew pointed to an open-doored hangar across the way that contained a ravished B–24. It was a wreck, with one remaining propeller, all the engine cowlings gone and parts of some engines missing. It was a so-called Hangar Queen, kept around to be cannibalized for parts.

"There's your plane," he said with a laugh.

They were the "Hangar Queen" crew from then on, and went to war as passengers.

As the year came to a close the 460th Bomb Group departed for its trek down the line to join the Fifteenth Air Force. "Down the line'" was a term for the route to North Africa via South America and Dakar.

While the 460th and several other groups were gathering for a southern trip to join the fold, the Fifteenth AF's headquarters moved north from its base in Tunis, Tunisia, to a new site in Bari, Italy, to be nearer its six bomb groups that had already been transferred to Italy.

That month the Fifteenth flew missions on sixteen days to over forty targets—most of the targets being airdromes, as they were called those days. Marshaling yards began to get some attention, in an effort to curtail transportation in the war zone.

As the 460th "Black Panthers" headed down the line, the "Hangar Queen" crew was split up into four planes. Co-pilot Rhodes and bombardier Newby were on the same plane, riding on the flight deck. As they were starting across the 100 mile wide Amazon, Newby decided to go back to the waist section where he talked someone into letting him go down in the ball turret.

When they closed the trap door over his head and lowered the ball to its combat position *outside* of the plane, he had never felt so out of everything as he was at that moment. The only thing holding him up was a couple of bolts, or whatever they used to secure the turret.

He swung the turret around, up and down, and all he ever saw was the bottom of the bomber and the Amazon River. It was just about the most frightening moment of his life, on a par with takeoffs at Davis-Monthan. He couldn't imagine a shooting match with an Me 109. The fighter can break it off anytime things get too hot, but the ball gunner is trapped where he is sitting. He finally yelled for help to get back into the world as he knew it.

The bomber took them as far as Fortaleza, Brazil, where they spent four days in the exclusive Hotel De Gink. The Air Transport Command (ATC) operated a huge chain of Hotel De Ginks all over the world. They weren't exactly Hiltons or Statlers, but they did offer beds and food, and the rates were attractive—free.

The fleet of ATC planes consisted for the most part of C-47s that featured a row of bucket seats along each side of the interior of the plane. A bucket seat was a 14 in. dimple in a ledge running the length of the interior. They were not only uncomfortable, but cold when the uninsulated plane got up to altitude. Everyone traveled tourist class.

The fleet also included C-87s (converted B-24s) for the transatlantic flight to Dakar.

All bomber personnel on the way to war received an A-1 priority pass, which was the best one available, and would bump any higher ranking soldier not a bomber crew member. A private could bump a colonel. What power!

When the weather broke they were put on C-87s for the night hop across to Dakar. The commercial airliner type reclining seats, with pillow and blanket, were comfortable, so the "Hangar Queen" crew had a better trip across than those in their own planes. Small consolation.

As the C-87 touched down at Dakar it sounded like it had been hit by a bomb, and startled even the jaded flyers aboard. The noise came from the Marston Mat landing surface. Marston Mats were perforated steel panels about 10x1 ft. The panels were welded together to form relatively smooth, but noisy landing surfaces.

While these flyers at Dakar were experiencing their first taste of war conditions, American ground personnel were right behind our advancing armies in Italy, rough grading and laying down more of these metal air strips. Thus were Fifteenth Air Force bases being constructed as the future occupants were en route from stateside training bases.

Active bomb groups were moving en masse from Tunisian air bases to the new Italian airfields as they were completed, without missing a beat. Vacated bases were turned into staging areas for the new bomb groups en route to war.

The logistics of the move were staggering: in January three new groups were staged at Tunis and moved on up to Italy; the new air force increased its mission count to seventy-four targets for the month.

During the boring, cold C-47 trip to Marrakech, Morocco, over the hot Sahara Desert Newby introduced Rhodes to chess, with a cheap 6x6 in. piece

Tail gunner's view—tight formation.

of cardboard, the reverse side of which had thirty-two round cutouts with chessmen pictures on them. This exciting pastime was interrupted by a stopover in the middle of the desert for gas. There the American tourists saw their first German fighter planes, wrecked as they were, and their first working swastikas—more indications of the war they had been reading about.

The souvenir prone Americans made straight for the pile of newly found prizes, but were told in brusque barracks language to stay away; the planes were still booby-trapped.

It was beginning to get exciting.

At Marrakech the two flyers checked in to the Hotel De Gink and were assigned army cots in a windowless former classroom of a bombed-out school building. The two army blankets were not enough to keep out the chill of a night on the other end of the temperature spectrum from the midday heat of the desert. During the night both men got up, put on their uniforms, placed overcoats on top of the covers and climbed back into bed.

The next morning they decided to test their A-1 priority passes by skipping the early flight to Algiers, opting for a leisurely mid-morning takeoff. Many others made the same decision so there were more passengers than seats when they arrived.

While hanging around the gate they heard a story about a man who made a career out of special passes. It seems he had a priority pass to anywhere. He traveled all over Africa, India and the Middle East having a ball: free meals, free lodging at the ubiquitous Hotel De Ginks and free transportation. He even managed to get paid once a month.

The chess players were about to find out how good their A-1 passes were. As the corporal at the counter checked off available seats he told the two full colonels just ahead of them that they were the last two for the flight.

Rhodes noted that while the Air Force field grade officers had two rows of campaign ribbons on their chests there was not a pair of silver wings included. Here comes the test, he thought.

He waved his A-1 pass at the corporal and said, "We would like those two seats." The embarrassed corporal had to tell the two colonels they had been bumped. The colonels were likewise embarrassed, and angry at being upstaged by two grinning shavetails with silver wings and no ribbons on their

110

chest. The two flyers, for one reason or another, hadn't even earned a good conduct ribbon.

Algiers was an interesting city. More evidence of war: wrecked tanks and airplanes strewn everywhere. This was the city where Rommel and Montgomery had it out. The contrast of pedestrians intrigued the flyers: modernly dressed people, American military and traditionally dressed Arabs, or A-Rabs, as the Americans disparagingly called them.

They ran into several crew members and one of them told of meeting an MP who had agreed to take some of them on a tour of the Casbah, the famed walled city of murderers and crime. It was off-limits to GIs, but Rhodes and Newby decided it was fair game for two enterprising air force men.

They met the MP and hired a horse-drawn cab for the stealthy incursion through a dark back alley. The MP removed his white helmet, arm band and white gun belt, but kept the gun in his hand. The two "Hangar Queen" crewmen, on their first mission together, removed .45s from shoulder holsters and got as ready as they could for the unknown. None of the three would have known what to do if challenged.

The Casbah street was not much wider than the carriage. The dark objects grouped here and there just a foot or two away may not have been noticed if it weren't for the small red glows near the tops. When the red glows suddenly moved about halfway down and then back up it meant the black objects were alive. They were men hanging around on the streets, smoking, just like back home.

The Americans were intruders; they were slumming, and probably not welcome. Mindful of the warnings about the murdering ways of Arabs the unauthorized expeditionary force held their guns in ready position as the driver brazened his way through the hostile crowd.

Suddenly a shower of red glows headed their way from both sides of the street. Was this an unprovoked attack on the Americans? Should they retaliate? They were all properly frightened, but had enough sense not to fire back.

The driver finally made his way out the front gate to safety, and the men of the "Hangar Queen" crew survived their first sortie into enemy land.

It is a truism that two people can sit down to the same army mess meal and view it quite differently. The man who has been at the base awhile feels it is awful; the new arrival, comparing it to his previous base, thinks it is pretty good, for a while.

When the flyers traveling down the line began eating their first meals at North African Transient Messes the food wasn't too bad, and they couldn't understand the grumbling of the regulars. After two days in Algiers they caught up with the regulars and learned to complain about the fare like the troopers they were fast becoming.

They still had a week before they were due at their staging air base in Tunis, so they decided to stay around a few more days. They could have a good meal at a swanky-looking restaurant they had cased earlier in greater downtown Algiers.

When Rhodes, Newby, Hammett and Wood were faced with tablecloths, six or seven pieces of silverware, tall glass tumblers, including wine glasses, real china and a strolling violinist, they weren't sure they had made a good decision. It was like no restaurant any of them had ever been in.

The formally attired waiter smiled, handed Hammett the wine list and said something in French. Hammett gulped and looked around for help, but found nothing but smiling faces, and shrugs. Hammett nodded and pointed to a selection. The waiter said something and looked quizzically at the others. They, of course, all nodded in agreement.

That was easy, but when the waiter handed each of them his own menu they were all on their own.

Someone figured out the salad and the entrée sections, but from there it was all guesswork. Rhodes mimed a person reeling in a fish and the alert waiter pointed to two selections, from which he gambled on one. Newby made like a cow and mooed in counterpoint to the violinist, figuring a French moo was the same as an American moo. The waiter obligingly pointed to two selections, and the pseudo thespian made his choice. The others merely pointed to a selection and took their chances.

Three of them were served something resembling food they had eaten before, but all Newby saw was a cow's black tongue sticking out at him from a bare plate, the wide part toward him. Grotesque was the only description he could muster in his surprised mind. He could envision the cow's face around it; big pleading eyes staring at him.

After calling for more wine, by waving his glass as he would in a neighborhood bar, Newby took a deep breath and pitched in. He felt like a cannibal, and it bothered the others to see him eating the tongue, but he persevered to finish his meal, insisting it was good.

That evening at the base bar they met a genuine war correspondent, who enthralled them with a firsthand accounting of the recent tank battles in El Alamein, Egypt, and Tunis. The war was rapidly becoming more than something they had heard or read about.

He gave them some gratuitous advice on a subject they had never considered to be a fighting man's problem, but apparently was a common ailment for foot soldiers.

They learned how to treat crabs without the benefit of a local pharmacy. Just lather up the afflicted area and let the soapsuds dry in place. He claimed it kills them all.

"Hey Newb!" resounded from across the wide main street of Algiers one day. The bombardier looked up, and there racing across the street was Bill McMahon, a wide grin on his Irish face, and waving three $10 bills.

Mac was also on his way to Tunis, to join his bomb group, and was pleased to see his buddy and repay his debt. They dropped in at a sidewalk cafe and had a cognac. The Algerians had never heard of bourbon. After a short visit they shook hands and went on their separate ways, never to see each other again.

The "Hangar Queen" crew managed to get together on a couple of occasions while in Algiers, and finally they all decided it was time to go to where their orders had sent them. On January 22 they bid farewell to the Hotel De Gink, flashed their A–1 passes and boarded an ATC plane to Tunis.

Upon arrival they read the bulletin board to learn the 460th was reassigned to Oudna No. 1, but it would not be ready for a day or two. Stand by for further orders.

Now they would get to sample the cuisine of a new transient mess. It was cold and they were hungry when they stood in the chow line, only to learn the main course was corned beef and cabbage. Newby had refused to eat cabbage all his life and now he was faced with that or nothing. He was so hungry he took some on his plate, and figured if he could go a cow's tongue he might make this. To his surprising delight he enjoyed the cabbage, and wasn't sure if he should tell his mother.

The crew decided to add a little culture to their laurels and went out to visit the aqueducts that carried water from the mountains to the great city of Carthage on the Mediterranean. The water traveled by gravity flow hundreds of miles across wide valleys and tunneled through hills. They stood in awe beneath the remains of a series of aqueduct archways that stood 160 ft. high; not far away the channel merged with the hillside where water was still running, and people were drawing water for personal use.

Finally, the bulletin board ordered them to their new staging base, where they met all the other crews and the sixty-two new bombers of the 460th Bomb Group.

At Oudna No. 1 the Group began a regimen of daily formation flying with skeleton crews. The nonessential flyers got to do hours of close order drill— just to let them know they were still in the Army Air Forces. It seemed cruel and unusual punishment to meet 6:00 A.M. reveille every morning, clean shaven, and nothing to do. Good for morale, they explained.

Everyone got a day off finally and most of the flyers headed for Tunis, about ten miles away. One's first trip to Tunis is a memorable event. The experience begins a mile or so downwind of the city, where a strange, unpleasant odor fills the air. After checking each other for the source the travelers decided it was coming from somewhere else.

The odor was stale urine and feces. The residents of that quaint city used the street to relieve themselves. They weren't subtle about it, either.

Concave street centers were part of the city sewage system; human wastes that were eliminated indoors ended up in the street. Women dumped garbage from second-floor windows onto the sidewalk. All things considered, the distinctive odor was certainly understandable.

Tunis was always an afternoon visit, never at night. After dark, GIs were fair game to have their throat cut, as a few found out—too late.

You weren't in danger of your life in daytime, but you could lose your wallet to a pickpocket. The "Hangar Queen" flyers were walking along a street when another GI passed them up walking the same way. His right back pocket was hanging down flopping as he walked. He was unaware that an Arab had cut across his wallet with a knife, and lifted out the prize.

The Seven-Eleven Club, a private watering hole for Allied officers, was a fairly ordinary bar by American standards. But the unisex latrine certainly was different. Along the left and far side of the room was a series of eight-inch holes in the floor. Straddling each hole was a pair of oversized shoe prints. Underneath the holes a water channel ran the length of the wall.

A peninsula jutted out from the right wall, an open trough along each side, and water running along the length of each trough. That was the extent of toilet facilities.

After a few drinks the crew filed into the latrine for some quick relief and lined up along the group urinal. Nothing strange about that, but when two British women officers came in, glanced along the row of standees, uttered a snide comment or two, straddled selected holes, stooped and dropped their drawers it was too much. The scene elicited a common reaction: I can't believe what I am doing and watching at the same time.

Life back at the base finally became exciting with a report of a 70 mph wind on its way. All hands turned out to secure the planes. They were all faced into the direction of the expected wind; the planes pushed so that the wheels went into small holes, dug for that purpose; the tails tied down with rope and stakes.

Tents were also tied down with extra ropes and stakes, but some did not fare as well as the planes, which survived the onslaught. The tent shared by the "Hangar Queen" officers and two others began to rise on one end, so all of the occupants ran outside and held on to the lifting ropes, until the emergency was over. They saved the tent. Another battle won by this downtrodden crew.

While the new bomb groups were gathering in the Tunis area, awaiting their turn to move on up to the real war zone and begin bombing the Germans, the Germans did a little bombing of their own.

On the night of December 2, 1943, in the harbor of Bari, Italy, seventeen ships were totally destroyed and eight others damaged by the Luftwaffe bombers. Thousands of bombs, flak suits, ammunition, parachutes, and other vital supplies went to the bottom of the bay.

The greatest tragedy was caused by the sinking of the USS *John Harvey*, which had on board one hundred tons of one hundred pound mustard gas bombs. The mustard gas spread across the harbor, mixing with the surface oil or evaporating and combining with the flame and smoke. Men in the water became contaminated with the mustard, and the gas moved into the city, contaminating and killing over one thousand civilians and military personnel. The hospitals, unaware of the gas involvement, were not treating victims properly. Those affected just suffered and died. (More information on this rare mustard gas bombing can be found in *Disaster at Bari* by Glen B. Infield.)

During this tiresome waiting period Col. Robert Crowder, CO of the 460th, flew up to Italy and went on a couple of missions as a co-pilot with one of the established groups.

In the meantime Sgt. Sid Woods had a little excitement of his own, right there in Oudna No. 1. Each of the enlisted men had to take turns standing guard duty all night, one for each plane. This annoyed the men of the "Hangar Queen" crew—standing guard over someone else's plane, after being denied one of their own.

One night while Woods was reluctantly standing his shift, the Officer of the Day received a report that there was trouble out at one of the planes. He grabbed an MP and they drove out to where poor old Sid was holding three loud-talking, arm-waving, flowing tattle-tale-gray robed Arabs at bay with his Thompson sub machine gun.

"What's up, sergeant?" said the OD as he alighted from the Jeep.

"They want *their* airplane. This afternoon someone sold it to them for six chickens."

Woods later said that even though he held the gun he was more scared than they were. They ignored his gun and were threatening, almost attacking him; he couldn't bring himself to shoot them.

On Valentine's Day the sixty-two new B–24s and sixty-eight bomber crews of the 460th Bomb Group set out for the newly built air base awaiting them in Spinazzola, Italy, located at about the ankle area of the Italian boot. The three other groups that had flown up in January would be on line this month, bringing the Fifteenth's total to twelve.

The 460th would take their place "on deck," as they say in baseball.

One of the arguments for establishing an Italian-based air force was the good flying weather available in the winter, when the England-based Eighth Air Force was standing down a lot.

Now that the Fifteenth was committed to Italy, planners were learning that European February bad weather was not restricted to England. The weather over Italy was so foul the Fifteenth could fly missions on only six of the first thirteen days of February, resuming increased activities on the fourteenth.

The sixty-two pilots of the 460th were flying over unfamiliar territory in barely marginal flying weather. Letting down through the rain producing clouds near Spinazzola was hazardous at best, and for two of the planes it was fatal—they crashed into the mountains near the new base.

At their new home the Marston Mat landing strip was in place; the ground crews who had come over by ship had set up the Group and Squadron Headquarters and their own living quarters; all that remained was establishing the living quarters for the flying personnel. If the 460th flying personnel thought they had been living a Spartan life the past six weeks, compared to stateside, they were in for a shock at Spinazzola. It had been raining for several days and the designated tent area was a quagmire.

The area was divided into four sections, one for each squadron, and scattered throughout were wooden stakes protruding from the mud, each with a small piece of paper containing an airplane commander's name. Each stake represented a tent site that would be the home of six men. The enlisted men of a crew would be intact, but the officers of crews without a plane had to split up.

So it was that Rhodes and Newby were assigned to live with Bob Holland and his crew; Hammett and Wood were assigned to live with Charlie Stevenson, the man who went to bat for Hammett when he and his crew were in disfavor with Major Ward and Colonel Harrison.

A truck pulled up and two indifferent privates dumped off a folded pyramidal tent into the mud and threw some poles, stakes, rope and six army cots on top, grinning as they drove away.

The mental picture suggested by the words of the Army Air Corps song, "Off we go into the wild blue yonder," didn't seem to fit the scene they were now in.

As they stood in ankle-deep mud, watching the leering yardbirds disappear from sight, any self-image they might have had of being a prima donna airman was quenched by their mucky trap.

There probably isn't a better way to get acquainted with new tentmates then erecting a large pyramidal tent in the mud. When they placed the cots in the tent the legs sank down several inches and just barely kept the canvas out of the mud. By the time the tent was up it began to snow. Such was the 460th's introduction to sunny Italy.

The local natives, who did laundry and other menial tasks around the base, kept telling everyone to wait until the Ides of March, when the sun would come out and the sky would be clear all summer. They looked upon March 15 in a manner somewhat like Americans look at Groundhog Day on February 2.

The planners of overall strategy had long been looking forward to a joint Eighth AF, RAF (night) and Fifteenth AF attack on the German aircraft industry. The code name was ARGUMENT, and they needed a week of good flying weather to put it into action. The week of February 20 was set for what would later be known as Big Week. The considerably larger Eighth Air Force would carry the brunt of the attack, but their little brothers to the south would carry their weight also.

The Fifteenth could not participate on opening day due to prior commitments at Anzio for the B-24s and icing conditions over the Alps for the B-17s.

On February 21 the Fifteenth stood down due to weather, but on February 22 a force of 183 bombers hit two Messerschmitt factories at Regensburg, Germany, losing nineteen planes. Other planes hit targets in other countries that day.

February 23 saw 102 of the heavies hitting the ball bearing works at Steyr, Austria, with a loss of seventeen planes.

On day five, February 24, they went back to Steyr to hit an aircraft component factory and industrial targets and marshaling yards in Yugoslavia and Austria. They lost seventeen that day.

On the final day, February 25, the Fifteenth sent 400 planes back to the Regensburg aircraft factories and suffered a loss of thirty-nine bombers.

Many of the losses were to fighters who were ferociously defending the womb from whence they had been spawned. Flak was heavy at both targets. The ninety-two bomber loss was high, but the Luftwaffe lost several hundred fighters on the wing and over 500 fighter planes in the womb. The German aircraft industry lost some sixty-eight percent of its factory buildings, and the ball-bearing industry a number of its facilities as 3,800 ARGUMENT bombers unleashed 10,000 tons of bombs during Big Week. To appreciate the enormity of this operation, the Eighth Air Force dropped 10,000 tons in its entire first year of operation.

Bomb tonnage on aircraft factories dropped to 2,400 tons in March, due to bad weather, and hit a record high of 12,000 in April. Despite this attention to the German aircraft production their monthly production rate stayed at 1,400 a month during that period. The reason was that Germany had begun dispersing their aircraft complexes early in the year. Obviously American bombing attacks were not really stopping the Luftwaffe in the womb. It would soon be evident that they would have to be stopped on the wing.

While the rest of the air force was engaging in Big Week, and its heavy losses, the only oblivious new recruits of the 460th were standing on the sidelines grumbling about the cold, the mud, the eating outside in the snow and that new insidious accommodation, the straddle trench.

For one who has never used a straddle trench before, it is an experience. A straddle trench, which makes an outhouse look like a gold-plated bathroom, is about 1 ft. wide, 2 ft. deep, and perhaps 20 ft. long. Any number of men can use this facility at the same time. Particularly exciting is to be downwind on a windy day. The flak gets rather heavy. What generally happens is the participants usually get to laughing so much at their plight some of them almost fall in.

The day the 460th arrived they had been greeted by Berlin Sally, who said, "Welcome Colonel Crowder and all the Black Panthers of the 460th Bomb Group. We almost got your ground crew on the way over, and we will be looking for you in the air. While you are being shot out of the skies over here, your girlfriends and wives will be having a good time with their civilian boyfriend back home. Wouldn't you rather be there?"

The visitors to Italy were not impressed with Sally, merely amused. After all, she did play good music; she couldn't be all bad. The listeners, far afield, were merely American youngsters just recently out of teenage status who still enjoyed their favorite big bands, even from this questionable source. It was cool. The only problem was the lack of radios at that stage of their careers. Later when they began flying missions, they would catch her show more often.

When these same young men were faced with a serious need for something, they showed an inherent trait called Yankee ingenuity. Even the southerners had it.

The obvious need was to be warm and to walk on solid ground inside their tents.

"Hangar Queeners" Newby and Rhodes seemed to fit well into their host crew's tent family. Pilot Bob Holland, co-pilot Bob Zorns, navigator Vince McCoy and bombardier Mo Wollan treated them as one of their own. After a week or so of slopping around in the muddy interior, tent boss Holland suggested they get modern like some of the other tents, and install a furnace.

Some enterprising tent groups had devised a simple tent furnace that burned raw 100 octane aviation gasoline. It was another of those new experiences that took some doing to get used to; a roaring cherry-red furnace about 5 ft. from your cot wasn't exactly music for sleeping. It took a lot of courage to close one's eyes in that environment.

The construction was simple. A ten-gallon can was the furnace. A small "rat hole" was cut out of the front near the bottom, about 3 in. wide. Inside the hole was placed a Planter's peanut can, which had several ¼ in. holes punched in the sides, about halfway down. Into the top of the can ran the end of some copper tubing, and out of the tubing poured raw gasoline. The tubing ran underground from a fifty-five-gallon drum located outside and up on a platform. The copper tubing was separated near the drum and joined with a short section of rubber tubing with a screw clamp on it. This was the flow control.

The chimney was a section of 3 in. piping extending from the furnace, along the main tent pole and out through the top of the tent. The lower couple of feet of the chimney would also glow cherry red, requiring a piece of metal to shield the pole.

Holland's gang scrounged all the necessary parts and assembled the furnace; Zorns started the siphoning action by sucking on the rubber tube before McCoy closed the clamp; then they looked around for someone to light it.

Lighting this monster was a feat of raw courage. Everyone left the tent except the one who drew the short straw. The trick was to get some flame into the peanut can *before* opening the flow control. If any of the gasoline arrived at the peanut can and became fumes before the starter flame was inserted, the man on lighting detail was in for a surprise. Once lit, it stayed on until warm weather.

Bombardier Wollan spoke up, "The honor of bringing this tent into the 20th century and lighting the furnace should go to the most important man on the crew, the bombardier. In all modesty I vote for our esteemed guest Ted Newby. All those in favor say 'aye.'"

It was an ingenuous ploy. No self-respecting flyer normally will admit any other position is more important than his, but the four other cowards meekly responded, "Aye."

After winning the election Newby found himself alone in the tent with his rolled-up section of *Stars and Stripes* and the awaiting furnace. Or was it a bomb?

Dusty Rhodes stood outside with the tent flap held high. "I'll hold the door open, Newb, in case you have to leave in a hurry."

"Thanks, *pal*," he replied.

The unhappy election winner lighted the end of his torch, stood to one side, ready to run, and gingerly inserted the flame into the rat hole. Nothing. With that he left the tent and said, "Turn 'er on." Holland unscrewed the clamp a turn or two; raw gasoline poured onto the lighted paper before deadly fumes could build up. The furnace was lit, and did not blow up. Then came the roar of flames filling the interior of the furnace—a roar that would last until warm weather set in.

Soon after most everyone had installed a furnace someone backed a truck up to a tent with an operating, red-hot furnace, in preparation for unloading a drum of gasoline. They managed to tip it over and gasoline cascaded in through the tent flap toward the roaring fire. When the tent exploded, the pajama-clad occupants went slithering out under the sides, leaving all their earthly belongings behind.

Others chipped in and donated clothing to the fire victims, who fortunately were not seriously injured.

Newby's first trip to the PX, ration card in hand, required an hour's wait in line. His reward was one Clark Bar. Later trips resulted in reasonable quantities of candy, beer, cigarettes and other items. Each tent received one candle every other day, and sixteen sheets of toilet paper per man, per day. Toilet paper was almost like currency. It was used in poker games and for bargaining purposes.

During Big Week the 460th was preparing for its entry into the war: pilots practicing formation flying; bombardiers out at the bombing range; gunners at the gunnery range.

March came in like a lion; the Fifteenth AF could mount an attack on only five days out of the first fourteen, just two days from the 5th through the 14th. The problem was Italian weather, not target conditions.

Then came the Ides of March. On March 15 the clouds went away, the sun came out and the Fifteenth AF flew missions the next five days, and again on six of the final ten days as March, except for one final mild snow, crept out like a lamb.

The "Hangar Queen" officers' crew celebrated the sunny day in a less exciting way than the rest of the Air Force; they visited the town of Spinazzola and went to a public bathhouse which was part of a monastery, run by busy nuns and smiling monks. A steaming bath in a big old-fashioned tub was a treat, compared to sponge baths out of a helmet.

The fellows were struck by the lack of young girls on the streets. Not a one! A number of mature women, though, were walking around with tall bottles balanced on their heads. They were fascinated by the sight of a woman balancing a three-foot-high bottle full of water or wine on her head, a little pad of some sort serving as a base. Even though she would use one hand to balance her cargo, it was quite a feat.

There was a constant lineup at the flowing fountain in the main square, women filling containers to take home and horses enjoying a drink a few feet away.

It was amusing to see chickens flying out of windows of residential houses, and downright astounding to see a horse walk out of one house.

They purchased two kerosene lamps, one for Hammett's tent and one for Holland's tent, which would make them the envy of others who had to share one candle for six men to write letters at night.

118

Later, one of Holland's tent mates swiped some sugar, cocoa and canned milk from the mess hall and they made fudge in a mess kit over the furnace. Best any of them had ever eaten.

Spurred on by that success they borrowed some bread from the mess hall, rounded up some K rations containing tins of cheese, and had toasted cheese sandwiches for a few nights—until they were caught.

Colonel Harrison had been chiding the Squadron Officers about their lazy acceptance of living conditions for the flying crews. He felt strongly that it was essential his people live well, and be proud of their surroundings.

His first directive for better living conditions had been his order in early March that all tents have a hard surface by a certain date. After much grumbling most tent units complied. Not Holland's gang. They had obtained the materials, but procrastinated the floor laying. A command appearance at the colonel's quarters late one evening was their reward for taking his order lightly. A long wait in the rain, followed by a stern lecture, convinced them to lay the floor by reveille. Then they had the comfortable home the colonel wanted them to have, despite the mud surrounding their tent.

Hard surfaces in tents was a start, but they could do better, he told them. Trucks would be made available for obtaining needed supplies. The chide was an order in disguise. His remarks were like fire to tinder.

The Group was destined to stand down for the next six days, and during that period a building boom started in the area that would please any real estate developer. Within a span of a few weeks a bivouac of pyramidal tents turned into a small village of white tufa block and tile houses, unique to Italian air bases. The Holland tent unit continued its policy of procrastination and half-heartedly began gathering materials, but made no real effort to join the others in bettering their living quarters.

Tufa, a native white stone resembling soft sandstone and cut into 18x12 in. blocks, weighing 80 lbs., was obtained from a local quarry. A 16x24 ft. house required about 800 blocks. Men from tent units hauled tufa blocks after dark, and local contractors and workers were hired. Red roofing tile and lumber were obtained to complete the roofs. A typical house cost about $180 to build.

The morale effect of Harrison's message was remarkable. Conversation in the chow lines at the mess tent was about tufa block houses, roofing tile and fireplace design, rather than the usual gripes about living conditions—despite a few smashed toes from dropped tufa blocks.

The Holland tent unit was conspicuous by its noncompliance, but they doggedly stayed with their ramshackle tent affectionately, or perhaps defiantly, called *home*.

About a month later the group would be heralding the newly built Officer and Non Com clubs and dining areas, which would become the envy of the Fifteenth Air Force.

The tufa block housing complex and clubs became known all over Italy as Bomber City, and even invited comments by Berlin Sally, who promised to reduce it to white dust. She never came through on that one.

On March 19 the 460th flew its first mission, a milk run to the marshaling yards at Metkovic, Yugoslavia. The Fifteenth offered this little patsy to all groups on their maiden mission. Holland's crew drew the honors for the historic flight. Newby and Rhodes heard the others shaving and trying to act nonchalant that morning, while they pretended to be asleep. The four empty, made-up bunks had a sort of final look to the late risers. Will they be back? Newby wondered.

The Group did a poor job of assembling and set out for Yugoslavia in a ragged assemblage that did not deserve the name formation. They were all over the sky as they joined several other Groups heading for the Balkans. Certainly not up to Fifteenth AF standards. Fortunately no planes were lost in the debacle.

Although three new Groups had gone on line for the Fifteenth this month, only two of them were allowed to fly in combat. The day after the Metkovic fiasco the 460th Bomb Group was ordered to stay out of the sky while the war was going on. They could go up in the air after the others had left for war, but get back on the ground before they returned. When they learned to fly in formation they could get back in the war.

Colonels Crowder and Harrison were dumbfounded at the severity of their reprimand, and took swift measures to correct the affront to their proud "Black Panther" Bomb Group.

For seven straight days half of the pilots went up for formation practice in the morning, and the other half in the afternoon. Colonel Harrison sat in the tail turret of the lead plane, with a formation sheet on his lap, lambasting, by radio, any pilot who strayed from tight formation. The frenzied pilots were actually tapping each other's wings on occasion.

While this electronic whiplashing was taking place in the air the other pilots and crews were marching in close order drill on the ground—just like in cadet days.

This regimen paid off. It got them back in good graces with the Fifteenth Air Force, and over the next few months saved countless lives; time after time the ultra-tight formation of 460th bombers would be bypassed by German fighters seeking less disciplined patsies to attack. Harrison was not very popular at the time, but many a crew thanked the good Lord for his insistence on a tight formation the Germans respected. The firepower of a tight formation normally is too much for just a few fighters to dare an attack.

On March 23 the "Hangar Queen" crew was scheduled for one of several practice missions following the ejection from the war, and while eating their breakfast out of doors the last diehard snow of spring was settling on their canned-milk-covered oatmeal. The result was not watered-down milk, but a gritty residue remaining in the mouth after eating the cereal—like when the dentist cleans your teeth. The cook got a lot of negative votes that morning.

On the way to briefing the snowflakes melted on bare necks and wrists, leaving a gritty deposit. At briefing the flyers were notified that Vesuvius had erupted and the volcano ash had traveled the 100 miles to Spinazzola during the night. That explained the grit, and also the reason to scrub the mission. They were concerned the ash would damage the engines.

Finally, on March 30 they let the "Black Panthers" try it again. This time it was the Hammett "Hangar Queen" crew's turn, and the milk run was to Mostar, Yugoslavia. The Group made a good assembly, and flew good formation to the target area where they faced a 10/10 undercast. They could not see the target, and were forced to salvo the bombs in the ocean.

The Group lost its first plane to flak the following day at milk run Mostar. Then the "Hangar Queen" crew visited Knin, Yugoslavia, two days later and laid their bombs on the marshaling yards—a big morale booster.

The Fifteenth Air Force now had fifteen groups in action, and thoughts were centering on the big prize, Ploesti.

Chapter 9

The Big Wink

The quest for Ploesti oil, the taproot of German might, took a dramatic turn when the Russians, fresh from military successes in the Ukraine and Crimea, advanced westward to threaten, and even penetrate Rumania's eastern border.

This new development changed the direction of the Fifteenth Air Force and resulted in new marching orders. German transportation facilities in Rumania now had to be destroyed; German eastern front resistance must be weakened.

Russia was in effect assigned the role of capturing Ploesti and the other important refineries in oil rich Rumania. The United States's more subtle role would be to choke Ploesti indirectly.

To accomplish this high-level objective, a new set of priorities was established for the Fifteenth Air Force in early April:

1. Destroy the Bucharest and Ploesti railroad facilities.
2. Bomb Budapest railroad targets.
3. Bomb other Balkan targets.
4. Attack rail communication centers also on the famed Orient Express route, which ran from southeastern Bulgaria through Sofia, Nis, Belgrade and Zagreb, and attack the rail lines attaching to it from the south.

Oil refinery targets were conspicuously omitted.

In keeping with the new directive the 460th bombed rail lines at Mostar and Knin, Yugoslavia, losing one plane (at milk run Mostar), and on April 5 were assigned the marshaling yards at Nis, their first brush with the route of the Orient Express. The mission started off badly and got worse. A plane crashed on takeoff, killing most aboard.

Bob Holland was scheduled to fly the No. 4 position, known as the slot, right behind the lead plane and far enough below to avoid its propwash.

As the bombers were assembling a few thousand feet over Altamura, Italy, a nearby town, Holland was edging his way into the slot, when his plane became ensnared in the lead ship's propwash. The force of the turbulent air flipped Holland's plane over on its left wing and slammed it into the front of Russell's plane, flying in the No. 6 position.

Neither pilot had a chance to avert the mid-air; none of the twenty men aboard had a real chance to jump, although one did manage to get out, but his chute failed to open in time.

The loss of three planes before the group got under way had a telling effect on the others. The shocked, not yet battle tested pilots could not hold formation; they scattered all over the sky. When they were still many miles from the target area a bomb fell from one of the lead planes and thirteen tense bombardiers toggled their bombs onto some open fields. Bombs were dropped all over the countryside near the target, located on the edge of Nis, but none on the marshaling yards.

The siege of Ploesti was on that day, despite the 460th's futile effort at Nis. General Arnold had informed General Spaatz that the Combined Chiefs had no objection to bombing Ploesti, as long as the bombing directive specified transportation targets only. It isn't easy to include a wink in a coded radio message, but somehow it must have been done.

The Fifteenth Air Force had been given (subtle as it was) the green light it had been waiting for. Ploesti's main marshaling yards were directly north of and adjacent to the Astra Romana refinery, White 4 target of TIDAL WAVE fame, and completely surrounded the Phoenix-Orion refinery.

Astra Romana's tank farm, consisting of 334 oil storage tanks, held 425,000 metric tons of oil and gasoline (over a month's production of all refineries). If you destroy the means of moving this supply to the German forces at the eastern front it might as well not exist. That logic would seem to be in keeping with the intention of the directive.

The Big Wink seemed to have trickled down to the seven bomb groups assigned to the first high-level attack at Ploesti. The entire force of 230 bombers was ordered on a heading of 135 degrees to hit the giant marshaling yards broadside; obviously any spillovers might accidentally land on the tank farm.

Fifteenth Air Force B-24 unloads 12 500 pounders through a 10/10 undercast.

A few bombs hit the marshaling yards, but somehow the majority landed on the tank farm, causing huge fires reminiscent of TIDAL WAVE days. Official communiqués reported heavy damage to the transportation facility, with some incidental damage to the Astra Romana refinery. All Air Force secret reports and documents solemnly perpetrated the charade. The rape of White 4 was on again, only this time it was a virgin target.

Thirteen bombers were lost on that maiden high-level attack on Ploesti. The uninformed may call this incursion a raid, but no veteran of Ploesti skies will accept that term. A raid suggests a stealthy, guerrilla type of activity.

There is nothing secretive about several hundred four-engine bombers flying into the deadly flak barrage box at the bomb release point. The hundreds of flak gunners rarely aim at individual bombers, they simply keep filling that big square in the sky with exploding flak shells. Red flashes are the ones that get you. Black puffs are death's calling cards, from earlier red flashes. The pilots just take a deep breath and send their souls into the invisible, for that staring match with death. Their orders are explicit: *no evasive action!* Fly straight in and straight out. Take it like a man. A raid indeed!

The members of the 460th knew nothing of the attack on Ploesti, they just knew their group had fouled up badly, and were concerned they would be kicked out of the air again.

That evening the war entered the tent Newby and Rhodes had shared with Holland's crew. They sat on their cots looking at the four empty, neatly made up bunks, pictures of wives or girlfriends in evidence.

Newby broke the silence, "Dusty, I know where they keep that jug of Johnny Walker's Red Label they've been hoarding for their 50 mission celebration. Won't do 'em any good now."

"It'll never get off of this base," said Rhodes.

"They would expect us to put it to an appropriate use now," Newby said.

"Right!" Rhodes agreed.

By the time the first visitors arrived a noticeable dent had been made in the bottle. Neighboring buddies had come in to help them commiserate, and toast the departed. Wasn't that the way they did it in the movies? Even Chaplain Dodds stopped in.

Life went on. Men came in, gathered up the dead mens' belongings and departed. Lt. H. P. Whitehead and his officer crew moved in, looking critically at the uneven, but hard, floor covering. They didn't know about muddy Italy.

The new tentmates had no sentimental feeling for their new crummy home, and insisted they get in step with the others. A contractor was hired, and the necessary materials were obtained to build a tufa house. Rafters to hold the roof tile were a concern, so they went out to a nearby mine and loaded a quantity of small-gauge rails onto a GI truck. The owner of the rails protested, but the Americans who came to save his country felt the rails were their due, and ignored his objections. Newby showed the man his ID card as authority for confiscation of his property. They had the man outnumbered six to one, which was perhaps the most persuasive argument.

They weren't as bad as the scroungers who earlier had taken the roof off a house while the protesting occupants still lived there.

Instead of the group being kicked out of the air again for the fiasco at Nis, they were pleasantly surprised to receive a commendation from the 55th Wing headquarters for destroying ammunition dumps with their wayward bombs. The Germans apparently thought they had them well hidden.

The group went to Zagreb, according to script, and bombed rail lines. One plane ditched in the sea on the way home. Seven men were rescued.

The Fifteenth Air Force would continue its relentless attacks on rail transportation throughout April, flying twenty-six such missions, while the RAF and a few selected Liberators dropped mines in the Danube River. This was effective as it stopped river traffic for a couple of weeks and jammed rail facilities, making them juicier targets for the high-level heavies.

One of the first of early replacement crews to arrive had a co-pilot named Lt. Thornton "Monte" Carlough, whose wife had given him a hand-tooled leather shoulder holster when he left Biggs Field in El Paso, Texas. On the way down the line he had acquired a pair of mosquito boots in Belem, Brazil, and while in Marrakech swapped four bottles of Four Roses Whiskey for a German Luger. He thought he was the group's answer to General Patton.

Arriving in Spinazzola he immediately wandered in to Group Headquarters and soon found himself in front of Colonels Crowder, Harrison and Campbell (the latter was Group operations officer).

Decked out in his boots, no blouse to hide his fancy shoulder holster and Luger and a proud smile, he threw a smart salute to the big three.

Colonel Harrison in his inimitable way told him, "This is no shootout at OK Corral, or an Al Capone underworld gang war. Wear Government Issue like the rest of us. Dismissed."

On April 15 the Fifteenth sent four groups of B–17s to wreak more havoc on the marshaling yards, while a strong force of B–24s including the 460th hit the Bucharest yards.

Heavy destruction of rail facilities was reported by the Fifteenth AF at Ploesti, with some incidental spillover damage to the refineries. Three planes were lost.

The 460th, on its first major mission, had been assigned the marshaling yards at Bucharest, some thirty miles south of Ploesti.

Colonel Crowder, the Group commanding officer, was leading the formation of thirty-six bombers. Hammett's "Hangar Queen" crew was flying Yellow "C" for Charlie in the No. 5 position of the lead box. Maj. Charles Ward, 763rd Squadron CO, was flying first pilot and Hammett was flying right seat.

The progression in the event of the loss of the leader's plane was for the No. 2 plane, immediately to its right, to assume the lead; the No. 5 plane then moved up to the No. 2 spot as deputy lead. This knowledge made bombardier Newby nervous, as he knew he was third in line to lead the group over the target.

About 100 miles from the IP the Group sighted a flight of enemy fighters. There was little concern because everyone felt the tight formation would dissuade any attack, but they underestimated the Goering "Yellow Nose" Squadron.

One of the problems of bombing Rumanian targets was that the bombers always flew into the sun: the morning sun on the way in and the afternoon sun on the way home. The sun at a fighter pilot's back is his greatest ally.

The "Yellow Nose" gang had the sun at its back as six of the Fw 190s dived head on at the bomber formation, 20 mm cannons and machine guns blazing. A cannon shell from the lead Focke-Wulf hit Crowder's plane in the nose,

124

exploded and enveloped the cockpit in flames. Gunners from the first three bombers converged their fire on the leader and his plane exploded, falling in front of the oncoming flight. The other German fighters continued firing as they flew right through the bomber formation.

When the bomber went into its death dive the pilot was last seen fighting to regain control of his plane so others might bail out. Three chutes were seen leaving the plane as it disappeared into the clouds.

The deputy lead moved up to lead; Major Ward moved *Yellow "C" for Charlie* into deputy lead. The "Hangar Queen" crew had flown *Yellow "C" for Charlie* the last two missions and even though a gas hog they kind of liked it.

Major Ward came on the interphone with, "Newby, I hope you have that bombsight warmed up. You'll be sighting for range."

"Yes, sir. All warmed up and I'm ready," Newby replied.

As they neared the IP someone said, "Look up north." It was the 460th's first look at Ploesti, where 137 of their brothers were flying into a flak barrage; a polka dot sky full of those calling cards of death.

The major said, "You'll get a firsthand look soon enough, pay attention to what's at hand."

The view down below was of more concern to the bombardier; the 10/10 undercast meant no visual target sighting. The lead plane would have to turn at the IP on ETA, to start the bomb run, and hope they would see some ground to pick up the target through some holes in the clouds.

No such luck. The bombs had to be dropped by ETA; when the navigator's watch read 1209 hours and 13 seconds he signaled the bombardier, who in turn flipped the toggle switch. Sixteen trailing bombardiers dutifully toggled their bombs when they saw the two lead planes' bombs fall. The second attack unit of eighteen planes suffered the same fate, so where the 340 500 lb. bombs landed none of them would ever know.

Clouds at the target were a gamble every bomb group in the European Theater often faced. You did your best under conditions as you found them.

Would-be cowboy Monte Carlough (complete with GI boots, shoulder holster and regulation Colt .45) was on his second combat mission, and when the smoke cleared from the shootout at Bucharest his trusty steed was limping; a feathered engine slowed them down enough that they could not keep up with the formation. At the junction of Bulgaria, Yugoslavia and Rumania, they were hit by fighters and forced to bail out. Except for the pilot, who was captured and spent the rest of the war in Stalag 3, the crew evaded capture and joined the Chetnik forces in Yugoslavia.

A few days later Colonel Harrison was made commanding officer of the 460th BG, and the disciplinarian who ordered his men to fly better, bomb better and live better was cheered.

The spirit of the "Hangar Queen" crew was reflected in their camaraderie and lighthearted banter in the air, despite some shortcomings in ground discipline. Bob Kaiser entertained the crew with his songs, and Danny Smith always brought along his lucky, stuffed donkey, on which he listed each target.

His contribution to their lucky ways was in printing on the names en route to the target. Smith had taken over as engineer when Dominic Minitti was taken off flying status due to ear problems.

Newby, who had never been out of Pittsburgh before joining the Air Forces, had difficulty understanding the three soft-spoken southerners: Charlie Hammett from South Carolina, Howard Thornton from North Carolina and Dusty Rhodes from Louisiana. He made it worse by asking them to repeat most everything they said, sometimes two or three times. It became downright funny when the pilot would call the bombardier to ask or tell him something and then have to repeat it. Somehow it didn't fit the picture of crisp interphone protocol on a flak-spiced bomb run over an enemy target. It infuriated the pilot when Newby asked him to spell out a particular word, a fact that probably spurred the bombardier on.

The southerners, in turn, thought he talked funny. One expression they enjoyed was the one he used when inquiring if someone had yet eaten, "Jeet chet?" Pittsburghers have many such provincial expressions.

A week after the Bucharest mission Hammett was given a plane of his own—*Yellow "C" for Charlie*. The crew promptly named it *Hangar Queen*, with a pretty girl in a skimpy bathing suit sitting in the foreground in front of an open hangar.

On April 23 the 460th joined hundreds of other bombers and fighter escort planes to hit aircraft factories and an airdrome at Wiener Neustadt and Bad Voslau, Austria. Thirteen bombers were lost, including two from the 460th, but fifty-one enemy fighters were destroyed.

On April 24 Hammett's crew flew *Hangar Queen* back to Bucharest where the group ruined the marshaling yards, and some spillover bombs blew up a roundhouse. It was like hitting a bull's-eye, as flames shot hundreds of feet into the air.

The "Black Panthers" had had a second sneak preview of Ploesti, when they earlier approached the northerly IP. The naturally clear sky above Ploesti was alive with a polka dot pattern of small black clouds. A formation of smaller dots was moving toward the mass of polka dots, which began to absorb the smaller ones like a sponge. Suddenly, the smaller dots and polka dots became one.

A black finger emerged from the polka dot clouds and slowly, to the observers, headed for the ground. Then another. It was too far away to see any parachutes.

A force of 290 bombers was hitting marshaling yards up there and the spillover was doing more incidental damage to the not yet officially bombed refineries. Eight bombers were lost.

The crew was proud of Hangar Queen.

Hangar Queen *on the way.*

126

The purpose of hitting Bucharest a few minutes after "bombs away" at Ploesti was to divide fighter opposition, as had been done on April 15. The plan was found to be effective.

Newby, Rhodes and Whitehead's four officers were sitting in their new Tufa house, each agreeing it was $30 well spent, when in walks a sergeant from headquarters and a familiar looking Italian man, with a smug look on his face. The sergeant counted the steel rails supporting the tile roof, turned to the occupants and announced, "Thirteen rails at $1 each is $13 you owe this gentleman." They were glad to round up the cash and get off that easily.

The monthly production at Ploesti had been 365,000 metric tons of fuel in March. As a result of the incidental spillover bombs during the three assaults on the marshaling yards, production for April was 172,000 tons—a fifty-three percent "accidental" curtailment of production. Astra Romana, the largest refinery in Europe, dropped from 170,000 tons to only 25,000 tons. The Fifteenth Air Force was having its proverbial cake and eating it, too. Still no mention in any official reports of an attack on Ploesti oil production.

Four more bomb groups joined the Fifteenth in April. Only two more to go to make the full complement of twenty-one groups.

The 460th Bomb Group ranked fourth in accuracy for the month of April, placing 21.9 percent of its bombs within 1,000 ft. of the briefed aiming point. The Fifteenth AF average was 16.3 percent.

POINTBLANK, the Combined Bomber Offensive (CBO), brought two widely held views of bombing priorities to a dramatic head. The British held that the widespread railway system in Europe should have first priority, long before Russia made its move in the Balkans.

Lt. Gen. Carl Spaatz, Commander, US Strategic Air Forces in Europe, wanted to destroy the Luftwaffe, mainly in the air. He wanted them to come up and fight, because he knew the US bombers and fighters could take them in direct battle. Bombing oil targets would draw up more fighters than bombing railroad lines and marshaling yards.

Gen. Dwight Eisenhower, US Army Commander, Allied Expeditionary Force, sided with the British, but left the door open for oil when he authorized bombing Ploesti marshaling yards.

On April 17 Eisenhower moved the German Air Force up to top priority for the United States Strategic Air Forces and that begged some interesting interpretation. The Luftwaffe used oil and gasoline, as the reasoning went, so attacks on oil installations could come under the general heading of POINT-BLANK without disturbing the Combined Chiefs or the British. There would be no change in the existing priorities. The destruction of fighters rising to defend oil refineries was certainly commendable, and in keeping with the intent of aerial combat.

Now the Eighth Air Force could destroy oil refineries, while pursuing POINTBLANK, and the Fifteenth could bomb oil targets under the guise of attacking marshaling yards. A cozy arrangement that made everyone happy. It would appear General Eisenhower was showing some of the political acumen that would mark his postwar career.

The three Ploesti incursions did not go without notice in Berlin, where Hitler was soon referring petulantly to the whining of the Rumanians about the air attacks.

The two teaser looks at Ploesti from high above Bucharest were viewed by the men of the 460th with mixed emotions. Ploesti was of course *the* target, and the macho side said, I want to be part of this. The practical side said, I'll never make fifty if I go there very often. None of them got a vote, so when the assigned crews assembled for briefing early on the morning of May 5, they learned they were elected to make the first "Black Panther" attack on Ploesti.

None of them knew about the game being played at top side. The lead bombardiers and navigators knew that their target was the marshaling yards (wink) adjacent to the tank farm at the Xenia refinery northwest of the city proper. It had been spared the low-level attack because of its small size, but due to the pasting of the four largest refineries, Xenia had been pressed into service in April. In addition, most of the crude from the gravity pipe lines from the many northwestern oil wells was processed through Xenia. While not a big refinery, it was significant. And flak guns didn't recognize the size of a refinery, just the size of a bomber.

As the flyers filed in to the converted barn that served as a church, movie theater and briefing room they saw the ever present curtain drawn over the large wall map that extended from floor to ceiling at the rear of the stage. Peeking out over the top of the curtain was the northern part of Europe.

Came the big sweat: Where to today? For those who had not yet been tipped off, the dramatic opening of their curtain on the war revealed the blue yarn running from Spinazzola, Italy, to the IP, twenty miles west of Ploesti, thence to the western edge of the city and back to Spinazzola. The familiar blue yarn triangled to every target.

A briefing officer gave them route out and route back headings and altitudes; a weather officer gave them wind velocity and direction aloft at the target; an intelligence officer gave the gloom report—increased fighter and flak activity could be expected.

Finally Colonel Campbell strode to the front of the stage. Campbell was a no-nonsense warrior who treated the occasion with due respect. No funny lines. No heroics. Just a cold appraisal of what was going on.

"You gentlemen have been in battle for over a month, and have seen some fighter action and some heavy flak at Bucharest, but what is in store for you today will make everything else pale in comparison. Oil is the backbone of the German war machine. Over a quarter of all Hitler's oil comes from the refineries at Ploesti. They will defend this target with the ferocity of a cornered rat.

"I know you will make us all proud before the day is over."

The room was so still the men could hear each other breathing. All of them knew that this could be their last day on earth. They knew of TIDAL WAVE's terrible losses at this target. They were aware of their own daily losses at the lesser targets they had been hitting. No one looked at the man to his side. They all looked straight ahead at the man on the stage. The air was filled with a strange tension.

After a short dramatic pause the colonel looked around and asked, "Any questions?"

Capt. George Bishop, squadron navigator for the 760th Bomb Squadron, raised his hand.

"What is it, Bishop?"

"Sir, are you coming along today?"

"Why yes. . . . I'm leading the mission."

"Then sir, I suggest you button your fly. It gets mighty drafty up there at 20,000 feet."

Tail gunner's view of Ploesti—high level.

Our feared enemy—a flak gun crew. Fourteen-year-old gunner on right is father of author's friend. Note wooden shoes.

The juxtaposition of the open fly and the somber speaker and his equally somber message had fascinated the audience, but no one had dared interrupt to tell the king he was naked.

Campbell was stunned. His face turned a beet red; his neck flushed past his open collar and crept down to his chest. If it had been quiet earlier, it was now beyond quiet. The group leader slowly looked down, with disbelieving eyes, and studiously buttoned his fly; not an easy feat with a couple of hundred subordinates looking on. He held for a dramatic second, then slowly raised his sober, but red face. When erect, the butt of this massive joke burst out laughing.

The audience exploded. Men were slapping each other on the back and pounding knees in emotional relief.

Colonel Harrison, sitting alongside the stage, leaned over to a major and said, "We needed that."

The major replied, "I think they are ready, now."

Hangar Queen was making her maiden flight to Ploesti and would have squadron operations officer Maj. Heberd "Heb" James in the left seat, Hammett in the right seat.

It was a typical pre-boarding ritual. Hammett walked up to the plane, kicked the left tire and knocked on the oleo strut; his normal regimen before each mission. "Charlie, are you superstitious?" he was often asked. "Not me!" he'd answer.

Navigator Sherman Wood was making certain the pitot tube was uncovered so the airspeed indicator would work.

Bombardier Newby was checking the cotter pins in the bomb fuses.

The others were on board checking their ammo and guns.

Finally the control surfaces were physically moved full range, and the engines were revved up.

When taxi out time came, Major James wheeled *Hangar Queen* out to take its place as deputy lead in the first attack unit of eighteen planes.

The three and a half hour trip to the IP was made without incident, and everyone aboard hid their inner concerns with light banter.

While still over the Adriatic Sea, Major James asked Smitty (Danny Smith) to see his little good luck charm. "Maybe some of it will rub off on me. Hey, you already have Ploesti printed on the side. That's really confidence," James chuckled.

"She's worked pretty good so far, major," Smitty replied.

When they cleared the Dinaric Alps in Yugoslavia Smitty climbed into his top turret, and everyone donned oxygen masks except Newby. He was out in the bomb bay removing the safety cotter pins from the nose and tail fuses of eight 500 lb. bombs. The sixteen pins safely in his pocket, he returned to the nose and donned his mask.

After awhile, the inevitable happened. Bob Kaiser began crooning over the interphone.

When he finished his song James said, "That was nice, but no more singing for a while. We are getting near fighter country, and we need the lines clear."

About an hour from the target Newby turned on the gyroscope of his bombsight to let it warm up in the minus-sixty-five-degree nose compartment. The little space heater wasn't working properly.

As they neared the IP, thirty-seven enemy fighters congregated off to one side out of range, but they passed up the 460th for another group flying sloppy formation.

James came on the air to say, "I hope you all appreciate what our ultra-tight formation means. But don't get too cocky. Keep your eyes peeled for fighters."

There had been a 10/10 undercast most of the way across Rumania, but it began breaking up into about a 5/10 coverage, a fact that made both the navigator and bombardier happy.

Finally, the big moment. "Navigator to bombardier, Ploesti is dead ahead at two o'clock. The IP is dead ahead at twelve o'clock. Be at the IP in two minutes."

Newby, who had been fussing with his bombsight, stood up and looked out the small right window. My God, I'm here! he gasped. Through the holes in the scattered clouds he could make out the nineteen-square-mile city about twenty-five miles ahead, and some of the black, mile-square refinery properties spotted around the perimeter.

More alarming was the sight high above the city. He was seeing a repeat of what he had seen earlier from the IP at Bucharest. The same polka dot sky soaking up the same little dots. Only this time he was not going to be a mere spectator.

His was one of thirteen bomb groups to test the guns of Ploesti this day. A pillar of black smoke billowed and curled up through the cloud cover reaching and clawing for the bombers. Others had obviously been there moments earlier.

"Major James, get ready to make a turn to a 77 degree heading at 1416 hours," announced navigator Wood.

At 1415 hours the lead plane dipped its wings and started its turn onto the bomb run. James followed suit, as did all the following planes. As they leveled out Newby had his head in the eyepiece of his bombsight and was turning one of the large knobs on the side.

He came out of the sight and looked hastily at a photo and said, "I think I see some tanks in the general area of our target, and marshaling yards to the right. We can get them both."

With that he sat back on his haunches and reached over to the bombardier's control stand which contained two large levers. He pulled the cold left lever full forward, and rubbed his bare hands together vigorously in the minus-sixty-five-degree compartment, announcing on interphone, "Bomb bay doors open."

He then pulled the equally cold right lever full forward, rubbed his hands and said, "Bomb release armed."

His left hand reached up to a panel of indicator lights and flipped a switch. Eight of the twenty-four indicator lights glowed amber. Another switch was flipped and he said, "Nose fuses armed."

He reached over to another switch at the left of the panel, located next to a large dial calibrated from 7 to 750, and moved it to TRAIN. Again he spoke into his mike, "Intervalometer set for 200 foot intervals. First bomb should hit the front of the first oil storage tank on the right."

An anonymous voice chided, "Idle boasting."

Newby ignored the rib and settled in for sighting on the target. As deputy lead his responsibility was to accept the course established by the lead plane, and sight just for range. The idea was that the two bombardiers should be releasing at practically the same time so if one bombsight or release system malfunctioned the other was there for a backup. The sixteen bombardiers following were instructed to toggle on the first bomb to fall from either plane.

As they proceeded down the five-minute bomb run the bombardier made a few corrections with his rate (range) knob, and glanced occasionally at the target photo showing rows of storage tanks two abreast, and fifteen deep. They were going in on the difficult thin axis. A bad course error would mean a total miss.

The bombardier suddenly came out of the eyepiece and looked at the target photo. Then back into the eyepiece, and back out. He shook his head and went back into the eyepiece once more.

Suddenly he bolted out of the sight, depressed his mike switch and said, in as calm a voice as he could muster, "Sherm, did we turn early?"

"Yeah, a minute early. Why?"

"This is the wrong target," he said, not so calmly.

Major James cut in with, "Right or wrong, this is the one we are bombing! We can't fly 18 planes all over Ploesti looking for your target. How do you know it's wrong?"

"The tank farm is the wrong shape. Should be two abreast and fifteen deep. This tank farm is more square shaped. It's wrong!" Newby said.

"Bomb it!" James demanded.

Into the sight went the worried bombardier, only to face a new problem. The lead bombardier was right on course for the middle tank in the front row, but the huge cloud directly over the target was drifting toward them. It would soon intercept his direct line of sight to the aiming point.

He had heard a lecture on offset bombing, but had never tried it. Now was the time for some on-the-job training. He set the lateral cross hair on the aiming point and synchronized it to his rate of approach as best he could from a minute away. Then he ran his eye across the hair to the far left of his scope of vision, where the sun was shining on the ground through a hole in the clouds. There he spotted a cluster of white buildings about a mile left of the tank farm. That would be his range aiming point when the tanks disappear under the cloud lid.

As he was not sighting for course he did not bother to locate a similar offset course aiming point.

He continued to refine the synchronization of his range hair, as any hair drifting would magnify as they got closer. Just before the tanks disappeared from view he picked out a corner of one white building and continued to synchronize on it. Finally the hair froze on the new offset aiming point. Synchronization! If the lead bombardier was synchronized on an offset course aiming point, a farm house or whatever, they would hit their aiming point and eighteen bombers would each string eight bombs 200 ft. apart across the tank farm. An exhilarating feeling—like bowling a 300 game.

The heavy flak activity along the bomb run was bothering everyone but the bombardier, who was too concerned about fouling up to pay any attention to the reality of the situation. While he was preoccupied, the others were watching two bombers in another group blow up, and spew out a few white chutes.

About twenty seconds before bombs away, a flak burst directly under their plane kicked it up in the air, and the familiar sound of gravel being thrown on a tin roof reminded the bombardier of what the others already knew.

In a euphoric mood, born of the successful sighting, Newby, who had been knocked away from his bombsight, depressed his mike switch and said, "Major James, will you please try and stay out of those potholes?"

"I'll try," James said.

Fortunately for the bombardier he was using a Sperry bombsight, with its electronic, self-leveling gyroscope. Had it been a Norden the gyroscope would have toppled and he probably would not have had time to right it manually before its computer determined the bomb release point. Such a violent disruption usually requires an additional refinement of the cross hairs in the synchronization process—with either bombsight.

A quick look into the eyepiece confirmed the need for a minor adjustment with the range and course knobs. The little warning flag appeared in his field of vision telling him he had less than eight seconds before bomb release. By then of course the cross hairs intersected the middle of a cloud bank, and hopefully the aiming point was directly below. The range hair held firmly to the corner of the white building a mile to the left of the target, so there was nothing more he could do.

Newby came out of the eyepiece, turned to his navigator and gave him the OK sign. They both watched the Sighting Angle Index pointer close in on the Dropping Angle pointer on the adjoining scales. Newby held in the arming switch with the palm of his right hand and waited for the audible click from the meeting of two electrical contacts and the lurch of the plane to tell him that the bombs had been released.

Those signals received, he then depressed his mike switch and calmly announced the famous bombardier line, "Bombs away!"

He moved the bomb bay door lever back to normal and followed with "Bomb bay doors closed." Then added, "Will one of you guys in the waist check the bomb bay and see if they all got away."

A moment later a voice said, "Bomb bay clear."

"*Red 'N' for Nan* is hit! No. 2 is on fire, and he is dropping out of formation," came a voice over the interphone.

"Tail gunner, keep an eye on him and report his progress," barked the major.

"Roger," responded Sid Woods.

As the plane went into a banked right turn the clouds continued to obscure the tank farm, so none of them knew if the target had been hit or missed.

All agreed that it was the worst flak they had ever experienced.

The crew was treated to a front-row seat for an exciting dogfight between the P–47s and Me 109s as they left the target area. Just like in the World War I movies. The *Hangar Queen* cheering section applauded two Me 109s going down in flames.

The damaged bomber slowly fell behind, but was picked up by two P–38s who were still escorting it as they went out of sight at the Danube River. The plane did not make it back to base.

Twenty-eight of the returning bombers suffered flak damage. Many had hundreds of flak holes by actual count. One plane could not get its right landing gear down and had to make a crash-landing on the dirt crash strip. Two others had a tire punctured by flak and had to follow standard operating procedure: shoot out the good tire with a waist gun, and then shoot the presumed damaged other tire to make sure *both* tires would be flat. One flat tire can cause an erratic landing. Two flats increase the likelihood of a successful landing.

This had been the biggest attack on Ploesti ever. The 485 bombers reaching the target inflicted heavy damage on several refineries despite the official reports stating damage to key rail centers and incidental damage to the refineries. Nineteen bombers were lost this day.

The Fifteenth sent 135 B–24s back to Ploesti the following day, but without the 460th. The "Black Panthers," including Hammett's crew, were sent to bomb the marshaling yards at Craiova in western Rumania. They had a good bomb pattern on the choke point, and suffered no losses, due to minimal flak and no fighters.

The Ploesti defenses, however, accounted for six bombers, as the near four percent loss rate continued. If every target were that bad nobody would ever survive fifty missions.

The morning of May 10 found the "Hangar Queen" crew asleep in their bunks as the Group took off to bomb a place called Wiener Neustadt, Austria. The correct pronunciation was something like "Viennior Noidstadt," but the Americans simply called it like it looks, Wiener Neustadt. As bad as Ploesti was, reputation and fact, this new addition to everyone's geography knowledge was worse.

Forty-two planes took off, in six boxes of seven, led by Colonel Harrison, and ran into severe weather over northern Yugoslavia, encountering mild flak on the way near Zagreb.

Uncharacteristically, fourteen planes aborted and went home, most claiming to have heard a radio recall code word.

One entire box lost the formation in the weather, six planes had engine or mechanical trouble and one had an inadvertent parachute opening aboard. Harrison would have a lot to say on that subject when he got home.

The lead navigator on Harrison's plane learned as they had started over the mountains that he had forgotten his oxygen mask, and so informed the colonel. By now, Harrison had learned of the high abortion rate, and was not to be trifled with. His reply was, "We are not turning back. Either get out or suck on the tube." He spent the next several hours bent over his work table with the oxygen tube in his mouth.

While on the bomb run the co-pilot's windshield was pierced by a piece of flak that dented his steel helmet. The distraught man, fearing lightning might strike twice, slithered down in his seat and pulled the helmet over his eyes. That was too much for the colonel. He pulled off his oxygen mask, looked over and shouted, "Sit up and take it like a man!" (at least that was the story told by the co-pilot later that night in the club, as he exhibited the dented helmet).

There was little fighter activity, despite the Fifteenth being there to bomb the local aircraft factory, and get a few in the womb. Others went for the airdrome to get some in the nest.

The Germans must have figured out the IP for bombing Wiener Neustadt because flak activity began several minutes before the IP and continued very heavy all the way on the run in. Ploesti was never this concentrated, as the men who were there a week earlier noticed.

Two planes were hit on the bomb run, caught fire, rolled over and went in. Nearby planes had to scramble to avoid a mid-air. The flak was doing what it was intended to do—disrupt the bomb run.

Navigator Sid Smith on Lt. Maurice Clark's crew was watching the demise of the two bombers and feeling and hearing the flak hit his own plane. He just knew this was the end of the trail, when co-pilot Walter Mahoney came on interphone with, "Co-pilot to navigator." Smith responded with, "Go ahead." Mahoney, who had recently read an article in a *Reader's Digest* his wife had sent him, came back with, "Did you know that over 50% of American married women sleep in the nude?"

Black humor was the hallmark of the young American flyers in the flak skies over Europe. This ability to keep their sense of humor as they held out their souls, eyeball-to-eyeball with death, helped them to avoid becoming flak happy, an aerial euphemism for shell shock.

Clark's plane received four direct hits on the bomb run: one knocked off the right rudder; one near the bomb bay left two doors hanging in the slipstream; two exploded by the starboard engines, starting fires on both.

Due to a lack of rudder capability the pilot dropped out of formation and headed in a generally south direction, to try to reach Italy. To add to their worries an oxygen fire broke out, so the pilot sounded the bail-out alarm. Before anyone could jump, two men managed to put out the fire, so Clark countermanded the alarm via interphone. They had one emergency after another for thirty minutes and with one engine feathered and virtually no rudder control Clark finally asked Smith for their approximate location so the men would have some idea of which direction to head when they hit the ground.

They continued to drop, and when they hit 8,000 ft. the pilot rang the bail-out alarm again, and they all got out.

Smith eventually wound up in Stalag 3, where en route, he was astounded when the interrogation officer recited his complete background: his college; his wife's maiden name; his dog's name; his civilian job; his commission through ROTC. The picture of his flying school graduating class was the crowning blow.

On the same bomb run Tech. Sgt. William Dale, radioman on Lt. Ray Woods's plane, received a minor flak bruise in the thigh, and several other more serious injuries. Woods was badly injured in the head and both feet.

The tail gunner's oxygen was shot out so he came up to the waist to plug into an extra station there. The mask hose, however, had been severed so he had to suck on the tube. Dale had to hold his mask plug in the socket with his hand. The bombardier's and nose gunner's oxygen systems were shot out, so the bombardier went up on the flight deck to an extra station; the navigator and nose gunner took turns on the remaining oxygen outlet.

All engines had been hit by flak: No. 4 had to be feathered; No. 3 was failing; the other two were smoking. There were hundreds of holes throughout the plane.

Dale was called up to the flight deck to help the wounded. He had to walk along the 8 in. wide catwalk, coated with slippery hydraulic fluid, and through both bomb bays with the doors open, to reach the deck. There he administered first aid to several men, pouring sulfa on open wounds, and injecting morphine where needed. Lieutenant Woods, though in great pain, refused the morphine.

They knew the plane would not make it to Italy, so they decided on the island of Vis off the Yugoslavian coast, an emergency field for stricken bombers. As they approached Vis they were surprised to see flak. It later developed that the flak was for two Me 109s who were there to intercept them.

The hydraulic system was shot out so they had to crank down the main landing gear by hand. The nose wheel tire was shot so they left the nose wheel up. The landing flaps were also lowered by hand.

Pilot Woods insisted on being placed in the pilot's seat, and it took two men to do so. Once there he was too weak to do anything, having fainted twice while on the flight deck.

As they came in to land, No. 3 failed, leaving only the two port engines operating. Co-pilot Lieutenant Nutter made a remarkable landing, skidding along on the nose until stopped.

They were met by American Rangers, British Commandos and Yugoslavian Partisans, and taken to the town of Vis.

A P-38 pilot had crash-landed before they had arrived and reported the '38s had shot down nine enemy fighters, which may explain why the crew did not see any fighters.

They learned much about the Partisans, who gave them food, wine and cigarettes. The Partisans were a band of communist resistance fighters led by Marshal Tito. They would give up ten Partisan lives to get a downed American flyer back home. When the Americans showed them on a map the places they had been bombing, the Partisans were ecstatic.

The P, though a rough, tough people, they had morals that all could envy. If a Partisan man or woman gets a venereal disease, they were shot. If a single woman gets pregnant, she is shot (by women). If a married woman, they give her a blanket and send her up in the mountains to take care of herself. If a Partisan soldier gets drunk twice, he is shot. This is total war, Partisan style.

Two days later the crew was put on a boat for Bari, Italy, where the pilot and Sgt. Rector Evans, another wounded man, received proper treatment. Then back to base, to fly more missions.

May 10, 1944 was not only the date of the Wiener Neustadt mission, but it was also Sergeant Dale's birthday. From that day on, though, May 10, 1944 was his *birth date*.

Island of Vis, Yugoslavia—a haven for Fifteenth AF bombers unable to make it to Italy.

May 10, 1944 was one of the bloodiest days for the 460th "Black Panthers." Three bombers were lost over the target. Two others were reported missing. One was so badly damaged it could not make it home, and landed at Foggia, Italy. And, of course, Woods's plane that landed at Vis.

Another plane received a flak hit at the target that exploded an oxygen bottle. Six men bailed out without waiting for the alarm, and before anyone else could leave the fire went out. The remaining four went back to work and flew the plane home.

German flak gunners fought hard this day to protect the Luftwaffe's womb and nest. The Fifteenth lost twenty-eight planes at Wiener Neustadt.

Another Ploesti?

Chapter 10

Oil Strike: Fifteenth Air Force

When the Non Com and Officer's clubs opened in mid-May it marked a milestone in the lives of the men of Bomber City. The gleaming white tufa houses in both the enlisted men's and officers' living areas were finally matched with white block buildings where the flyers, and others, could relax in the evenings. The adjoining dining room (no longer called a mess hall) made this a world-class operation, at least compared with the transient messes of North Africa and South America.

They had a nice arrangement in the Officer's Club for drinks. All officers gave up their whiskey ration to the club and then bought their whiskey or "Gin and Juice" by the drink. One problem was that ferry pilots who brought over new planes would gobble up drinks for which they did not contribute a bottle. Near the end of each month the club went dry for a few days.

Another good deal was the privilege of bringing a warm beer to the bar and trading it for a cold one.

May 18 marked another milestone when the Fifteenth sent 206 bombers to bomb the oil refineries at Ploesti. The charade was over. Oil was proclaimed the No. 1 priority target.

The 460th went to Concordia Vega, White 2 of TIDAL WAVE, where their target was a refinery, and they did a fair job. One plane was damaged at the target and on the way home was shot down as it fell behind the formation. Many planes received flak damage.

The prime target, however, was Romano Americana, which had been baptized on May 5 with some marshaling yard spillage.

The Luftwaffe repeated its relatively new tactic of drawing off fighter escort for air battles so the bombers would be prey for other fighters. It was cat and mouse, as seven groups lost fourteen planes.

Dan Smith was adding names to his little donkey's side at a rapid rate. The "Hangar Queen" crew flew consecutive missions on May 22, 23, 24, 26, 27, 29, 30, and 31. Their mission count stood at twenty-three. Eight of the Squadron's original seventeen crews had been shot down so far. Will we ever make fifty? was the question on the crewmen's minds.

The "Hangar Queen" crew looked upon the May 24 mission to Wiener Neustadt with much concern. Worse than Ploesti? Their target was the Wollersdorf airdrome, and when the P–38s showed up at the rendezvous point everyone cheered.

So much for the Luftwaffe. Now, what about flak? The only defenses against flak are a 10/10 undercast and "window." The former was a good news/bad news situation (while they can't see you for visual sighting [the best kind], you can't see the target, and someone has to come back another day). The latter pits common Christmas tree tinsel against sophisticated radar sighting equipment. It is remarkable how this old-time Christmas trimming can defeat modern electronics. Each bomber is issued a carton of window, which contains dozens of smaller boxes of the tinsel.

Waist gunners are supposed to throw the strands out one at a time every few seconds. A group of bombers dispensing window properly will actually fool the ground radar by cluttering up the screen and hiding the bombers. Bombers and window look alike on the screen. Clusters of window, however, plummet and accomplish nothing. In the heat of battle it is difficult to restrict window tossing to one strand at a time. If one is good, two is better. Then, so the frenzied logic goes, four is better yet and so on.

Before they ever reached the western edge of Lake Neusiedler—the Fifteenth's favorite IP for this target—the clouds closed in for a solid 10/10 undercast. That took care of visual sighting for both the offense and defense.

Although the turn onto the bomb runs was made by ETA, there was little question they had turned at the right place, as evidenced by the black polka dot sky near them. As they made the blind run in, flak seemed to follow them, so the window tossers had their chance to shine.

Hangar Queen's waist gunners Homer Luke and Johnny Woodland were tossing their window, but the flak seemed to be getting closer despite their efforts. Soon Luke was throwing out several strands at a time. Then as the flak intensified, he began ripping the entire contents out of the small boxes and throwing window out by the handfuls.

Woodland looked over, began laughing and hollered, "Hey, just one strand at a time!"

Luke pointed excitedly out the window, and said, "Looka that! A guy over there just threw out a whole carton!"

Halfway down the bomb run the lead ship closed its bomb bay doors, and the others did likewise. Finally, it veered about twenty degrees left and suddenly the clouds opened up to reveal a city, with a factory on the edge of town. It was the secondary target shown at briefing, NeunKirchen, Austria, a few miles south of Wiener Neustadt. The Group reopened its doors and bombed it visually with excellent results. Whatever they were making there the day before, they wouldn't be making any the next day.

As the Group was leaving the flak zone they began seeing red flak clouds, instead of the customary black clouds. All flak starts out with a red explosion, but the *new* red cloud worried everyone. Some kind of poison gas? It was later determined the red flak was a signal the flak was over so fighters could come in at the bombers. German fighters didn't like flak any more than the bomber crews. Unlike the last trip to Wiener Neustadt, the Group suffered no losses on this one.

Major Ward, CO of the 763rd Bomb Squadron, had a harrowing experience on the bomb run. He looked down at his parachute harness and saw two D rings on it. He checked his parachute pack and saw two D rings. One of the sets of D rings should have been snap fasteners—a male and a female connection. There was no way he could use that parachute with two female connectors.

When he got on the ground he raised Cain with his supply people and learned that the new replacement crews were arriving with opposite connectors than the original crews had on their harnesses and chutes. All chutes were

Anatomy of a perfect sighting—I. In this first of a remarkable series of five bomb strike photos the bombs of lead bombardier Capt. George D. Williams are seen just after leaving his plane. His aiming point is a cluster of oil storage tanks and a key building in Le Pontet, France a week before the southern invasion. The aiming points are hidden by the tail fins of his top bomb shown leaving the photo at the top.

intermingled in a squadron pool. At Ward's orders they color-coded everyone's harness with the appropriate chutes.

There were a lot of discussions about parachutes that evening in the tents and huts. Rhodes and Newby obtained a D ring chute pack and experimented with how one could somehow hook it onto their harness. It could be done by hooking it to the mid-chest connection and a leg connection, but the opening shock might break your back. If it didn't, you would be coming down in a horizontal position and would hit the ground on your side.

They also experimented with how two persons might use one parachute. This was more practical, but no one knew if the single connector would hold, and also if the no doubt greater velocity would make landing dangerous. Considering the alternative, it was worth a chance. After all, if there are two men for one parachute and the plane is falling, do you flip coins? Pull rank/serial number? Or . . . shoot the other guy!

None of the men in that hut had ever used a parachute, so they reminded each other of tips each had heard. It was generally agreed that a long free fall is desirable from 20,000 ft. It has the advantage of quickly getting out of the extreme cold and rarified air, as well as the bursting flak, if any.

One of the men mentioned two ways you can tell when it's time to pull the rip cord. When you see the general ground area turn from a dull gray to a greenish color you are about a mile from the ground, and time to pop your chute. Another clue is the sudden temperature change that occurs about a mile from the ground.

The matter of carrying a gun provoked many inter-tent/hut discussions. One school says you will do more harm than good with a gun, if shot down. You can't shoot your way back from 400 miles behind enemy lines with six bullets. The other side says they want something to defend themselves with.

Quite a few of the men Newby and Rhodes had come over with had gone down, and they were of course concerned with how they had all fared. The parachute discussion brought to mind the possible fate of Mark Smith, the bombardier on Swayze's crew, who went down at Wiener Neustadt.

Smith had told them during a bull session that he had traveled all over Germany hiking and bicycling in the late thirties, and he was a marked person. If he ever got shot down in Germany he would be executed immediately, and not taken to a prison camp like other crew members. No explanation was given why he would be given such special attention if captured.

While the flood gates were open on Ploesti oil, other strategic targets got their share of the Fifteenth's attention. In a three-day period, May 25–27, the fourteen most important marshaling yards in southern France were hit with 3,171 tons of bombs.

On the afternoon of May 26 Major James, operations officer of Hammett's 763rd Bomb Squadron, held a meeting with all the pilots, and chewed out several of them who had landed at Corsica for frivolous reasons. Namely, the large-busted girl tending bar at the officer's club. He had noticed too many landings there for gas or repairs. He told them no more Corsica landings. Fly it home to Spinazzola!

The "Hangar Queen" crew stood down on May 27, but bombardier Newby was assigned to fly with Major James to lead the second attack unit to bomb the marshaling yard at Nimes, France. The plane they flew was a new replacement B–24J, the newest Liberator built. It looked like an H model, but had some subtle internal differences. This would be the longest flight for the Group so far, nine hours.

As the Group neared the IP area the navigator on Newby's plane came on interphone with, "Bombardier, get ready to turn, the first attack unit is starting their turn onto the bomb run."

Anatomy—II. The aiming point 35 seconds later just before the bombs—some 22,000 ft. below—begin impacting. Looks peaceful enough. The second attack unit's aiming point is a pair of buildings located about five o'clock from Williams's target.

Newby shook his head and said, "Major James, they are turning at the wrong railroad junction. It's the next one."

"Are you sure?" questioned James.

"Yes sir, we have 20 miles to go," Newby affirmed.

"You'd better be right," replied James.

Lucky for Newby a railroad junction showed up as promised and they turned north, made the bomb run to the west side of the briefed target, and headed for home. The first attack unit had discovered their error and veered over for an angled run on the east side of the briefed marshaling yard.

James was of the school that believed in not transferring the 200 gallons of reserve gas, from each of the "Tokyo tanks" located in the wingtips, prior to the target.

He knows transferring from these tanks en route to a target means taking two empty, fume-filled gas tanks into the flak and fighter zone.

The other school feels you should get the reserve 400 gallons into the main tanks as soon as possible, in case something happens that you can't get to the Tokyos later.

From the events that followed it would appear that Major James may have gone to the wrong school.

Soon after leaving the target the engineer informed the major that he could not transfer the fuel from the Tokyo tanks. The basic 2,300 gallons was not enough fuel to make it home on this long flight.

The pilot announced that he was going to redline the engines all the way home. Redlining means letting the cylinder-head temperatures rise above the red line on the gauge. This higher cylinder-head temperature is accomplished by reducing the gas-to-air ratio of fuel fed to the cylinders. This obviously saves gas, and it increases power which translates into higher speed. Get home quicker on less gas. This sounds like the answer to a low-fuel situation, and it *is* the only choice. However, the flip side of this decision is the danger of an engine blowing up. How long will an engine last under this stress? You don't know. You simply try it and see what happens, or fly it normally and either ditch or bail out in the middle of the sea.

Formation flying is fuel consuming so James dropped out of formation and headed home alone, pulling away from the others.

Everyone was justifiably nervous riding this B–24 that was living one of its nicknames—The Flying Time Bomb.

As they approached Corsica, the co-pilot, wearing a sardonic smile, looked over to the pilot and said, "Why don't you land at Corsica?"

"After my little speech yesterday, I don't have the guts."

The pilot, navigator and engineer were in constant touch as they checked on gas consumption and availability and miles to go. They kept comparing the ETA for Spinazzola with fuel availability, and the numbers were coming out frightfully even.

Newby learned about faith that day, faith in his pilot. Major James dropped to under 3,000 ft. when they reached the Rome area, and dropped even farther as the plane started through some mountain passes. It is an eerie feeling to look out the windows of an airplane and see trees lining both mountainsides. Even more so when you look up and see a cloud lid over the valley. You don't have to look down to know the ground, which is more trees, is close below you.

Anatomy—III. The thrill of a bombardier's life is when his stick of bombs brackets his aiming point. Take a look! The second attack unit's bombs are beginning to impact around their aiming point.

Factor in the knowledge that the gas tanks are approaching empty and you know you are playing a real life game of Russian roulette. Who needs flak and fighters?

As this realization swept over the bombardier a new horrible thought entered his mind. He thought of himself and the plane being like a rat in a maze. When they come to a fork in the valleys, what if the navigator chooses a blind alley?

The navigator knew his trade. Just as the red light appeared on the instrument panel, signaling nearly empty gas tanks, the bomber broke out of a pass onto a flat stretch, and the home base landing strip lay a few miles dead ahead.

A straight-on landing was possible because the Group had not yet arrived, and was made routinely. The taxi back to the hardstand wasn't so routine, though. Just after turning off the runway all four engines sputtered out, despite 400 gallons of fuel being just a few feet from the engines.

It was learned later that this new J model had an ON/OFF switch on the bomb bay side of the flight deck bulkhead, which housed the fuel transfer controls. The switch had been wired OFF. No one aboard was aware of this drastic change.

Bomb strike photos confirmed that the briefed target had been hit on both the west and east side sections.

That evening the badly shaken bombardier, despite flying a milk run that day, felt he had to celebrate his resurrection—as he termed his escape from seemingly certain death.

When a stand down was ordered for the following day the club bar sold a drink called No Mission Tomorrow. It was made of several kinds of rum and other spirits, something like a Zombie of civilian days.

A stand down had been ordered for the following day, so the Officer's Club had its bar signs up proclaiming "NO MISSION TOMORROWs ON

SALE—25¢." It was a much-appreciated amenity offered the flyers on stand down eves.

On the back bar was a caricature of a drunk black panther, tail tied in a knot, red testicles, pilot's wings and a Good Conduct Medal on his chest, and a near empty bottle to the side. Rookies were always told that's what they will look like after fifty missions.

Newby, Rhodes, Wood and Hammett walked up to the bar and squirmed into a space meant for three; each removed his Cairo ring and threw it on the bar so it would come apart. A Cairo ring consisted of four silver, odd-shaped, thin circular sections, intertwined like a Chinese ring puzzle. When assembled they form a finger ring that looks like the parts are woven into one. Some of the fellows had flown to Cairo and brought back a supply of these interesting rings.

Throwing the rings on the bar was an unspoken challenge to see who could assemble his ring the quickest after a start signal was given. A completed ring was held up and the palm on the other hand was slapped on the bar. The contestant still fumbling with his ring when all other palms have hit the bar pays for the round.

The four crew mates struggled feverishly with their chosen weapons in this four-way duel; Hammett pounded his palm on the bar, followed by Rhodes and Wood. Newby reached into his pocket and threw a 100 Lira note onto the bar, shaking his head and saying, "Jever see anythin' like it? I ollies lose."

"Now, say it in English like Dusty and I talk," laughed Hammett.

The crew of *Hangar Queen* suffered through two embarrassing consecutive aborts to Wiener Neustadt, a spent shell through the pilot's windshield, and an inoperative tail turret being the causes.

A few days later on May 31 the "Hangar Queen" crew was up for the day's mission and the four officers were all in a row in the chow line waiting for their turn at the new cocoa server. Each man was allowed only half a canteen cup of cocoa, which is equal to a regular cup, but Newby had a little trick he would use when a new Italian server was at the station. He held out his cup and raised

Anatomy—IV. More bombs from other planes are added to the target areas.

it to meet the lip of the pitcher held by the server. As the pouring started he exerted a little upward pressure. Just as the pourer began to lift the pitcher Newby lowered his cup, and cocoa kept pouring to fill his cup.

As Newby walked away with another triumph Rhodes said, "Someday one of those guys is going to pour the pitcher over your head. And I hope I get to see it."

At briefing they learned it would be Ploesti, where fourteen groups would hit the beleaguered target. *Hangar Queen* was the lead plane of the second attack unit for the 460th, with Squadron CO Major Ward in the left seat. Dusty Rhodes would be flying replacement on another crew.

All of the major refineries were targeted that day, with the 460th ticketed for the Concordia Vega refinery on the north edge of the city.

Colonel Harrison led the group of thirty-six planes for its 0642 rendezvous with the 465th BG between Conosa and Spinazzola, and with the two other groups of the 55th Bomb Wing at 0657. Fifty miles off the Yugoslavian coast they rendezvoused with their P–38 fighter escort for the trip across the unfriendly skies of the Balkans. Three planes aborted, but thirty-three pressed on.

The offense and defense planning for the continuing battle of Ploesti was interrelated: American planners selected either Ploesti or another target; the defenders had to *expect* an attack each day. The refineries' daily regimen was based on historical fact. The American bombers always came about noon, so all refineries operated from 5:00 A.M. to 11:00 A.M. After the refineries were shut down and the workers went home, the key operators sat around and read or played bridge. If no alert came within a reasonable time they took off for swimming, tennis or some other activity.

An ironic overview of this situation is the thought of refinery operators casually playing cards while at that very moment some 5,000 American airmen were in a state of apprehension and fear for their lives as they approached that dreaded graveyard of bombers.

An alert gave the operators about forty-five mintues to make final adjustments and get to a safe place. Often they would go to a hill at a safe distance and watch the bombings. There was a certain fascination to the occasion, quite like an American Fourth of July fireworks display. After all, they *were* Rumanians with no real love for the Germans.

When a day's bombing ended, the refinery managers phoned each other to compare damages, not unlike Americans checking on the day's ball scores.

About ninety percent of employees at the Romano Americana refinery had worked with Americans before the war, so there were diverse feelings about the bombings. Their refinery was inadvertently spared by TIDAL WAVE, and as George Suciu sat down for a hand of bridge he commented that local citizens no longer flocked to his refinery for safety. "The Americans wouldn't bomb their own, would they?" they had said. They learned. The Yanks came after their own refinery just two weeks earlier, and would be back. The night-bombing RAF had already been there on May 26 and 27 (with seventy-four Wellingtons; they lost seventeen). The RAF had also hit Campina on May 5 and 6 with forty-three bombers, losing three.

Suciu told his friends about the recent downed American flyers he had been asked to interrogate. He couldn't get over the confidence shown by those young men. Some were carrying tickets to an evening theater performance scheduled and dated for *that* night. "Imagine," he said, "buying a theater ticket for that night and going off to bomb Ploesti that day! I can hardly believe it, except that I know Americans from when I lived over there." He looked all around. "They are quite different from our German comrades."

Suciu was wound up on the subject, and continued, "I went up to the prison camp at Sinaia to translate confessions between the prisoners and the priests, and was amused to see American bomber pilots acting as altar boys during mass."

Hooters soon broke up the bridge game.

Newby was to see his first serious smoke screen, which would be used so successfully from now on. The Gerstenberg defense included a network of 2,000 smoke pots scattered in an area about 6x6 miles with the nineteen square miles of the city located off center, to make it difficult for bombardiers to guess where the refineries were. The entire thirty-six square miles would be one big maze of white covering the ground.

Each smoke generator consisted of three elements lying in a shallow hole about 10 ft. square and 2 ft. deep. A fifty-five-gallon drum containing the smoke chemicals had a 6 ft. nozzle sticking out of it, and had a hose connecting it with a pressure tank. Somebody had to run around and open all the valves, but it was worth it as this was the best defense they had—even though it ensured more civilian losses.

The sight of this large white mass on the ground on a day when the undercast was nil was frustrating for a bombardier. He couldn't really tell where the city was, let alone Vega.

All Major Ward could do was follow the first attack unit when it turned at the IP onto the briefed heading. The Group ahead had dropped its bombs into the white area and the flak all around them suggested they were at least in the right county, so to speak, if not the right city. Suddenly the familiar pillar of black smoke sprouted out of the white protective covering and rose to 16,000 ft.

Anatomy—V. This bombing was considered one of the best examples of pinpoint bombing in the Fifteenth Air Force. The Norden bombsight reportedly could put a bomb in a pickle barrel from 20,000 ft. What do you think?

"Major, give me eight degrees to the left, I think we have a target here," requested the bombardier.

"Roger," replied Ward.

The major made a slow turn to the left so the trailing seventeen planes could follow without any whip action. Newby got into his eyepiece and aimed for the base of the black pillar. A pushover, he thought.

After bombs away they followed the 180 bombs moving in a straight line for the black bull's-eye. He could not see the impact for the smoke screen, but everyone knew the unit's bombs were on the mark.

The flak had been heavy and fairly accurate as twenty-seven of the planes would later report flak damage. As they left the target one of the Group's planes was on fire, and the pilot dropped out of formation, but still under control. About ten miles south of Ploesti the flames got worse; it flipped over and headed straight down. Returning crews reported seeing seven chutes, and seeing the plane hit the ground with a huge explosion. By now everyone had seen his share of nearby bombers burst into flames, flip upside down and go into a death dive, sometimes ripping the wings off while still in sight. Chute counting became a habit. Rarely did they count more than seven or eight, if the plane went down over a target.

Hangar Queen suffered a lot of flak holes but no damage was done and no one aboard was hurt. On the way home, as they dropped down from altitude, Smitty began passing out K rations for those desiring a delectable snack. Co-pilot Hammett couldn't resist calling Newby on the interphone and asking, "Hey Newb, 'jawl eachet?"

Thornton came through with his North Carolinian drawl, "Y'all got him there, Charlie."

Major Ward looked over quizzically, but said nothing, thinking to himself: This is the raunchy crew I nearly kicked out of the Squadron back in Chatham. But they are still alive and that's more than eight others can say.

Ward then looked back on the flight deck where the bombardier and engineer were sitting, and said, "Let me see that donkey I've been hearing about."

A grinning Dan Smith handed it over to the CO, who looked it over and said, "They're right, you do show the mission on here before you make it home."

"We're damned good, sir," said Smitty.

"You're alive," Ward retorted.

"And baby, it is you," came over the interphone.

"Harrison told me about that crooner you have aboard. Who is that?" asked Ward.

Smitty, still grinning, said, "That's Kaiser, the one you caught up in the overgrown tobacco plant."

The major laughed so hard he had to wipe his eyes, and looked over to Hammett.

"I think this crew is going to make it," said Ward.

The following day's report by the P–38 recon group caused much embarrassment to several bomb groups. The 460th learned that the black pillar of smoke they used for a target of opportunity was a decoy—part of Gerstenberg's clever defense. The crafty Germans had set oil fires out in the fields a mile or two from some refineries to sucker bombardiers into wasting their Group's bombs. It was another learning experience for many.

The Fifteenth lost sixteen of the 481 planes that bombed Ploesti that day. Score a big one for Gerstenberg.

One of the crews shot down the day Colonel Crowder got it had spent some time with the Chetniks in Yugoslavia, and was flown out of that country by the RAF and returned to Spinazzola the day before the Ploesti mission. Lt. Monte Carlough was the leader, as the pilot had been captured and was a POW.

The Chetniks, led by Draža Mihailovich, were another group of Yugoslavian resistance fighters, as much at war with the Partisans as with the Germans. Both the Chetniks and the Partisans would befriend American flyers, but would kill each other on sight. Such befriended flyers would feel obligated to fight with them. It was sometimes an ironic situation when the two anti-German factions would be fighting a close-up battle, with American flyers in both front lines.

The final two groups joined the Fifteenth in May so the full force of twenty-one heavy bomb groups would be available to curtail Hitler's war machine behind the lines, and make it easier for the men fighting in the mountains of Italy, and those about to invade the mainland from the north and the south.

The Ploesti campaign, now out in the open, had further reduced Ploesti's oil production from 172,000 metric tons to 156,000 tons. The great Astra Romana's May production was *zero*. Small Dacia Romana and Xenia, pressed into service, went from just 4,000 tons up to 23,000 tons. Steaua Romana, barely hit in April, dropped from 37,000 to 4,000 in May.

Ploesti was hurting. All of Hitler's oil plants were hurting.

Losses at Ploesti for May were fifty-five bombers.

The 460th BG moved up a notch in the accuracy ratings to third place with 29.2 percent of its bombs within 1,000 ft. of the aiming point. The Fifteenth AF averaged 23.4 percent.

Albert Speer, Nazi Minister of Armaments and War Production, would later say that the May oil attacks by the Eighth and Fifteenth Air Forces brought about the decision of the war.

An ETO press release dated June 4, 1944 stated, The oil offensive is on! No one knew just who the ETO was talking to. The Germans knew, though. The men of the USAAF had certainly noticed where they had been going lately. The British had begun to realize what the oil pounding meant.

Another offensive was quietly taking place in early June. The "Hangar Queen" crew was issued a two-day pass to Bari. The 763rd Squadron had leased a small hotel for use by all flying personnel on Bari leave. The rates were as good as the Hotel De Gink—free—and there were about ten rooms on three walk-up floors, with a bathroom on each floor.

On the sixty-mile GI truck ride to town three of the officers who seemed always to be betting on anything decided to bet on the ETA to the front door of the hotel. The truck had a governor on it so there was a reasonable basis to figure arrival time.

It was the old con game. The pigeon announced 1000 hours. Another picked 0959 hours and his accomplice announced 1001 hours. Everyone had a good laugh at the sucker's expense. When the truck pulled up and the brakes were applied it was exactly 1000 hours.

Hammett & Co., as they occasionally called themselves, rented bikes and rode all over the waterfront area and were impressed with Mussolini's pride and joy, his showplace lineup of beautiful new modern office buildings and apartments. At the Red Cross Center they met some P–38 pilots and found out they were not gods; just young flyboys like themselves. Some of them did photo recon and told of how much damage the heavies were doing to Ploesti. Nice to have confirmation that your work has been effective.

The bikers decided to visit the Peninsular Base Station Officer's Club that evening where all the action was reported to be. Only problem was transients, flying personnel that is, were not eligible to join, or even walk in off the street. The only way to get in was to bring a girl. One girl, one entry. Apparently girls were scarce, and they certainly added something to a dance. The club had a five-piece band that played all the American popular songs of the day.

As it was turning dusk, with the blackout-imposed darkness about to surround them, the foursome met four young ladies at a fountain. The ages were about right and they were nice looking. The boys and girls gravitated to pairs even though none of the fellows knew any Italian. Newby lucked out; his girl was an English teacher in a local school, so she became the spokeswoman for the girls.

She shyly admitted to knowing about the entry requirement at the club but, no, they had never been there. The food, drink and dancing appealed to them so it was no problem selling them on being their tickets of admission.

They entered and joined several other opportunistic flyers and their dates at a big table. They danced and drank champagne all evening, and enjoyed their first hamburger in over five months.

About midnight Maria, Newby's girl, said she had to go home. Now what? It was blackout black outside, no light whatsoever. A closer look revealed dim blue crosses moving along the street. It was headlights of horse-drawn cabs or autos. The headlights were blacked out except for the bluish cross.

Along came a horse-drawn cab with its blue cross up where a lantern would be. Newby somehow managed to hail it without being stomped on by the horse. Maria gave the cabbie some directions and they took off. He felt his gun for reassurance; the one he never carried on a bombing mission.

As the cab left the downtown area and crossed a small bridge his eyes began to get used to the darkness. The partial moon crept out from under a cloud so one could navigate fairly well.

Unknown to the adventurer the cabbie had told Maria he would only take them across the bridge. He learned this when the cab stopped and the cabbie asked for his money, a few Lira.

Maria said, "This is all the farther he will take us."

"But where do you live?" Newby asked.

She laughed and said, "Oh, just two miles up that road," pointing to a moonlit cobblestone road.

Shades of Casbah! I'm supposed to walk up that road with a girl and back down alone, when a cab driver won't go up there? he shuddered.

He took Maria's hand, more for his own comfort than hers, and they started up the slight grade to what would prove to be "the hill" where affluent folks live. It was all there: huddled groups of men on the narrow sidewalks; red glows near the top; an American out of his element, and with a girl to protect. Or was she protecting him?

At the top of the hill they emerged into a new world, at least in the eyes of the intruder. Instead of common walled houses on a narrow cobblestone street he saw large estates with vine-covered walls, and beautiful mansions located back about fifty yards.

Seeing the startled look on her escort's face in the moonlight, Maria explained that her father was a government official. After some small talk the young man's courage picked up and he held her and kissed her. She did not resist, but after a proper interval she dropped the bomb.

"My father does not like me associating with American officers. We'd better not be seen together, so I can't invite you to walk up to my house," she said.

This cooled the young man's ardor, so they parted by the entrance gate and he began his solitaire walk back down the gauntlet. The street was so narrow he was just one leap away from the spectators on the sidewalk.

Out came the .45 from its shoulder holster, and into the right-side blouse pocket. Someday I'm going to use this thing and then I'll be in real trouble, he said to himself.

The trip down to the bridge was made without any attacks en route, so he breathed easier as he crossed over and back into downtown Bari.

Finding the hotel seemed impossible at night, but an MP with his white arm band and helmet showed up and escorted him to the hotel. So much for his Bari romance.

On June 6 General Eisenhower told the invasion forces under his command, "If you see fighting aircraft over you, they will be ours." He was not fooling them; the Luftwaffe did not show up for the invasion!

That same day the Fifteenth sent eleven groups to Ploesti, including the 460th. This time the 460th had a Pathfinder bomber in the lead, the Air Force's answer to the smoke screen. Pathfinder planes were equipped with an H2X bombsight that used radar to pierce the smoke and show the target outline on a scope, which the "Mickey Operator," as he was called, would use in his sighting.

On this particular mission the Mickey equipment was not functioning properly, so the lead ship had to drop on ETA, a frustrating experience for any highly trained bombardier. Bombing by wristwatch, indeed.

George Garrett, a replacement pilot, was on his first mission flying as a co-pilot, and didn't know enough to be afraid as they neared the IP. His naiveté was evident when he asked the pilot, "What are those black puffs?"

As they started down the bomb run a plane exploded in a nearby group and he commented to the pilot, "I didn't know we had orange parachutes."

The pilot would have laughed if his answer wasn't so serious: "We don't. Those chutes are on fire." With that, a piece of flak came through the windshield and glanced off the rookie's helmet. He had officially entered the war. He was now a combat veteran, and he hadn't even left the target area.

After bombing on ETA into a sea of white the Group was rewarded with a black pillar of smoke rising to 15,000 ft. A lucky hit? A phony hit? Who knows?

At least the Group lost no planes, which was well under the average for the day. The Fifteenth lost fourteen of 310 planes making the run in.

Two days later General Spaatz issued an interesting order to both the Eighth and the Fifteenth: That from this day on their primary strategic goal would be to deny oil to the German war machine. The Fifteenth AF was assigned the crude-oil refineries around Ploesti, Vienna and Budapest, as well as synthetic petroleum plants in Silesia, Poland, and the Sudetenland: Brux, Czechoslovakia; Oswiecim, Poland; Bleckhammer South, Bleckhammer North and Odertal, Germany. The Eighth AF was given a similar list of oil and synthetic oil targets in its territory. The RAF was assigned ten targets in the Ruhr Valley, and instructed to continue mining the Danube.

The leaders of the Fifteenth AF were no doubt somewhat surprised at the decree, as that is just what they had been doing for quite some time.

Within a week after proclaiming oil as the number one objective, the Fifteenth AF clobbered all of the major Hungarian refineries, all of the Yugoslavian refineries and all but one of the Italian refineries. The prime target of them all, Ploesti, was reeling so from the pre-season action that it could be rested through much of June. But its turn would come again.

The premature attack on Ploesti and other oil suppliers in May and the added emphasis in June had a telling effect on Germany's conduct of the war at all levels. The training program of the air force was curtailed, resulting in a shortage of pilots and causing higher casualties. Panzer divisions occasionally found themselve reduced to the humiliation of using horses. The Allied sweep across France would be aided greatly by Germany's lack of oil. Reinforcements for the front would set out by truck and arrive on foot.

In the month of June Hitler's 34th Infantry Division was ordered to stop all journeys not absolutely essential. Gasoline-driven vehicles were to be towed by diesel vehicles, which could burn kerosene.

Spaatz's June emphasis on oil would cause Commandant Sperrle, of the Western Front Air Force Area, to issue orders that motor transport was to be curtailed and violations punished severely. Officers of the 21st Panzer Division were required to submit daily gasoline reports, even under battle conditions.

The price in airmen and bombers was high for the denial of oil to Hitler, but considering the help provided American ground forces in their race to Berlin, it was worth it.

The *Stars and Stripes* gave the flyers a good overview of the war, but also created some reactions that in civilian life would have resulted in letters to the editor. If the paper stated relatively light losses for a particular mission to a major target, and men reading the item knew their group lost heavily that day, it would provoke a lot of paper shaking and finger pointing to the offending article.

On the other hand, one day the paper told a horror story that got the attention of thousands of men who thought they had seen it all. It seems a B–17 from the 5th Bomb Wing in Foggia had the tail section shot off by a flak blast. That in itself was not news to anyone, but the news angle was that the tail gunner never knew about it.

The empennage of the B–17 was still intact, and apparently the big piece of thin aluminum shaped like the rudder and elevator was so well balanced that it glided down like a falling leaf to a perfect landing in a field. The tail gunner opened his rear door to go back and congratulate the pilot on a fine emergency landing, and was dumbfounded to step out onto grass. The rest of the plane was nowhere to be seen.

Mail call was a big event every day. You may go several days with nothing, and then you hit the jackpot with several letters from home. So it was one nice day in mid-June, when stateside mail reaction to D-day arrived. Everyone who ever wrote to anyone wrote about the big day. "The war's days are numbered!" seemed to be the theme.

In among several letters from Newby's mother, girlfriends and parents of old friends was a letter with the writer's name printed on the envelope: Shirley Ross.

150

Now he would be vindicated for his idle boasting about knowing a movie star. She wrote a nice newsy letter with just enough suggestion of romance to titillate his friends. They can believe what they want to believe, he shrugged. One of his buddies who had a real relationship with another movie star just smiled when Newby tried a little name dropping with him.

The smoke screen defense at Ploesti was bothering the Fifteenth AF top people, so on June 10 they sent thirty-eight P–38s in at low level, each with a 1,000 lb. bomb, to try and get under the smoke. They were ambushed on the bomb run and lost twenty-three planes, including escorts, in the attempt. They never tried it again.

Ploesti was struck again on June 23 by only 139 planes, losing six. US fighters shot down 243 defending planes. The following day they sent in 135 planes and were met with a staggering loss of fourteen, the worst percentage loss since TIDAL WAVE. Smoke screens again made life miserable for the bombardiers.

Meanwhile the 460th bombed the oil refinery at Giurgiu, some seventy miles south of Ploesti. One plane was hit and lost a propeller. As it neared the coast it was attacked by five Me 109s. They shot down one fighter and limped across the ocean with considerable new damage from the fighter attack, and made it back to base.

Hangar Queen paralleled the Fifteenth Air Force's wide range of effort to destroy Hitler's oil; from the Russian front in Rumania to the Spanish border within a two-day period when it went to Sete, France, to bomb their oil tanks on June 25.

Chapter 11

Summer of 1944

What follows is an excerpt from a copyrighted true story titled "The Ring," written by William Blocker, co-pilot on *Honey Chile* the day it was shot down over Vienna, and is used here with his permission.

"Adolf Reuter was starting another week—it was Monday June 26, 1944—just like any other week for more than a year now. As far as he was concerned, the beginning of the end for his German Luftwaffe, as well as the entire Third Reich, started back in North Africa where he was a fighter pilot, trying to slow the devastating British and American war machines. Before the war, Reuter had been the youngest licensed pilot in Germany, flying gliders and what was described as small, low powered sport aircraft. He had established a good record from the moment he entered the Luftwaffe back before Germany had invaded Poland. Although he preferred just to fly, he had been put into some Administrative work, and in North Africa when he wasn't flying missions in support of the Wehrmacht, he was busy training new German pilots shipped across the Mediterranean from the homeland.

"Now, the German Army and the Luftwaffe, after having been pushed back across the Mediterranean to Italy, held only the northern part of Italy. He had been relieved of all combat flying duties and was made commander of a pilot training field on the outskirts of Vienna. It had become a common sight—Liberators and Flying Fortresses of the American air forces flying up from southern Italy, bombing any target they chose. In spite of the fact that a reasonable number of fighter planes were still somehow being produced in Germany, lack of fuel kept many of them grounded. Also, the American fighters so thoroughly controlled the skies, even as far as Vienna, that the loss of German fighter pilots had created a critical shortage which his training field, plus a few back in Germany, could not overcome. In fact, American fighters occasionally swooped down on his air base at D. Wagram and shot down his students flying training planes as they circled in the traffic pattern.

"On this beautiful, partly cloudy June morning in 1944 he wondered how long Germany could go on—and more specifically, how long could he go on. The air raid alarm had sounded several minutes ago, and he had gone outside his office at the airfield to see the now familiar sight of hundreds of bombers approaching from the south and an ugly black cloud of bursting anti-aircraft shells over the city of Vienna.

"First Lieutenant Jack Weller Smith, a spit and polish West Point graduate, Class of 1943, and his motley crew had found their way down the line to South America, across the Atlantic to Dakar, up to North Africa and across the

152

Mediterranean to their new base near Spinazzola, Italy in early May 1944. By the time they had arrived at the 460th Bomb Group's new base they had selected a name for their shiny new B-24—HONEY CHILE. The name came from a pet they had during training, a honey colored cocker spaniel. The picture selected to go on the nose of their airplane was from *Esquire* magazine—a Varga girl holding a honey colored cocker spaniel.

"Unfortunately, after landing at the 460th and being assigned to the 760th Bomb Squadron, they never saw their new B-24 again. They found that a replacement crew had to work its way up on the seniority list before being allowed to claim its own airplane. It was good news/bad news when they learned it wouldn't take long to earn the right to claim their own airplane—it seems the loss rate would move them right on up the seniority ladder in a short time.

"Smith had tried unsuccessfully to shape up his raunchy crew from the day he inherited them until the day they shipped out for combat. They were a loose, carefree but lovable assemblage of men who just before they did ship out presented their leader with a 12 plaited leather whip.

"The pilot carried his whip coiled on the back of his seat on every mission, and by late June the HONEY CHILE crew felt like old timers, having survived 23 missions, including three over Ploesti. After a nice weekend in Naples, they were now on their way this Monday June 26 to Vienna. Vienna was like Ploesti: one of the three most heavily defended targets in Europe. They would be approaching the halfway point for their ticket home.

"Jack Smith was an excellent and courageous pilot. This, plus his West Point background, was beginning to get the attention of the senior squadron and group officers. Evidence of this recognition could be found on this June 26 mission to Vienna in his assignment to lead the high box of six B-24s in his attack unit. By now, they had reclaimed HONEY CHILE.

"Due to flak damage before reaching the IP, HONEY CHILE's superchargers became erratic, reducing power on the four engines to the point where the airspeed fell below that flown by the group. Lt. Smith signaled his wingman to take over the box lead, and he pulled HONEY CHILE out of formation.

"The superchargers' operation became worse. Smith ordered the bombardier to salvo the bomb load to reduce weight, and asked the navigator for a heading calculated to intercept the group on its return from the target. A steady descent had to be maintained to keep sufficient flying speed to compensate for the reduced power being delivered by the four engines.

"At about 19,000 feet on the way down from the original 21,000 feet altitude, four twin engine Luftwaffe ME-110s dived on HONEY CHILE from 11 o'clock high. The B-24 vibrated and shook momentarily from several 20 millimeter cannon shell hits. A quick interphone survey told Smith miraculously there were no injuries, and crewmen in the nose and tail reported no obvious severe damage. The only critical damage was that which could easily be seen by the pilot and co-pilot. On the flightdeck bulkhead, a few feet directly back of the first pilot, where the visual fuel gauges and some oxygen lines had been severed, was a hot fire of bluish white flame.

"It was obvious the fire could not be controlled with the onboard fire extinguishers, so Lt. Smith gave the order to bail out. After sufficient time for the rest of the crew to be out, Smith told the co-pilot to leave. On the way down in his parachute, the co-pilot, apparently the last one to leave, counted

Eight 500 pounders fall toward a Vienna refinery.

just seven parachutes, including his own, which was the last in the line of seven floating down.

"The seven crewmen—co-pilot, bombardier, navigator and four gunners—were captured and brought together within a couple of hours. They all agreed that since the two missing gunners and Lt. Smith had all been observed to be uninjured and performing normally after the attack, that the two gunners must have refused to jump or couldn't jump due to some chute trouble and Smith saw this, returned to his seat and attempted to land HONEY CHILE. The seven survivors spent the remainder of the war in prison camps.

"Commander Adolf Reuter noticed one B–24 coming down in a tight spiral, trailing heavy smoke, and it appeared that it might even strike him where he stood by his car. But the Liberator veered slightly away from him, and he noted a parachute leave the doomed airplane about 200 feet before it struck the ground. He quickly got into his car and drove the few hundred meters to the crash site. When he arrived at the scene, the airplane was in full flames and could not be approached. Several meters from the burning wreckage was an opened parachute on the ground. Beside it lay an American flyer who could not move, but he spoke slowly to the German, 'Please, after the war tell my family. My name is in my ring.' Reuter did what he could to make the American comfortable on his parachute, but realized it was too late to help him. Adolf Reuter took the American's heavy gold ring and made arrangements for him to be buried in a local cemetery. He paid the expenses of the burial, but his military regulations did not allow him to be present.

"After the war Reuter held important positions in the reconstruction of Germany's transport system. One day he showed the ring to an American Army of Occupation officer and asked for help in locating the family of Jack Weller Smith, West Point Class of 1943.

"Subsequent communications involved the co-pilot, Bill Blocker, of Olive Branch, MS, who in 1982 finally made contact with Reuter. Blocker had been trying unsuccessfully since 1945 to have his pilot recognized for valor for voluntarily staying with the plane to save two crew members. 'Too speculative' was the reason given for not accepting Blocker's proposal.

"In 1984 the co-pilot flew to Marburg, West Germany to spend three days with Reuter, a visit which included January 26, the 40th anniversary of the day HONEY CHILE was shot down and an occasion for which Adolf Reuter proved that human love, in many instances, is stronger than the cruel passions of war.

"Reuter not only volunteered to give a notarized statement in support of Blocker's cause, but he went to the American consul in Frankfurt and sold him on starting an effort through the State Department to put pressure on the Air Force to make the award. Reuter phoned Blocker regularly from Germany to see how the campaign was going.

"Reuter's statement was forwarded to the Air Force to supplement and validate Blocker's earlier claim.

"In 1985 the Secretary of the Air Force posthumously awarded Lt. Jack Weller Smith the Distinguished Flying Cross.

"A bomber pilot and a fighter pilot, enemies by edict, had touched each other in an act of human love during battle, and again 41 years later when the fighter pilot proved to be the key to the Air Force's decision to make the deserved award."

Lt. Jack Smith's *Honey Chile* was one of the group's three planes shot down that day; two others crash-landed back at the base; eight were badly damaged by flak.

The "Hangar Queen" crew had spent that brutal day lolling around at the beach on the Isle of Capri, and thinking about that night's dance at the deluxe hotel where the air force was putting them up on their week's R&R. After surviving thirty-five missions they finally got the coveted week in the sun at

Capri. The night before, dressed in their Class As, they made decorative wallflowers at the nightly dance, where the men outnumbered the girls about twenty to one. This night would be no different.

After lunch Charlie Hammett and Sherman Wood took a donkey ride up to the ruins of Tiberius's Iovis Villa. From that location you could see across to the Gulf of Naples. Ted Newby and Dusty Rhodes felt they couldn't stand all that excitement and begged off, so they could relax at a sidewalk cafe in the Piazza Umberto.

Over his cognac highball Rhodes mused, "How we all gonna get a date tonight? All the local Red Cross gals and nurses have been latched onto by majors and colonels; us second louies don't have a chance."

"The 1500 hours steamer will be bringing another boatload of nurses, Waves and Wacs. Somebody has to get 'em," reminded Newby.

With that, he slammed down his drink and said, "SMOE is the answer!"

"Waddeyall mean, SMOE?" asked Rhodes.

"Remember those CIC guys we met last night at the dance?" said Newby.

"Yeah, those spies," recalled Rhodes.

"They told us about their training in sneaking into places; the little face with the big ears and nose looking over the top of a straight line was their signature. That was their SMOE. You and I know him as 'Kilroy was here.'"

"Yeah, SMOE is an acronym for Surreptitious Mode of Entry," said Rhodes.

"Well, you know those goodies coming over on the boat? We're gonna get us two of them," Newby said confidently.

"I don't get it," said Rhodes.

Newby ordered two drinks and said, "Now, here's my plan. . . ."

As the steamer pulled up to the pier about fifty yards from shore two men dressed in local garb, including stockingless sandals, wearing sunglasses, one with a coil of rope over his shoulder and the other carrying a bucket, strolled past the MPs who were holding back the army of GIs.

"That part was easy, Newb. Now comes the test," whispered Rhodes.

As the two interlopers waited at the gangplank the mainlanders bounded off the ship, smiles of anticipation on their faces and looks of wonderment in their eyes. Finally, two good-looking Army nurses came tripping down the gangplank, each carrying a small suitcase. The tall brunette had sharp features on her beautiful face and a nice figure. Her pretty blond companion was shorter and more full bodied.

Newby whispered back to Rhodes, "Your little blond isn't too bad either."

"Who gave you first choice?" Rhodes retorted. Then quickly added, "But I'll take her."

The two bums at the end of the gangplank held out their hands, as Rhodes said, "Me carry bag?"

"Why, how nice," said the blond second lieutenant, as she handed Rhodes his ticket to a night of dancing. Newby's brunette followed suit, and the two porters fell in behind the girls as they marched along the pier toward the horde of awaiting would-be suitors with smiles of anticipation on their faces. The smiles on the two dock workers were smiles of pending victory.

Rhodes whispered to his buddy, "We better make our move pretty soon."

He spoke quickly, "Say, girls, you ought to know, we aren't really native dock workers. We're two flyboys who would like to take you all to dinner tonight, and to the big dance later."

The nurses stopped, spun around, looked at each other and burst out laughing.

"I thought I had seen it all," exclaimed the blond, "but this is wild." They looked at each other, big grins of approval on their faces, and the brunette said, "How can we say no? You're on!"

They exchanged names, set a time to pick them up for dinner, helped the girls into a carriage, threw their bags onto the rear baggage rack and climbed on the back.

As the carriage pulled away the winners waved to the losers, who in turn shook their fists in a mixture of admiration and anger at being outwitted.

The dinner and drinks at the sidewalk cafe were great and the dance went well for Rhodes, who kept his date in tow throughout the evening. His bombardier didn't fare as well, however. After a couple of dances a full colonel, with pilot's wings and several rows of campaign and battle ribbons on his chest, cut in during a dance. When the colonel and the girl came back to the table she said, "This is my cousin I haven't seen in years."

The colonel added, "You won't be needed any longer to entertain my cousin." After being shot down in flames this evening Newby hoped he would do better on his next fifteen missions.

Rhodes kept his blond away from any long-lost relatives.

The next day's trip to the Blue Grotto was highlighted by the singing gondoliers. In the boat next to the "Hangar Queen" crew's a man who looked like Chico Marx was singing the "Beer Barrel Polka" in bad English as he poled along. In their boat the man was trying for the "Isle of Capri."

Once inside the large grotto, with its brilliant blue glow, the flyers stripped off their clothes to reveal swim suits and dived into the water.

The secret of the blue cast inside was the fact that from about nine to eleven each morning the sun's rays went through the water under the rock cliff

A postcard painting of the Blue Grotto on the Isle of Capri.

and entered the grotto through the water. The water filtered out all but the blue portion of the color spectrum, resulting in this world-renowned spectacle. The swimmers all glowed like long fluorescent lamps.

The week at Capri had been fun, and the opportunity to get away from the war was great for morale. As they headed for the base they all contemplated the real world they were about to reenter. Ten of the original seventeen crews in this Squadron had been shot down, and they had fifteen more missions to go before they earned their tickets home.

The men of Capri were unaware of the events of June 30 when their Group dispatched thirty-five planes to a place no one had ever heard of, until the curtain was pulled revealing the blue yarn going to the southeastern corner of Germany to a place with a mean name—Bleckhammer South synthetic oil refinery. (The name suggested there was another one, and there was— Bleckhammer North.) Bleckhammer sounded evil, and the Fifteenth would soon learn that it was well named.

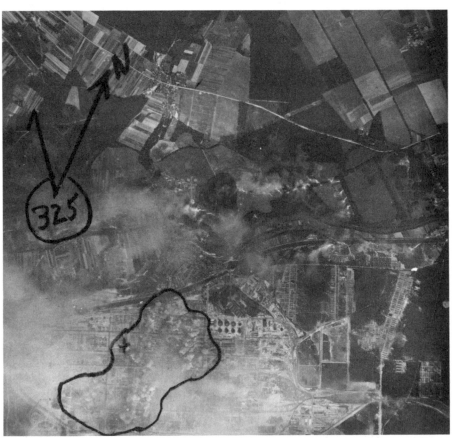

Bleckhammer North. The name even sounds evil . . . and it was! The smoke screen was ineffective this day, but the bombing accuracy was "on target." This strike photo shows the impact area outlined. An obviously high percentage of bombs landed within 2,000 ft. of the aiming point—an oil refinery, as usual. This is the measure of a group's efficiency.

As the 460th approached Lake Balaton they began seeing Forts, Liberators and fighters flying south; they soon learned why. Cloud banks were so fierce that the entire Fifteenth abandoned briefed German targets and headed home, bombing targets of opportunity on the way.

The 460th split up and bombed six different targets. The high box of the first attack unit, consisting of only five planes, was attacked by thirty-two Me 210s. The fighters came in from seven o'clock high in eight waves of four abreast and closed to within fifty yards. Seven others came in from six o'clock.

Misfortune, piloted by Erfeldt and Barrowcliff was hit by machine gun bullets, killing the tail gunner, ball gunner and the left waist gunner. Gasoline was gushing from the tanks located over the bomb bays as bombardier Mike Brown noted with horror that his chute pack was on fire. He smothered the flames and snapped the chute onto his harness, not knowing if it would still work. Had the heat fused the nylon panels? His hesitation was not understood by the man behind him, who pushed him out. The chute worked. The other six men got out before the bomber exploded.

Another bombardier in that fateful box, Jerry Conlon, was wondering why none of the men on the flight deck or cockpit was not hit when the thirty-some fighters came at them. They all felt the impacts from the many bullets raking their plane. When pilot Bob Evans saw Conlon standing over his right shoulder he turned partway around and hit him in the chest with a backhand, shouting, "Get out of here!"

Conlon popped on his chest pack and went down to the bomb bay, where two others were struggling to get the bomb bay doors open with a hand crank; the hydraulic system had been shot out. They gave up and went up to the nose section and went out through the nose wheel door.

The bombardier went through the bomb bay to the waist section where he discovered a terrible mess: the tail gunner was sprawled backwards half out of his turret, and dead; the left waist gunner was bloodied and dead; the right waist gunner had his chest partly ripped away and his right leg severed—he was obviously dying. Only the ball gunner survived the attack on the rear of the plane.

Bob Evans rang the bail-out alarm, and after ordering the co-pilot to leave he stayed at the controls to enable the others to get out. Evans was not seen by any of the survivors and was presumed to have gone down with the plane when it crashed near a farm not far from where the navigator had landed.

Two other planes from that ill-fated high box went down under the fighter assault, but one plane survived in one of the strangest encounters of the war.

The other planes had been scattered by the clouds and were flying in singles and twos or threes. One plane came out of some clouds to face a frightening sight: an Me 109 was stalking the remaining bomber of the high box, just fifty yards behind. It was obvious there were either no live gunners aboard or no operating guns to challenge the German. The bomber had one engine feathered, and another smoking—truly a helpless cripple. The German was toying with his prey.

The pilot of the B-24 coming upon this scene was enraged at the cruel sight, and from his 1,500 ft. height advantage he racked his four-engine bomber into a sharp diving turn and roared down from out of the sun, fighter style. The fighter pilot never knew what hit him as the steep-diving B-24 poured sixty-nine rounds per second for several seconds into the hapless Messerschmitt.

It was man bites dog, as the Me 109 burst into flames and plummeted to earth, to the applause of a happy bomber crew.

One of the downed bombers made a wheels-up landing on a farm at Csaktornya near Pecs, Hungary. The local newspaper later showed the demolished bomber, its four curled propellers and crushed underbelly as witness to its hard landing. The picture showed a dozen helmeted soldiers and civilians standing on or around the plane; conspicuously in the foreground on the nose section was the black panther, bracketed by two onlookers. It was poised and ready to strike, but it had been declawed and never would strike again.

June was not that busy a month at Ploesti; only three missions, but they were effective in that production was about half that of July. No doubt some of the May damage was cumulative and affected June production.

The Eighth AF and Fifteenth AF, combined, dropped over 20,000 tons of bombs on German oil in the month of June. The Fifteenth had hit twenty-nine of its sixty oil refineries in its territory.

High German officials were appalled at the vulnerability of Ploesti and other refineries, as well as the dozen or so synthetic oil plants, and sought measures to maintain the flow of fuel to their armed forces.

Albert Speer would later declare that the concentrated oil attacks made real what had been a nightmare for more than two years. He correctly feared they were the beginning of a planned campaign to wipe out oil. Hitler was upset that the synthetic oil plants, and their intricate structures so vulnerable to attack, were built in clusters, which the Allies could bomb with ease now that the Luftwaffe was faltering.

Both the Fifteenth AF and the 460th BG's bombing efficiencies increased for June, but the 460th fell out of the top four.

Near Pecs, Hungary, German soldiers pose for a news photographer as civilians inspect a downed B-24 of the 460th BG (note "Black Panther" insignia on nose section), one of the group's four bombers lost on June 30, 1944 in an attack on Bleckhammer oil.

May would prove to be a busy and important month for the Fifteenth AF as preparations for ANVIL, the long-awaited southern invasion of France, began to increase in intensity. In between oil and aircraft factory strikes the heavies from Italy would lend tactical support to the infantry as it advanced through northern Italy by hitting rail lines and marshaling yards. It also stepped up its activity in bombing French ports and marshaling yards.

As the "Hangar Queen" crew was winding down its week at Capri, the Eighth Air Force had just completed a shuttle mission in which they bombed German targets en route to a safe haven in Russia. From there they bombed some Balkan targets on the way to Italy. Then on July 3 the Eighth's heavies joined the full offering of the Fifteenth for the first 1,000 plane attack on Balkan oil, with effective hits on Bucharest and Belgrade, but with less success on Giurgiu, Rumania.

Upon arrival back at Spinazzola the crew was pleased to hear that their pilot, Charlie Hammett, had been made a flight leader.

On July 5 some American bombardier scored the shack of his life when he and his group hit the bull's-eye on the German battleship *Dunquerque* in the Toulon harbor. Fires leaped high in the air and the mighty battlewagon began to list as the formation departed the target area. Less demonstrable were the important hits on the nearby sub pens.

Two days later the Eighth and Fifteenth AFs made a major attack on synthetic oil plants, with the Fifteenth including Bleckhammer North and South in their effort. The Fifteenth was met by 300 fighters as Germany fought desperately to forestall the inevitable, and the Luftwaffe knocked down twenty-five of the invaders.

The 460th sent twenty-two planes over the target at Bleckhammer South: two were lost to fighters, sixteen suffered severe battle damage from flak and fighters and one plane that had a bomb go through its wing barely made it to Vis, its crew having thrown out everything that wasn't bolted down. The crew commandeered a just repaired B–24 of the 485th BG and flew it home, and were able to spend the night in their own bunks.

The smoke screen was heavy at Bleckhammer South so the "Black Panther" lead bombardier used the offset bombing technique to nail his aiming point, for a successful mission.

The next morning it was the "Hangar Queen" crew's turn, and while standing in line at breakfast Newby approached a new cocoa server, intent on tricking him into a double portion of cocoa. Another Italian spoke to the server, so when Newby held out his canteen cup the server took the cup out of his hand and poured it half full. With a big grin he handed the cup back to the defeated bombardier.

Turning to his buddies, Newby said, "How do you say touché in Italian?"

Hammett was leading the high box of the first attack unit, and was assigned the marshaling yard at Floridsdorf oil refinery at Vienna. They were told at briefing that additional flak guns had been brought in to Vienna, due to the job being done on oil.

As the Group approached the IP one of its planes was having supercharger trouble and had difficulty maintaining altitude. In order to stay with the formation it dropped two of its bombs before the bomb run. The loss of 1,000 lbs. enabled it to make its bomb run with the formation.

The flak was fierce, as usual at this flak hole, and two planes were hit and trailed fire after leaving the target. One went down a few miles south of Vienna, and the other one was listed as MIA.

Newby's box hit the marshaling yards and spilled a few bombs onto a refinery building, for a successful strike. Ten of the returning planes had battle damage.

Before and after the bomb run the 55th Bomb Wing, of which the 460th was one of four members, was attacked by 100 Fw 190s who were in turn engaged by many P–38s and P–51s. The aerial dogfights were enjoyed by bomber crew members; eighteen enemy aircraft were shot down by the fighter escort and the bombers.

During the fighter attacks Dusty Rhodes saw a lone fighter daring to come in at the 460th from two o'clock high and said over the interphone, "Let's get this guy in a Heinie Box." Hammett looked over and shook his head. Back in the waist the replacement left waist gunner hollered over to Homer Luke, "What's a Heinie Box?"

"Tell you later," shouted Luke as he lined up the oncoming fighter in his gunsight. Soon all the top turret twin fifties and Luke's guns were blazing at the oncoming Heinie. They didn't box him, and he broke off his attack and dived away.

When things calmed down Luke, with a straight face aided by the oxygen mask, told the visiting gunner, "Dusty is a good Christian man and dislikes hurting anyone, even the enemy. He knows our gunners are as good as they come, as we have shot down a number of fighters. So he has devised the concept of a Heinie Box, where our gunners will bracket the oncoming plane with tracers, top, bottom, and both sides. The fighter pilot knows he will be shot down if he moves out of the box, so the gunners escort him out of range."

The gunner shook his head, just like Hammett did every time Rhodes talked about his Heinie Box. The Heinie Box was Rhodes's contribution to keeping the crew loose.

Hangar Queen was on final approach and all crew members were in landing positions. The four up on the flight deck were taking turns looking at Smitty's little stuffed donkey and kidding him about having Vienna printed on it before they got home. The four back in the waist section were engaged in more worldly pursuits. Each had an empty .50 caliber shell balanced upright in front of him, and along in a nearby pile were four 10 Lira notes. A bet seemed to be in progress.

Holt Thornton said, "We have a strong crosswind out there so we may have a winner today." When the plane's wheels touched the ground three of the shells toppled over, and a grinning Sid Woods picked up his winnings; his shell survived the rough landing. Hammett was blissfully unaware of this game, and would not learn of it until forty years later at a crew reunion.

The next day the Fifteenth sent 222 planes to Ploesti and lost six.

With a stand down scheduled for two days Ted Newby decided to visit John Crippen, a friend from his hometown of Crafton, Pennsylvania, up in Foggia. He hitchhiked the fifty miles with no trouble and had a nice visit. Crippen, a sergeant in the Weather Section, took him around and he saw his first B–17 up close. He had never seen anything except the bottom of one, as they always flew two miles above the B–24s. There was a friendly rivalry between B–24 men and B–17 men, each plane having its advantages and disadvantages. Newby decided to keep his B–24.

Over a couple of beers Crippen told Newby of a mutual friend, Bill McKee, who was a bomber pilot in Crippen's outfit and had been shot down. Newby knew McKee had gone down, but did not know the particulars.

VE 71/44   (VE = VERMEHMUNGS EXTRAKT = INTERROGATION EXTRACT)

TB/RA   26.7.44

                    " LIBERATOR B24H"

HIT NUMBER: SO-U 312 8.7.44   1300 HRS

HIT LOCATION: SOUTH OF AGRAM (ZAGREB, YUGOSLAVIA)

760 (B SQN)   SPINNAZZOLA (ITALY)   460. (B) GROUP

INTERROGATED WERE: BOMBARDIER & ENGINEER

ATTACK ON VIENNA ON 8.7.44:

MAJOR TARGET: RAIL YARDS, 3 MILES NORTH OF VIENNA, IN THE VICINITY
                           OF HYROWORKS (HYDROGENATION PLANT)

ALTERNATE TARGET: RAIL YARDS NEAR AGRAM.

BOMB LOADS: 10 X 225 KILOGRAMM EXPLOSIVE BOMBS

TIMES: START: 0700 HRS
                           ON TARGET: 1030 HRS (PLANNED! THE FORMATION WAS
                                      10 MIN LATE)
                           RETURN: 1415 HRS

MISSION STRENGH: 760 (B) SQ - 9 AIRCRAFT
                           460 (B) GP - 36 AIRCRAFT

FIGHTER COVER: "P-38" PLANNED, BUT NOT OBSERVED.

WEATHER: CLEAR. EVEN THOUGH THE BOMBARDIER BELIEVES THAT A
                           "PFF" (PFADFINDER = PATHFINDER ?) WAS USED.

ALTITUDE: THE "B" GROUPS OF A WING FLY WITH AN ALTITUDE
                           DIFFERENCE OF 1000-1500 FT, WITHIN THE GROUP THE
                           ALTITUDE DIFFERENCE IS 1000 FT. THE 460. (B) GROUP
                           WAS SUPPOSED TO FLY AT 7000 MTR (20,000 FT) ALTITUDE.

IP: EAST OF THE TARGET, OVER A FOREST, ABOUT 12 MILES
                           FROM THE TARGET.

DEFENSE: THE INTEROGATED WERE VERY IMPRESSED BY THE
                           UNEXPECTETLY STRONG FIGHTER DEFENSE. THE BOMBARDIER
                           INSISTED THAT HE COUNTED NO LESS THAN 55 GERMAN
                           FIGHTER AIRCRAFT. AT AN ATTACK, ABOUT A MONTH AGO,
                           GERMAN FIGHTERS SHOT DOWN 5-6 AIRCRAFT OF THE
                           760 (B) SQUADRON. THE ATTACK OF THE FIGHTERS
                           CAUSED THE UNIT TO ABANDON THEIR TARGET. (REMARKS
                           OF THE V.O. (VERNEHMUNGS OFFIZIER = INTERROGATION
                           OFFICER): IT WAS PROBABLY THE ATTACK ON 16.4.44)
                           THE FLAK DEFENSE OVER THE TARGET IS DESCRIBED AS
                           VIERY STRONG. AT THE ATTACK ON WIENER-NEUSTADT ON
                           10.5.44, THE PILOT OF THE INTERROGATED WAS SO
                           SEVERELY WOUNDED, THAT HE WAS TRANSFERRED TO GROUND
                           PERSONNEL.

                           THE TARGET ACQUISITION OF THE ATTACK ON 8.7.44
                           WAS DESCRIBED AS UNUSUALLY GOOD.

                           THE INTERROGATED MENTIONED THAT EVEN IN THE AREA
                           OF PLATENSEE, THEY ENCOUNTERED STRONG FLAK DEFENSES.

FORMATION: THE AIRCRAFT FLEW AS NO. 4 IN THE LEADBOX OF
THE 2. ATTACK UNIT.

COURSE OF FLIGHT AND
FATAL HIT: AFTER "BOMBS AWAY" THE AIRCRAFT WAS DOWNED BY FLAK
                           AFTER IT HAD TO ABANDON THE FORMATION.

THE 760 (B) SQ LOSSES: ON 30.6.44 THE SQUADRON LOST 3 AIRCRAFT.

                           SIGNATURE
                           CAPTAIN AND DEPARTMENT HEAD

Crippen then told him the story. They were bombing Genoa and the lead bombardier on the bomb run was so far off course he had to abort the run and go around. A bomber was shot down on that run. He aborted again on the second run in, and another plane went down. On the third attempt Bill McKee's plane went down.

"I would hate to have been in that bombardier's shoes when they got back," said Newby.

When a lead bombardier hits his target his buddies can't buy him enough drinks that evening. But when he misses, he is treated badly, with snide remarks thrown his way. Not a pleasant experience.

A swim in the Adriatic, however, was a pleasant experience as long as it was down at the Manfredonia beach, and not out in the middle. The well-shaped girls in their skimpy swim suits were a welcome sight to the landlocked bombardier, but they all talked funny.

Bunking his visitor was a problem, but Crippen was up to it. He knew his boss, Capt. Joe Green, was away on an overnight pass, so he took Newby over to his tent and offered him the captain's bed. He climbed into bed and went to sleep.

When Green's roomie came in he was surprised to see Green's bed occupied.

"I thought you were off base tonight, Joe," he said.

The interloper pulled the covers up over his head and grunted a couple of times. The roomie didn't pursue it any further.

Newby got up early, shaved and got out of there as fast as he could, chuckling to himself over the thought of the next conversation the two room-mates would have.

At breakfast Newby mentioned the B-17 tail gunner that floated down in his tail section. Crippen knew the man.

"What was his reaction?" asked Newby.

Crippen laughed, and said, "Well, he never flew again."

"What's he doing now?"

"He transferred to the tank corps."

"Out of the frying pan. . . ." Newby responded.

Hitchhiking back was not as easy as the trip up. The adventurous bombardier finally got a ride out of camp and was left off at a crossroads in the middle of nowhere. That didn't bother him at first, but when US Army trucks and Jeeps passed him up one after another he couldn't understand it. They all had room for one more.

After several hours an officer came along and gave him a lift to Pantanella, a small village about fifteen miles north of Spinazzola, and the home of the 464th and 465th Bomb Groups of the 55th Bomb Wing. It was late in the afternoon and the bombardier was becoming a little concerned about being AWOL for the next day's mission. He stopped in at a little corner cafe to do some planning over a cognac and saw another flyboy at the bar. After introductions they both removed their Cairo rings and threw them onto the bar. Newby paid for the drinks.

His new friend, also a bombardier, had a simple solution to his problem. He would take him to his 464th air base and from there he could catch something in to Wing Headquarters in Spinazzola.

The first truck to Spinazzola was a laundry truck, so Newby finished his mission to Foggia sitting on top of a pile of dirty laundry.

The crew flew three days in a row and thought they would get a day off, like *Hangar Queen*, which was laid up for battle damage repairs. Instead they got to go back to Ploesti with a borrowed plane on July 15, when the largest force ever to hit that number one oil target, all twenty-one groups consisting of 607 bombers, hit four refineries and a pumping station. The 5th and 47th Bomb Wings, consisting of ten bomb groups, concentrated just on George Suciu's American refinery.

When the hooters sounded forty-five minutes before the arrival of the American heavies, the citizenry ran for their favorite bomb refuge, or left town. Mr. Grigorescu packed his wife, Ioan and the other son into their auto and headed out of town to a favorite vantage point on a hill about five miles out of the city. It was a familiar sight: all roads were one way—out. A two-lane road with wide berms became a four-lane speedway with wagons and autos vying for space. Woe to the vehicle coming the other way.

They watched the smoky, fiery spectacle from afar, counting the falling bombers and wondering if their house would survive again.

The entire target area was covered by the smoke screen and, coupled with a 7/10 undercast, bode a difficult day for the bombardiers. The 460th's first attack unit used a Pathfinder (H2X) plane and the results were not known. The second attack unit lead plane had two generators out and the H2X could not be used, so they bombed on a column of black smoke in the target area. A second column of smoke arose and went to 20,000 ft. as they rallied off the target. The formation was on course on the run in and on course on the rally, so with the new black smoke column it was presumed the target was hit.

Flak was heavy and accurate. Three planes suffered serious hits: one went down on the way back and all men parachuted safety; one ditched forty miles offshore from Bari and only five were rescued. Hammett's plane had a harrowing experience. His plane lost three superchargers and had its No. 3 engine shot out; he could not feather the propeller. The unfeathered prop windmilled all the way across the Balkans as the crew dumped everything they could, including the bombsight, to stay in the air.

As they came in for a last-ditch effort to land at Vis, the propeller came off. There was a biplane taxiing down the runway and as they could not go around they had to land in front of the plane, which left them only 1,500 ft. of runway—with a cliff at the other end.

The No. 3 engine operates the hydraulic system so the brakes were suspect. Chutes were tied to both waist gun mounts and popped outside on cue after the wheels touched. The heaving bomber ground to a final stop just inches from the edge of the cliff, with rocky seashore 200 ft. below.

When the Grigorescu family returned home there was a hole in the ground where their house had been.

The Fifteenth AF lost twenty at Ploesti, the heaviest so far on the high-level missions.

The next day the crew was on a small steamship bound for Monopoli, a seaport some twenty miles south of Bari.

At that same moment the 460th BG was en route to Vienna for a flak ride not to be forgotten, as it attacked the Neudorf aircraft engine factory. Vienna had the second heaviest flak concentration in the world, after Berlin. The heavy accurate flak began well ahead of the IP and continued through the rally off the target.

Lt. Ben Haller, a veteran from the 761st Squadron, was assigned to fly first pilot with a replacement crew to check out the new pilot. Several minutes before turning onto the IP for the run in, the plane shuddered like a car hitting a bump at high speed. There was no comment over the interphone from the stunned rookies on their first combat mission, and after a few seconds of silence Haller said as calmly as he could, "Just a little prop wash."

Two "Black Panther" planes were shot down on the bomb run as the flak intensity increased, and they experienced several more near misses. As his plane was safely away from the target a voice came on the interphone, "That was some prop wash, lieutenant."

Fighter activity had been heavy before the target and again on the way home. The attack on the wing continued as the Fifteenth AF shot down forty-five more enemy fighters, while losing nine.

The following day the crew hitchhiked a ride to Bari on a naval LCI (Landing Craft, Infantry), where they enjoyed a real meal.

Meanwhile the Fifteenth feasted on some relatively easy marshaling yards and railroad bridges in southern France as part of the softening up for the coming invasion.

On July 18, the Fifteenth's biggest air battle of the war was taking place as the "Hangar Queen" crew rode the GI truck from the Bari hospital, where they had stayed overnight for delousing, to Spinazzola. Over 500 heavies bombed the aircraft factories at Friedrichshafen, and the airdrome forty miles north at Memmingen.

The 483rd BG took the brunt of the tenacious fighter defense when it became separated from the others on its way north to its target. Two hundred fighters arose to defend their nest at Memmingen, Germany, and took on this valiant group of thirty-five B–17s, who closed to a wingtip-to-wingtip formation. No one had to order this reaction, the pilots knew what had to be done. The Germans attacked in wave after wave, but the gunners met every attempt with their own withering fire, and when the smoke cleared they had sent sixty-six fighters down in flames, or damaged beyond continued fighting. Thirteen bombers were lost in that battle. The decimated bomb group continued on to the target where it damaged thirty-five more fighters on the ground.

The 483rd BG was awarded the Presidential Unit Citation.

Munich, Germany, once famed for its beer halls, acquired a new meaning for the USAAF in July. The Eighth AF had flown down from England on July 11, 12 and 13 to inflict tremendous damage to their aircraft factories. As a result many new AA guns were moved in to the area, bringing this new flak alley up to near the firepower of Vienna. Thus was born the warm welcome for the 460th as it went back again to Munich on July 19 to bomb the Allach aircraft engine factory.

A bombing mission is an intricate thing. Some thirty-six pilots have been assigned their part in a well thought out plan of action, but the verities of execution can tear asunder the best laid plans. Murphy's law has now entered the picture.

What happened that day at Munich is another example of what happens when a bombing plan goes awry, as the men of TIDAL WAVE had learned a year earlier.

Colonel Harrison led his group of thirty-one planes to the IP; both attack units were led by Pathfinder (H2X) planes so the smoke screens or undercasts should not have been a serious problem. As the two attack units started down the bomb run the lead ship in the second attack unit lost its No. 4 engine to flak, and the pilot salvoed his bombs so as to try to stay in formation. In the excitement of all the extremely heavy flak, the planes behind the leader toggled their bombs. As they were far short of the bomb release point all of the second attack unit's bombs fell far short of the aiming point.

In the meantime, the Mickey (H2X) operator in the first attack unit could not find his target (different one from the second attack unit) through the smoke screen so the leader decided to go for the first alternate target, the marshaling yards. As the flight was passing over the center of the city the smoke screen cleared and the yards could be seen far to the left, impossible to reach.

As the plan began falling apart each individual was forced to make adjustments as the situation looked to him. The No. 3 plane was hit and two engines set afire; the pilot salvoed his bombs so people could have room to bail out. Murphy again. All of the planes except No. 2 (deputy lead), just off the lead ship's right wing, toggled their bombs on what they thought was their cue.

The lead ship pilot, unaware his other planes had dropped their bombs, decided to go for the second alternate target, oil supplies at Trieste, Italy. When they got to Trieste the two planes (lead and deputy lead) dropped eight 1,000 lb. bombs and set fire to the oil supplies. The Group's other sixty-two tons of bombs had been dropped somewhere in the city of Munich.

Low-level bombing was difficult, but high-level bombing wasn't easy either.

The flak gunners took a heavy toll that day. Four planes went down over the target. On one the No. 4 engine caught fire, and ten men were able to bail out. Another went down in flames and only four got out. Yet another caught fire in the bomb bay and eight managed to bail out before it blew up. The fourth caught fire and was out of control leaving the target, as four chutes trailed behind.

Three other planes were listed as MIA. One went into a dive just before the target and two men bailed out. The plane recovered and headed for neutral Switzerland. One was hit at the target and was on fire as it too headed for the neutral haven.

A third plane, piloted by Kennon Sorgenfrei, was hit over the target. The No. 1 engine was feathered; No. 4, smoking, had to be feathered a few minutes later. The crippled plane was last seen, under control, on a 240 degree heading that would take it to Switzerland, a very popular spot that day.

As they neared Switzerland a third engine quit and the pilot ordered everyone to bail out. (A *Reader's Digest* article, "Saga of the Sorgenfrei Crew," in the September 1984 issue, tells the exciting story of what happened after they bailed out.)

Four planes were so badly damaged they had to land at friendly fields, one of which was Vis. Of the twenty planes returning to base, fifteen were heavily damaged.

Bomber City suffered its first fighter attack one day when a P–47 buzzed low over the encampment, not once but several times, nearly destroying some of the still remaining tents. It was learned later that it was one of the local bomber pilots, a frustrated fighter pilot at heart, who had borrowed the plane from a buddy at a fighter field and was having a good time. He was later persuaded by the colonel, in his not so subtle way, to stop such activities.

The next afternoon a USO troop staged an excellent show, complete with girl singers and jugglers, but climaxed by the appearance of Heavyweight

Champ Joe Louis. A ring had been improvised and the champ, wearing boxing gloves, was brought to the center amid hearty applause and yelling. Then came the surprise. From behind a truck strolled the contender. It was Capt. George Bishop, of flybutton fame, dressed in long johns, a flak suit, a holstered .45 at his side, a flak helmet, catcher's shin guards, and of course wearing boxing gloves.

They squared off, and Louis was laughing so hard he barely fended off the windmilling arms of his opponent. Then the champ extended his right arm from its defensive position and barely tapped Bishop in the face. Bishop did an exaggerated spiraling fall and flopped onto his back, as did so many of his predecessors. Louis then walked over, put one foot on Bishop's chest and clasped both hands over his head in self-congratulation. It was a humorous side of the man that few have been privileged to see.

Occasionally the evening discussions got fairly wild as the bunkmates tried to outdo each other, and one time Ted Newby dropped the matter of an ice mine on his buddies from the south: Whitehead (pilot from another crew) from Birmingham and his bombardier Art Shiflett from Virginia; Rhodes from Louisiana. He told them of the Ice Mine at Coudersport, Pennsylvania, where there was this big cave with a large pool of water in it. A large grotto like at Capri. In the summer the water froze solid, and years ago someone made a living selling ice. A true seller's market. However, in the winter the ice melted into just another body of water in a grotto.

It was a tough sell for Newby, but it was true. "One explanation was," he said, "the extremely cold winters in this north central mountainous area enabled large deposits of subzero air to be captured in deep crevices, above the grotto. The cold air froze over some holes in the grotto ceiling and in the summer the warm grotto melted the ice plugs and let the cold air drop into the grotto, causing the water to freeze. Anyone not accepting that explanation was free to offer their own. Scientists from around the world have visited the ice mine and cannot figure it out. All it does is happen every summer without fail."

After they choked on that one he told them about the ducks that walk on the backs of fish at the spillway of Pymatuning Dam a hundred miles north of Pittsburgh. He was banned from telling stories for a week.

The "Hangar Queen" crew went back to the land of smoke screens its next outing July 22, flying *Hangar Queen*. It was part of a twelve-group assault on Romano Americana, a seemingly favorite target of the planners. Twenty-four bombers went down that day out of the 495 making the run. The oil defenders were dying hard.

By then the officers of the crew had been promoted to first lieutenant and the enlisted men upgraded one rank. Their little mascot showed forty-three missions, and word had gotten around about Smitty printing the city's name on it on the way to the target. They were tabbed "The Lucky Crew" by envious others, many crewmen having left a standing request at Squadron Headquarters to fly as replacement with them if available. Much of the luck, of course, was really the skill of the pilots, two of the best in the Group, and the performance of the engineer, gunners and navigator.

As part of the continuing assault on the nest of the Luftwaffe, the 460th joined the Fifteenth AF on July 26 to hit three airdromes in the Vienna area, the 460th's being the Zwolfaxing airdrome. The twenty-four bombers reaching the area were attacked by thirty fighters, but the tight formation caused the fighters to break off their attack at 1,000 yards.

Heavy clouds obscured the target, but Colonel Harrison, despite a large hole in his wing from a penetrating shell and two damaged engines, signaled his flight to drop to a lower altitude to be under the clouds for visual sighting.

Although they did severe damage to their target, three of the planes were shot down in flames on the bomb run. Two more were so badly crippled they had to drop out of formation and limp home alone. Fourteen others had severe battle damage. *White "M" for Mike* had taken a direct flak hit that twisted off the waist and tail section at the bomb bay. The front and rear of the bomber fell to earth in two parts. Two men bailed out safely. An Associated Press wire photo of the plane, its two parts circled, appeared in newspapers all over the United States. The 460th was awarded the Presidential Unit Citation for the mission.

When a man completes his fifty missions and gets his ticket home it is always a moment of mixed emotions for the others still seeking that prize. They are happy for him and of course envious, wondering, Will I live through four more and be smiling like that lucky dog?

The crew of *Hangar Queen* were in just that position when they all stepped from their plane on July 30 after having successfully bombed the

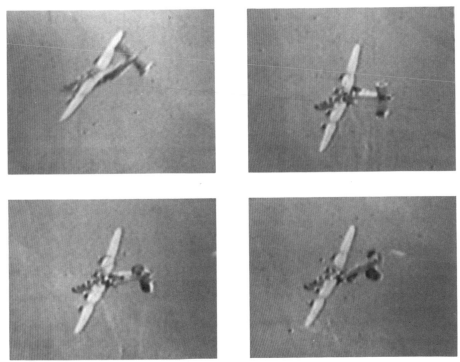

Ben Crawford, flying co-pilot in the lead plane, took a split-second 8 mm shot of a 460th BG B-24's tail twisting off, and did nothing with it. Forty-five years later he produced a video entitled, "White Mike." The Afterlog *contains some still shots from the 17 frames of the historic movie shot. The photos shown here were taken from the TV screen; while the picture quality is not the best, the results give us one of the most remarkable aerial sequence photos of the war.*

Marshaling yard bull's-eye. The 464th BG scores a shack on the marshaling yard at Szajol, Hungary.

Budapest/Duna aircraft factory. Navigator Sherman Wood ducked out from under the bomb bay and gave the ground its ceremonial kiss, as his happy crew mates looked on in envy. They all had two more to go.

The following day the 460th stood down and the flyers spent the day playing softball and cards, letter writing or just visiting. Rhodes and Newby got into another discussion with their roommates; this time it wasn't tall tales, it was a serious discussion about war. Speculation was about how soon we would go to war with Russia. Everyone felt Uncle Joe (Joseph Stalin) wasn't like the typical nice uncle. He was out to get us, when we finished off Germany—a fact of which there was no doubt. All the men knew Hitler was on his last legs and the end was in sight.

That discussion led into an even deeper one: when did World War II get its name? When they signed the Armistice on November 11, 1918 did the term World War I appear anywhere in print? In anyone's mind? Perhaps Corporal Hitler's? When did the Second World War get far enough into the planning stage to label it World War II?

Hangar Queen's final mission. Four engines quit in the landing pattern; in the resulting crash, two crewmen were killed on their 50th mission.

Preparing Hangar Queen for mission 50.

The Spanish War of the mid-thirties got a lot of votes for naming the new war coming up, but no one could guess as to the first time the term World War II appeared in print.

In a red brick schoolhouse in downtown Bucharest sat a group of Americans known to their jail keepers as The Italians. These men had come to bomb Ploesti and Bucharest from Italy. The Americans who came to bomb Ploesti from Africa a year earlier were held in a prison camp not too far from Ploesti, and were known as The Africans.

The Africans were looked upon more kindly because little damage was done to houses and few civilians were hurt or killed in their attack. The Italians, forced to bomb through smoke screens and clouds, did inflict considerable damage to residential areas, and many civilians were killed. The RAF Italians came at night and bombed the city proper. The American POWs were not discussing the philosophy of war on the last day of July, for the air raid alert had sounded a half hour earlier and smoke pots had been lit—this was the reality of war.

Roy Meyer of the 463rd BG and some others were looking out their windows at the scattered clouds and hoping they would open up so the American bombardiers could see their military targets on the city's edge. Meyer turned to a buddy and said, "At least the high surface winds will blow some of that sickening smoke away so our guys can find their targets, and not us."

They knew from their own briefings that the presence of American POWs in a nearby red brick schoolhouse was not known to the bombardiers, nor was the enlisted men's POW camp location next to the marshaling yard. Was this a form of subtle punishment for The Italians?

Bombing attacks on cloudy days, or when smoke pots were used, was a frightening time for the POWs. The night attacks were so spectacular: searchlights and bursting flak in the sky, an occasional flaming bomber falling to earth, and the dreadful exploding bombs nearby. Fortunately, none of the American POWs were ever hurt by Allied bombs.

Astra Romana, rested since June 6, got the full attention of the aerial predators on July 28, when twelve groups put 349 bombers over its much patched up facility. It was costly: twenty planes lost, for a 5.7 percent loss rate.

171

Due to the pounding on Astra Romana, Romano Americana, Standard Petrol and Concordia Vega, little Xenia, the next to smallest of them all, became the No. 1 priority target. It paid for that honor by being the sole subject of the Fifteenth AF's effort on July 31, when 154 bombers of the 5th Wing made a visit. The loss of two was the smallest of the campaign so far.

Other groups dropped pamphlets over the city stating, "Rumania under a Smoke Screen," and urging them to revolt. The citizens were generally aware that the Americans, beginning with TIDAL WAVE, had made a genuine effort to bomb only military targets. They were beginning to catch on that ever since the annoying smoke screens began the residential center of the city was being hit more frequently.

The smoke, however, was annoying to more than the civilians. The flyers unfortunately were not privy to the knowledge that flak gunners got seasick as they rocked in their gun seats amid the smoke. They thought the flak gunners were having a good time down there.

The loss rate for the 4,375 planes attacking Ploesti on the high-level campaign so far was 4.2 percent.

July showed the worst bomber loss ever, when the Fifteenth AF lost 318. However, a record 339 German fighters were shot out of the air during that period.

The two smashes at Friedrichshafen deprived the Luftwaffe of 950 jet aircraft. The Me 262 jet and Me 163 rocket fighters were new and frightening threats just coming on the scene. They were capable of flying 100 mph faster than our P–51, the fastest propeller-driven fighter in World War II.

Attacks on the Memmingen airdrome destroyed 350 aircraft in the nest.

Despite record assaults on Ploesti in July, oil production more than doubled over June; many thousands of slave laborers working twenty-four hours a day cleaned up the American mess as it was created; a well-trained, and *very* experienced fire-fighting force of 500, sometimes resorting to the ancient bucket brigade technique, quenched the flaming tanks quickly after each attack.

It was a good month for the 460th BG as they vaulted into first place in bombing efficiency for July with 53.7 percent.

As the summer of 1944 began to wind down, so did the crew of *Hangar Queen*. With Sherman Wood on the sidelines, the crew went to Friedrich-shafen to execute the coup de grace on that important womb of the emerging German jet fighters.

As the intensity of the softening up process for ANVIL increased, the Fifteenth began hitting bridges and the beach areas of southern France, so bombardier Newby with only one mission to go for his ticket home chose a so-called milk run to Arles for his finale. It was the custom of the 460th to offer a man on his fiftieth mission a choice, within reason.

This soft touch, where flak was light and never very effective, required him to fly with another crew. He was mildly concerned when his pilot turned out to be a rookie on his first mission.

The veteran's club was a tough one for a rookie to crash. Most men still surviving after thirty-five or forty missions had seen close friends go down in flames, or blow up over a target—perhaps a buddy from aviation cadet days. They resented a new man coming in and presuming to be one of them. He wasn't! Not until he proved himself by living through several missions. Sometimes a rookie would fly off on his first mission and never come back.

Pilot Lt. Parker T. Brown was attending his first combat mission briefing. He was apprehensive about facing combat, as his thoughts went back to his days as a Boy Scout, and then those glory days of football and basketball at Gould Academy in Bethel, Maine, skiing in the mountains and the crazy but harmless scrapes he always managed to get into. Some had called him a real hellion, but he knew he never got into any trouble with the law or at school. Fun days.

He thought especially about his mother, Edith, with whom he corresponded regularly throughout flight training and who was so worried about his flying these war planes. "Old Tom," his dad, was less vocal, and kept his concern bottled up. Brown's thoughts were on the folks back home: Wonder what my folks thought when I buzzed my house early that morning in my new B-24. If they could only see me now! Nothing will keep me from bombing that bridge today!

He thought, too, about his older brother Norris, an officer somewhere down in the South Pacific fighting that other war.

Now I will join him in the fighting! he thought proudly.

Brown also wondered where his replacement bombardier was. He had been told a man seeking his fiftieth mission was replacing his regular bombardier because this was such a milk run. Lucky guy!

When Brown jumped off the truck at the hardstand he saw a group clustered around the No. 3 engine, which had its cowling removed. Men were on a raised platform working on the engine. Wonder what's wrong, he thought.

Ted Newby didn't even bother to look up his pilot at briefing, so deep was his prejudice about rookies.

At the hardstand he alighted from a Jeep to see the crowd around the plane's cowlingless No. 3 engine.

"What's up?" inquired Newby of no one in particular.

"Minor problem with the engine. Be fixed in a few minutes," answered a slightly built young man with gold bars on his shirt collar, in a decided Maine drawl. "You must be my replacement bombardier."

"Yeah, I'm Newby," he answered.

"I'm Parker Brown. Call me PT," the pilot said.

"Glad to meet you, Brown," replied Newby perfunctorily, adding, "I don't like this," as the beginning of his campaign to scrub the mission.

"Don't worry, they'll get it fixed OK," said the eager rookie, anxious to get to war.

The radioman approached with some news: "Lieutenant, the interphone is not working right. The pilot's line is dead, and there is bad static on the other lines."

Newby grabbed on to that one with, "Brown, we should scrub this mission. I've been taught never to fly a combat mission with faulty communications."

"We are not scrubbing this mission!" Brown insisted.

A Jeep pulled up with a captain aboard, a clipboard in his hand, looking very official. Seemed to be a starter, or something.

Elated, Newby rushed over and explained the situation, requesting the mission be scrubbed.

"You're crazy, lieutenant," the starter said. "Go ahead and fly the plane. We won't scrub a mission for one little old faulty interphone. Where's the pilot?"

When the pilot walked up, the starter continued, "Brown, the group left 45 minutes ago. The engine, I'm told, is OK. You are to rendezvous with the group at these coordinates out over the Tyrrhenian Sea." He handed Brown a slip of paper.

"Thank you, captain," said the obliging pilot.

The frustrated bombardier was cool to the rookie pilot from that point on, and boarded the plane under silent protest.

At the rendezvous point Brown began sliding his plane up to the tail-end Charlie spot in the low box of the second attack unit, known as purple heart corner.

The co-pilot heard the unbelievable words on his static-filled interphone, "Bullets coming through the plane back here in the waist!"

"Say again!" replied the co-pilot.

"Bullets from the No. 5 plane coming through our waist!" repeated the voice.

"I smell smoke," chimed in the tail gunner.

The co-pilot unfastened his oxygen mask and leaned over to the pilot, who was unaware of their problem, and shouted, "We've been hit and something is on fire."

"Ask for a station check," said the calm pilot.

The co-pilot's interphone negated the need for a station check as the fearful words entered his ears, "Our right wheelwell is on fire!"

"PT, our right wheelwell is on fire. Must have hit a fuel line."

"Tell the bombardier to jettison our bombs. Lower the landing gear. It may blow out the fire."

A moment later the co-pilot shouted, "Fire getting worse, let's shut down the starboard engines." Brown nodded, and cut the throttles to No. 3 and No. 4. The co-pilot pushed the two feathering buttons.

The engineer by now was out of his top turret and was busy at the fuel transfer valves. He ran up to the pilots, unhooked his oxygen mask and shouted, "All starboard fuel lines shut off. Maybe we can starve the fire."

Parker Brown was extremely calm in his first trial by fire as he turned the burning bomber southeastward, the Italian shoreline not far in front of him.

Ted Newby came up to Brown and said, "Go due east, so we can bail out over land." He feared a bail-out over water.

"No. We are going to land at the Rome airport. That is enemy territory ahead."

"Brown, B–24s don't usually burn over ten seconds before blowing up. We are way past that. I'm telling you, take a 90 degree heading."

"No!"

"I'm pulling rank on you, Brown. Head straight for land."

"No one outranks the man in the left seat, Newby. You know that."

"Pleeeeease, Brown, we're gonna blow up."

With that, Newby snapped on his chest pack and went down to the bomb bay, frustrated, scared and aware of the consequences of heading for Rome, many miles to the south. He hollered at the radioman, busy keying May Day messages in Morse code. "Knock it off. Put on your chute and get down here!"

The loyal radioman shook his head and continued.

"Your IFF emergency green switch is ON. That's all we need. They're tracking us now and'll find us if we go down. Get your chute on *now!*"

The loyal radioman ignored the best advice he had ever received in his life.

174

Meanwhile the men in the waist had watched the bubble on top of the wing grow; slowly at first, then rapidly as the superheated metal was stretched from the raging fire below.

They had attempted to convey this development over the static-filled interphone, but in their excitement the message was not getting to the cockpit. The pilots did not know of the time bomb they were riding in. Suddenly, in front of the waist gunner's wide eyes, the bubble glowed a dull red. In one last effort to warn the co-pilot, he shouted into his mike, "It's gonna blow!" and then followed the other three out the open camera hatch.

On the floor of the deserted waist lay rumpled flak vests, steel flak helmets and two sets of earphones crying out, "Say again! Say again!"

When the right wing exploded, Newby reached across the door opening and hit the bomb bay door lever. Even though the doors slid open he was unable to move, the centrifugal force of the bomber rotating on its longitudinal axis pinning him to the door frame. Suddenly a reversal of forces popped him out through the open bomb bay door.

The chutist seemed to be above the flames, so in his confused state he pulled his rip cord to keep from falling into the fire. It worked.

He counted seven chutes in the air. As the stricken bomber fell away into its flat spin below him, the right wing several hundred yards away, the sound of its two port engines roaring and throbbing in a weird Doppler effect played a tune of death. His inner thoughts supplied the words, Go ahead and fly the plane, we won't scrub a mission for one little old faulty interphone.

He watched the three rookies, devoted to duty but who would not listen to experience, end their first mission; the fiery coffin crashed into the bay at the mouth of the Tiber River. The music stopped, as death refused to blink.

The bombardier and navigator landed in the bay near the circle of oil that marked the grave of the others. Five other chutes landed in the sea, not too far from shore. Only six of the seven were picked up by the Air Sea Rescue PT boat. It and the circling airplane had been summoned by the IFF automatic May Day signal, and went right to the spot where the signal stopped.

At the precise moment the bomber crashed into the bay, Edith Brown awoke with a sharp pain in her chest. She told Old Tom their son was dead.

The Group continued to the target where surprisingly heavy and accurate flak shot down one of the planes. Five planes landed at friendly fields and of the ones that returned to base one crash-landed with a faulty nose wheel. Eight required extensive repairs. A simple milk run to southern France.

Newby caught a C-47 for Spinazzola and beat his group back, where he was handed his ticket home by Capt. Dean Snyder, squadron flight surgeon. The piece of paper read:

FLYER'S COPY

To: the Commanding Officer 763rd Squadron.
It is recommended that Lt. Newby, Leroy W.
0-754756, Bomb. be removed from Flying Status.
Diagnosis Flying Fatigue   (date) 8-6-44
                        Signed D. C. Snyder Capt. MC

One man, commenting on Newby's miraculous survival, said, "If you are born to be shot, you won't be hanged!"

Two planes landing on a 460th BG air strip. Four landed planes, right, are taxiing to hardstand. The camp is at left center. The large dark area at right center is the site of Hangar Queen crash-landing. Valley is off the picture to the right of the taxi strip.

Lt. Parker Brown in front of his B-24 prior to his first and last mission, where he gave his life to save his crew.

Bombardier Newby's "ticket home."

The game of cat and mouse between the adversaries went on; this time it was the offense's move. They stole a page from the future when they employed the modern NFL's practice of using the quarterback audible to change the play after the defense has been revealed.

On August 10 a P–38 Weather Plane (WX), call sign "Tailpiece 48," was sent ahead to Ploesti where, when the bombers were twenty minutes from the target area, it radioed back in clear text: (1) cloud coverage, (2) cloud height, (3) direction and approximate velocity of ground wind and smoke screen, and

(4) targets by number that were visible. Wing commanders then radioed a change in target to their groups, if indicated, using call signs and code words.

The night before, the RAF had made another of its night attacks, this time to help finish off Romano Americana, and lost eleven of its sixty-four planes. As the American refinery, which local people thought would never be touched, was still smoking, the 5th Bomb Wing sent in 154 B-17s to bring it to a near standstill.

That same day Hammett & Co. took *Hangar Queen* to Astra Romana for its farewell trip to that terrible place, and the flak gunners exacted their usual toll; a plane in *Hangar Queen*'s box blew to smithereens on the bomb run.

On August 12, 13 and 14 the Fifteenth AF blasted bridges, railroads, ports and beaches along a wide front of potential invasion points. On its fiftieth mission the crew was sent on August 12 to bomb gun emplacements at Sete, France. The mission was a milk run, as expected, but as the Group began its landing procedure *Hangar Queen* was on its downwind leg, with gear down, when suddenly all four engines quit.

Quick-thinking Charlie Hammett instinctively shoved the control forward and called for all four engines to be feathered. Two thousand feet above the ground is not enough altitude for a power-off landing in a B-24. They would have crashed if their famed luck had not held out; they were approaching a valley near the air strip. Hammett dived the dead-engined bomber into the valley and soared up to a lower plateau for a perfect dead-stick landing.

When the engines quit the replacement bombardier, who had requested flying with the lucky crew on his fiftieth mission, eschewed the reason for joining the crew and took to his parachute. His body was found just a few feet from the edge of the first plateau where *Hangar Queen* had escaped into the valley, his partially opened chute fluttering in the wind.

Bob Kaiser had crawled up to the nose to get his chute and was on the way back to make his jump when the plane made its dramatic landing in a farm field. The landing was smooth, but the pilots were unable to stop in time to avoid plowing into a small earthen mound. The impact crushed the underbody of the fuselage, and the man who had brought so much cheer to his crew mates in their times of stress and tenseness died from the collision.

Clyde Gilbert made his bail-out a few seconds after the bombardier's, and his luck held as he escaped along with the plane into the valley. He landed hard, but survived.

American forces invaded southern France on August 15, with the full support of the Fifteenth AF, which pounded invasion beaches prior to, during and after the successful landings. Ploesti was given a welcome six-day rest during that period.

The night before Ted Newby departed for Naples he was at the Officer's Club bar when a pilot walked up and introduced himself as Monte Carlough, and said, "I understand you were with Parker Brown the other day."

"Right. Tough luck. I really didn't get to know him and I feel awful about how shabbily I treated the guy before we took off. I gave him the old I'm-a-hot-veteran-and-you're-just-a-rookie treatment, and made no effort to be friendly," Newby replied.

"Too bad. You missed out on knowing one of the finest, most fun-loving guys you will ever meet," said Carlough.

"Really? Tell me about him," prompted Newby.

Carlough told his story to an about-to-be-humbled bombardier:

"I went through cadets with PT. He was from Bethel, Maine, and had been logging in the Maine woods just before joining the Army Air Forces, and was the most unforgettable character I have ever met. My first experience with him was returning from open post in Nashville pre-pre-flight. As a young inexperienced guy, I settled for a couple of beers. Singing and coming back through the gate we were challenged by the usual MP guard, and I was completely unaware that PT had a Coke bottle filled with Four Roses. That would have been the brig if we had been caught, but he led a charmed life.

"We roomed together at Maxwell Field pre-flight, and the upperclassmen had a habit of coming in after open post, bursting the door wide open, and putting the underclassmen in a 'Brace, Mister!' Brownie contrived a bucket over the door that gave the Cadet Adjutant a soaking when he kicked the door open. From that time on he was a marked man. At any opportunity PT would love to mimick the Cadet Adjutant crying out in his long Maine drawl, 'Squad-r-o-o-o-o-n-n-n, teeeeennnn-HUT!' He occasionally got caught at that one, but the other upperclassmen thought it so funny they made him do it every so often in the mess hall.

"Guess who became Cadet Adjutant when we became upperclassmen? I can still hear him dragging it out before formations across the Parade Grounds."

Newby gulped his drink and cringed a little, thinking regretfully, And I didn't give this man the time of day? He is my kind of guy.

Carlough continued: "We were taking our Physical Fitness Requirements tests and I think we had to do something like six chin-ups to pass. PT struggled through four chin-ups, and barely made five. The instructor had a smirk on his face as he was about to fail this cadet, when PT switched to one hand, the other hanging by his side. It looked like he was about to fall off, when suddenly he flexed his muscle and did a one-arm chin-up as the instructor gasped. He then proceeded to do one-arm chin-ups until well into the high twenties. The red-faced instructor finally ordered him down. Remember, he was cutting logs by hand, and had wrists and forearms like Popeye, but a small waist and skinny legs, leaving him little weight to lift up to the bar."

By now Newby was totally chagrined: How could I misread someone like that? I'll never get a chance to make it right. And, the guy saved my life by getting me near shore before I had to go out.

Carlough wouldn't quit: "On our way by train to take our high-altitude chamber test, just before we graduated from advanced school, Brownie made a play for an attractive girl and ended up sitting with her for several hundred miles. I never thought any more about it, and never even knew her name. When I saw him here a few nights ago, just before your mission, he told me he had become engaged to the girl. PT was quite a guy. He was my good friend."

Newby was shaken by the meeting, reflecting on his boorish behavior with a man he would love to have called *his* good friend.

As American invasion forces landed in southern France, Ted Newby was lolling around in his tent located in the infield of the great Naples Race Track, where hundreds of others were awaiting assignment to a boat bound for the United States.

Ploesti's respite was over on August 17 when planners introduced a new wrinkle in their offense. Three bomb wings, 47th, 49th and 304th, would attack Ploesti at thirty-minute intervals. Three WX planes would hover over the target, each assigned to a bomb wing, and feed them target selection information. Stringing out the wings would take advantage of the relatively short life of smoke coverage, due to ground winds.

Astra, Standard and Romano Americana were thus dealt out to the oncoming wing commanders, who in turn assigned specific targets to their own groups.

Of the 245 bombers on that mission nineteen were lost—a high 7.8 percent rate.

The day before Newby's last mission Maj. Ray Whitley brought his replacement crew to Spinazzola, and got in a few missions before flying the Ploesti mission on August 18.

The previous night the RAF had bombed Ploesti, in an effort to immobilize the city and put an additional drain on the smoke supply, in preparation for the next day's USAAF attack. The night bombers lost three of their fifty-one planes.

On Whitley's mission, thirty minutes before the IP the oil pressure on No. 3 dropped, forcing him to shut it down while it still could be feathered. He could not hold formation, and rather than go home he went on to the target to bomb it alone. A near direct flak burst knocked out No. 1, and it too had to be feathered. As he and co-pilot Chuck Thornburgh fought trims and controls to keep the plane on an even keel, a voice came over the interphone screaming, "I'm hit!"

Whitley told bombardier Harry Holliday to go back and see who was hit, and help out. Holliday grabbed a walkaround oxygen bottle and headed back to the waist, where he came upon a raging fire in one of the waist ammo boxes. A piece of red hot flak had cut a hydraulic line and ignited the fluid. Bullets were exploding. Holliday and a waist gunner beat out the fire with flight jackets and went back to the injured tail gunner, Danny Gordon, and hauled him out of his turret. A large piece of flak had entered just below his right hip, shattered the bone and came out his knee.

The man was in extreme pain so they gave him a shot of morphine and applied a tourniquet as high as possible on his leg. Gordon began screaming, "No, no. Don't do that! Stop! You're killing me."

Gordon had good reason to yell, for the tourniquet was around his testicles.

The crew members jettisoned everything they could find to throw out, to try to stay airborne. Fortunately the two good engines had their superchargers in full working condition. The crippled bomber was at about 8,000 ft. as they crossed the Adriatic, but was losing altitude. Just as they reached the coast No. 4 began sputtering, so Whitley ordered No. 3 back into service. No. 4 died, and No. 3 was living on borrowed time.

The pilot offered the crew the opportunity to bail out; the two pilots and engineer would bring it in on two engines. They all knew Gordon could not survive a parachute jump so they declined to leave their buddy. As their now rapidly descending plane with landing gear down approached the Spinazzola landing strip from the north, landing north to south, No. 3 quit and was hastily feathered. Only one operating engine and a reasonably good glide approach was not the best of situations, but it was workable for a one-shot try. There could be no go-around for a second attempt. Not with three engines feathered.

The glide in was perfect, but just before touchdown Whitley was horrified to see another B-24 about to touch down on the same runway at the other end landing *south to north*. The engineer was watching it through his binoculars and cried out, "He has No. 1 feathered."

Whitley said, "I hope he can count to three. Fire a red flare," The engineer fired a red flare, the recognized demand for emergency priority landing. The other plane fired a red flare at the same time.

The stakes were high as they raced toward each other in this deadly game of chicken. Whitley knew he had no choice but to play on. The other pilot may have had the same determination, until he counted Whitley's three dead engines and yielded to the logic of the moment. The pilot who had been minding his own business and trying to bring his crippled bomber down on the prescribed approach pulled up and over the thankful winner of the contest.

After landing, the last engine quit and the plane had to be towed off the runway.

The Fifteenth AF had sent 373 planes and lost seven.

On August 19 the 5th Bomb Wing sent sixty-five B–17s to hit Xenia and Dacia, another small late-bloomer. Not a fighter was seen and not a plane was lost on this final mission, as Ploesti was written off as a Fifteenth AF target. Ploesti kaput!

The Fifteenth Air Force sent 5,479 heavy bombers into Ploesti skies and lost 223 to its flak and fighters. Add the losses by the dive-bombing P–38s of June 10, the night incursions by the RAF and the catastrophe of TIDAL WAVE and Gerstenberg extracted a high price for destroying Ploesti oil—339 bombers were lost at Ploesti. It *was* a graveyard of bombers.

A few days later Newby, along with about 600 other flyers and 500 wounded men from the invasion, boarded the USS *General Meigs* for the long-awaited trip home.

After two days out to sea the giant engines of the troopship quit cold, and the returning warriors spent a nervous twenty-four hours on a becalmed sea, as naval planes patroled the waters for German subs.

That same day, August 23, Rumania's King Michael quit the war and surrendered unconditionally to Russia. Ploesti, the city that had emerged from the king's glorious ancestor Prince Michael the Brave's campsite, had been delivered to the Soviets. It was the first of several historic events that would plague the United States for years to come.

For the next three days thirty German Junker 88s and Stuka dive-bombers flew from the nearby Bucharest/Otopeni airdrome and ruthlessly bombed the defenseless city of Bucharest. The brick schoolhouse, home of the American POWs, was flattened and the nearby hospital was damaged. Five American POWs were killed in the attacks. Four POWs were in a city restaurant enjoying a celebration meal when German soldiers burst in and machine gunned them to death. It was the worst three days of the war for Roy Meyer and his comrades.

Ploesti oil production was shut down on August 24, when the last five operating refineries were still pumping out their product at twenty percent of capacity. Six days later the Russian troops moved in and found the five diehards still connected by Gerstenberg's pipeline.

The Russians were dumbfounded to find the American-owned refinery totally destroyed. *What kind of people are these Americans?* they must have wondered.

Gen. Alfred Gerstenberg spent the next eleven years in a Russian prison.

The Ploesti campaign was over, and a high German official would state at war's end that the bombing of Ploesti was the most significant contribution of the Allied Air Forces to Germany's defeat.

After the Rumanian surrender all of the POW camps were open and the former Rumanian guards began treating the Americans and Britons with more respect. One prisoner, Col. James A. Gunn III, was determined he and his buddies were all going home. With the help of Princess Caradja he obtained the services of Capt. Constantine Cantacuzene to fly him to Foggia in an Me 109, with a crude American flag painted on its side. He had been promised a P–51 for his efforts. Gunn was stuffed into the empty radio compartment, and the external panel screwed on.

A surprised group of Americans watched an enemy fighter plane, with swastikas painted over and an American flag on its side, come in for a landing as wary, itchy-trigger-fingered flak gunners tracked it to the ground.

When the plane landed and pulled up to the parking ramp at Foggia, the Rumanian hopped out and casually asked for a screwdriver. The grinning Rumanian pilot then removed four screws from the large panel on the side of his plane. When it was removed, two GI boots emerged, followed by an equally grinning American pilot in an American uniform. The happy Rumanian pilot was sent home with his prize, a P–51 Mustang, to help pave the way for what would follow.

Starting August 31 and for two more days thirty-eight B–17 Fortresses, outfitted as transport planes, flew a round-the-clock airlift into Popesti airport. With the sound of Russian and German gunfire in the background they evacuated over a thousand American POWs.

At Bari airport 1,100 American youngsters, veterans of the unfriendly skies of the Balkans and the unforgiving prison camps of Rumania, walked, limped or were carried in stretchers off a different plane than the one that took them to Rumania. They were met by top Air Force officials and handed their tickets home.

On September 1, 5,000 miles to the west 1,100 American youngsters, veterans of the unfriendly skies of the Balkans or the bloody, unforgiving beaches of southern France, tickets home in their pockets, walked, limped or were carried in stretchers down the gangplank of the USS *General Meigs* to the dock at Norfolk, Virginia.

Part Four

All the World's a Stage

Chapter 12

River City

> *All the world's a stage,*
> *and all the men and women merely players.*
> *They all have their exits and their entrances:*
> *And one man in his time plays many parts.*
> —William Shakespeare, *As You Like It*, act II, scene 7, lines 139–142

Monday, Oct. 15, 1984

"Mr. Newby, you have a call from the State Department in Washington," interrupted Mrs. Steig.

The marketing team at Webster City Products, a producer of domestic laundry equipment, was in the midst of its weekly staff meeting when the marketing secretary made the startling announcement.

"Who?" asked Ted Newby.

"Better not keep them waiting," said Bob Kepler, Marketing vice president.

As Ted Newby departed he couldn't resist, "I wonder what they want *this* time!"

"Mr. Newby," said the voice, "this is the Visitor Program Service of the US Information Agency. We have an invited guest of the United States who wants to come out to Iowa and visit you."

"Visit *me?*" he inquired.

"Yes, Mr. Ioan Grigorescu, a Romanian writer, is doing research on TIDAL WAVE and saw your book, *Target Ploesti: View from a Bombsight*, at the Library of Congress. Mr. Grigorescu was a thirteen-year-old boy living in Ploesti when the low-level bombers came over."

"Wow, this is something. I give lectures on TIDAL WAVE and the Price of Freedom all over, and I am scheduled to give my TIDAL WAVE lecture at

182

the Friends of the Library at Mason City next Sunday. Why don't you send him there to join me on the program? I'll tell 'em about the planning of the mission, and what went wrong in its execution. He can come up and tell what it was like under our bombs. I hope he speaks English."

"No problem on the English, we will send along our US Escort and Interpreter, Mr. Paul Hiemstra. Sounds like a good idea, I'll get back to you," said the caller.

Sunday, Oct. 21, 1984

Ted Newby's TIDAL WAVE lecture included charts showing the planned routes of the five bomb groups and the targets to be destroyed. Other charts depicted the navigational error and resulting mixup over the targets.

He cited several personal examples of courage of men in their twenties in the 1940s, and told the incredible story of the man who was reading Shakespear's *As You Like It* on the mission.

At the conclusion of Newby's chart lecture on TIDAL WAVE, Ioan Grigorescu and his interpreter came front stage for one of the most unforgettable moments the audience of one hundred would ever experience. The diminutive Romanian with his dancing blue eyes, receding hairline—bushy in the back—and walrus mustache captivated the group in the first minute.

He opened with, "I am especially pleased to be here in this fine library, as my life has been devoted to books ever since childhood, when I had a home library second to none among my friends.

"To visit the mythical site of 'River City' is exciting for me. Meredith Wilson's *Music Man* has always been one of my favorites. I love Mark Twain too, but he, of course, isn't a local writer.

"We in Romania have fought for and cherish freedom just as you do, and where is the embodiment of freedom more evident than in a library?"

His words were met with applause.

"An event occurred this summer," he continued, "that I am sure many of you witnessed, but may not have realized its full significance. As you know, Romania broke with Russia on its ban of your Olympic Games. And when the small band of Romanian athletes entered the Coliseum in Los Angeles thousands of Americans rose for a standing ovation.

"Through the miracle of television and satellites millions of Romanians were touched by that gesture from America's heart. The Olympics is competition and medals, but that expression of love was the finest medal one people can give another."

The prideful audience was respectfully silent at this unexpected tribute. Perhaps they all looked inward for a moment. Americans know about fighting for freedom.

Then he told the hushed audience, "The reason I decided to write a book about TIDAL WAVE and come to America for research is to find out what makes you Americans tick."

"I saw those skimming bombers," he continued, his bright blue eyes flashing above his giant mustache, "flying into the heavily defended refineries, so low they were pulling the roofs off houses. I saw bombers on fire, with young Americans trapped inside. I saw a river on fire from a crashed bomber. I saw a dead American in a walnut grove looking up into the sky, not far from his burning bomber. Why were they here? I learned later Americans have their Statue of Liberty, just as we do."

Lecturer Ioan Grigorescu, Ploesti resident under fellow lecturer-bombardier Newby's bombs, sees his first Norden bombsight.

Bombardier Newby and 1944 Ploesti resident Ioan Grigorescu can smile with each other 40 years later.

His gestures and demeanor were in amusing counterpoint to the young interpreter's cool, deadpan, unemotional retelling of his words.

He went on: "Ten years ago my brother phoned me, all excited. He said they were digging up the area around our old homestead that had been destroyed by the high-level bombers and they found something I should see. I went at once.

"When I arrived my brother was standing beside a rusty old pipe. He held it up as I pulled out several pieces of damp, deterioriated rags. Then reached in, up to my elbow, to extract a mass of partially deteriorated sheets of paper."

When the interpreter repeated that statement the audience edged forward in its seats. It was no longer an audience of one hundred, *it* was an audience of *one*. It *knew* what the next statement would be.

The audience did not understand the dozen or so Romanian words preceding, but when the Romanian got to the word *Shakespeare* it grasped the significance of the literary bombshell exploding in its midst.

The gasp of the audience preceded the interpreter as he repeated in English: "When I examined the contents more closely I saw it was a book. I could barely make out the title to be Shakespeare's *As You Like It*."

"When I had come upon that dead flyer," he said, "my mind was a whirl. I saw a small book nearby and wondered what it was doing there. I picked it up and ran home, to add it to my library collection. My mother told me the book was in English and would be considered subversive if the German soldiers saw it. She told me to destroy my treasure. But instead, I buried it. When our house was later destroyed by a bomb, I thought my prize was gone."

184

Grigorescu then said: "Digging up that book and learning its contents impressed me. It was crazy. Life never offers this kind of metaphor. I was taken with the audacity of an American youngster who flew into the face of death reading this particular classic. And then to think it fell into a forest of walnuts.

"I had to learn more about Americans, so I began research on a bombing mission that brought many of you to my city at 250 mph, just 10 or 20 feet off the ground. I learned only today," nodding toward Newby, "the identity of that young man."

A lady in the audience spoke up, "Mr. Grigorescu, how does it feel to be sharing the stage with a man who was dropping bombs on you forty years ago?"

"Mr. Newby did not come to destroy my house," he replied, "but rather to shorten the nightmare our earth was going through."

The little Romanian then walked over to the American and embraced him in a big Balkan bear hug.

Theater was never more alive than in that one electric moment in the library at River City.

The man from Stratford-upon-Avon had reached nearly 400 years from out of the past to touch three lives from diverse world arenas, spanning several decades and two forests; to form a phantom quartet and provide a real-life scenario for the immortal words of Jaques:

All the world's a stage, and all the men and women merely players.
They all have their exits and their entrances: And one man in his
time plays many parts.

Faces of Hope

Sweet are the uses of adversity,
Which, like the toad, ugly and
venomous,
Wears yet a precious stone
in his head:
And this our life, exempt from
public haunt,
Finds tongues in trees, books
in the running brooks,
Sermons in stone, and good in
everything.
—William Shakespeare, *As You Like It*, act II, scene 1, lines 12–17

War was impersonal to us bomber crews flying over German-occupied countries. We fought things and machines—not people. We dodged flak and fighters, never seeing our faceless enemy.

A reader wrote, "You probably did not see a small American-born boy waving to you on the way to his Budapest bombshelter on July 30, 1944."

We also never saw the upraised faces of oppressed people living under German tyranny—faces that saw in us tangible evidence that help was on its way. We were not privy to seeing the love and gratitude in those faces for American youngsters flying to their potential death.

An Austrian wrote that he watched from his Vienna basement window on July 26, 1944 as our 460th Bomb Group hit the Zwolfaxing airdrome.

A Czechoslovakian wrote that he has visited nearly eighty-five crash sites of downed American planes, and has devoted his life to lecturing young people on how hundreds of American youngsters gave their lives for the freedom of Czechoslovakia.

A twenty-eight-year-old Canadian wrote and said, "Obviously your effort and the effort and sacrifices of untold others was all for the correct pursuit. To me, living the life I do, with my children and wife, is only possible through the commitment of persons such as yourself over 40 years ago. I am indebted to you and all others who made that effort!"

Several years ago while appearing on a Pittsburgh TV talk show a lady phoned in while I was back in the green room and told me, "I was a young girl in Yugoslavia and used to pray for you American boys flying over on your way to Ploesti. This is my first opportunity to thank one of you for saving my country. God bless all of you American flyers."

Author Newby, addressing Bi-Annual Reunion of Fifteenth Air Force, passes along the gratitude of a Yugoslavian lady: "Thank you, for saving my country. God bless all you American flyers."

Old aerial gunners never die; they just turn to latch hooking 40 years later. Sid Rotz re-created the "Black Panther" in fighting trim.

Alex Sonkoly latch hooked a portrait of what he looked like after 50 missions.

I was so moved by the words of the Yugoslavian lady that I shared her thanks with a fellow member of the Caterpillar Association of the United States, Vice President George Bush, a man who became a Caterpillar when he bailed out of his plane after being shot down in the Pacific.

He replied, "Thank you for sharing the salute to the American armed forces from the Yugoslavian woman. Her words are still meaningful after forty years.

"We in America must continually rededicate ourselves to the cause of human dignity and freedom, a cause that goes to the heart of our national character and defines our national purpose. Our country was always meant to be the champion of the oppressed.

"We owe much to the men and women of our armed services. They are the ones who have been in the front lines of our march to freedom.

"All who cherish human rights and individual freedom owe much to these men and women for their achievements."

May the faces of hope always look up to America.

—*Leroy W. Newby*

Acknowledgments

Thanks to all who wrote in appreciation of *Target Ploesti: View from a Bombsight*.

I am especially indebted to those who flew the unfriendly skies of Ploesti and shared their story of those exciting and terrifying times. Many of your narratives appear in this book as examples of the human side of the bombers' war; space does not permit using them all—but your stories are in my heart, if not in print.

Much statistical data was needed for the cold side of our shared experience and I want to thank Tom Britton, past president of the American Aviation Historical Society, for the loan of *Air Battle of Ploesti* with its detail on each of the high-level Ploesti attacks.

A small boy named Bill Polcsa waved to me on his way to a Budapest bomb shelter on July 30, 1944; forty-four years later he sent me an astounding book on the work of the US Engineer Model Makers Detachment during the European war. They were the people who made the scale models of Ploesti, Normandy, Sicily, Remagen Bridgehead, Peenemunde and other strategic targets of the USAAF so that aerial views could be produced for use by bombardiers.

Dr. Jerome Klinkowitz, Professor of American Literature at the University of Northern Iowa and an authority on the air war in Europe, critiqued my manuscript, which I gratefully appreciate.

Thanks to Mr. and Mrs. Norris Brown for the touching background on Parker Brown, the pilot who died trying to save my life on my fiftieth mission.

In addition, I would like to thank the following for their contributions: Norman C. Adams, Edward C. Baker and Wilmer H. C. Bassett, 93rd BG, Eighth AF; Harry Baughn, 98th BG, Ninth AF; George P. Bishop and William Blocker, 460th BG, Fifteenth AF; Merle L. Bolen, 98th BG, Ninth AF; Mike Brown, 460th BG, Fifteenth AF; Richard Byers, 376th BG, Ninth AF; Thornton "Monte" Carlough, Jerry Conlon, Bob Cutler and William C. Dale, 460th BG, Fifteenth AF; Julian T. Darlington, John A. Ditullio, Stuart L. Floyd, John Fontenrose and George W. Fulfer, 98th BG, Ninth AF; George Garrett, Clyde Gilbert, Benjamin E. Haller, Charles M. Hammett, Henrick B. Hanson and Bertram C. Harrison, 460th BG, Fifteenth AF; J. L. Hinely, 44th BG, Eighth AF; W. Heberd "Heb" James, 460th BG, Fifteenth AF; Harold F. "Harry" Korger, 98th BG, Ninth AF; Harry Lasco, 44th BG, Eighth AF; Worthy A. Long and Floyd Mabee, 93rd BG, Eighth AF; Roy Meyer, 463rd BG, Fifteenth AF; LeRoy B. Morgan, 98th BG, Ninth AF; Andrew W. Opsata, 98th BG, Ninth AF (on loan from 389th BG, Eighth AF); Russell Page and Wesley N. Pettigrew, 98th BG, Ninth AF; William G. Pimm, 98th BG, Ninth AF (on loan from 389th BG, Eighth AF); Earnest L. Poulson, 389th BG, Eighth AF; Felix Rameder, Vienna resident during bombings; Manuel "Manny" R. Rangel, 98th BG, Ninth AF; Edward R. "Dusty" Rhodes, 460th BG, Fifteenth AF; Albert A. Romana and James J. Sedlack, 389th BG, Eighth AF; Danny Smith, Sid R. Smith, Lyle C. Spencer, John F. Staehle, Robert C. Stephens and Ray Swedzinski, 460th BG, Fifteenth AF; Milton Telster, 93rd BG, Eighth AF; Howard H. Thornton, 460th BG, Fifteenth AF; Charles N. Wallace, 389th BG, Fifteenth AF; Worden Weaver, 44th BG, Eighth AF; Earl C. Wescott, 389th BG, Eighth AF; Rayford B. Whitley, Jim Wilkenson and Sid R. Woods, 460th BG, Fifteenth AF; and Larry Yates, 93rd BG, Eighth AF.

For contributing photographs, I would thank: Al Blue, Mrs. Norris Brown, "Monte" Carlough, Bob Cutler, Ben Crawford, Julian Darlington, Lee Decker, Norbert Dunkel, Ioan Grigorescu, L. B. Groover, Dorothy McDonald Harrison, Bob Kraus, Floyd Mabee, Bob Mathews, Hugh McClaran, Sam Page, Bill Pimm, Bill Polcsa, Sid Rotz, Dan Smith, Alex Sonkoly, Warren Tucker, Bob Wachowiak, George Williams and John Woodward.

Finally, for giving their time to grant personal interviews, I would like to thank Ioan Grigorescu, Ploesti resident during bombings; Paul Suciu, son of a Ploesti refinery official; and Mrs. E. W. (Dorothy McDonald) Harrison, Red Cross employee at an Eighth AF base.
—*Leroy W. Newby*

Bibliography

AAFRH–3. *The Ploesti Mission of 1 August 1943*. Historical Research Center: Maxwell Air Force Base, Alabama.

Air Battle of Ploesti. 941st Engineer Battalion, 1945.

Birdsall, Steve. *Log of the Liberators*. New York: Doubleday, 1973.

Byers, Richard G. *Attack*. Winona, MN: Appolo Books, Inc., 1984.

Cheatham, Dean. "Raid on Ploesti Still Vivid Memory," Benton County *Daily Democrat*, Aug. 6, 1982.

Cochran, Alexander S., Jr. "Low As We Could Go," *Military History*, Leesburg, FL, August 1985.

Dugan, James, and Stewart, Carroll. *Ploesti*. New York: Ballantine Books, 1962.

engineer(sic) M.M. Modelmakers Detachment. U.S. Army Engineer Service, 1945.

Fifteenth Air Force Association. *The Fifteenth Air Force Story*. Dallas: Taylor Publishing Co., 1986.

460th Bomb Group. Historical Research Center: Maxwell Air Force Base, Alabama.

Freeman, Roger. *B–24 Liberator at War*. London: Ian Allan Ltd., 1983.

Frisbee, John L. "Into the Mouth of Hell," *Air Force Magazine*. Arlington, VA, Sept. 1988.

Grigorescu, Ioan. *Ploieste*. Bucharest: Meridiane Publishing House, 1964.

Infield, Glen B. *Disaster at Bari*. MacMillan, 1971.

Lovell, Jan. "Terrors of War Unite Two Men," Mason City *Globe Gazette*, Oct. 22, 1984.

Newby, Leroy. *Target Ploesti: View from a Bombsight*. Novato, CA: Presidio Press, 1983.

Pringle, Henry F. "What Happened at Ploesti?" *Saturday Evening Post*, Jan. 6, 1945.

Rust, Kent. *Fifteenth Air Force Story*. Temple City, CA: Historical Aviation Album, 1976.

Rust, Kent. "War Diary of John R. "Killer" Kane, Out in the Blue Part IV," *Journal American Aviation Historical Society*. Garden Grove, CA, Spring 1983.

Steinhardt. Telegram to Secretary of State. Ankara, Turkey, Aug. 8, 1943.

Untermeyer, Louis. Introduction to *The Rubáiyát of Omar Khayyám*, by Edward Fitzgerald. New York: Random House, 1947.

Wolff, Leon. *Low Level Mission*. New York: Berkley Publishing, 1958.

Index